ROADMAP
to Success

AMERICA'S TOP INTELLECTUAL
MINDS MAP OUT SUCCESSFUL
BUSINESS STRATEGIES

Insight Publishing Company
707 West Main Street, Suite 5
Sevierville, Tennessee 37862

Roadmap to Success Copyright © 2013
Published in the United States by
ISBN 978-1-60013-043-4

Disclaimer: This book is a compilation of
ideas from numerous experts who have
each contributed a chapter. As such, the
views expressed in each chapter are of
those who were interviewed and not
necessarily of the interviewer or Insight
Publishing.

MESSAGE FROM THE PUBLISHER

The interviews in this book were conducted by David E. Wright, the President and founder of Insight Publishing

I'VE DONE A LOT OF DRIVING IN MY LIFE and one thing I have been smart enough to have is a dependable road map. If you don't have a good plan to get from where you are to where you want to go, you will get lost.

I've known many people who have started out in business and thought they had a good plan, but did not achieve the success they wanted. A major problem for many of these people was that they had not sought good advice from people who had achieved success. If you don't learn from the experience of others, you might achieve success but you will probably get there the hard way. You might get lost down many side roads before you find the right one.

ROADMAP to Success, is a mini-seminar on how to plan for your success. The successful people in this book have the experience that will help you find what you need to create your ROADMAP to Success. These perceptive businesspeople were fascinating as they unfolded their own personal road maps and told me about their various success journeys.

I invite you to set aside some quiet time and learn from these exceptional authors. I assure you that your time won't be wasted. It's not often that you can access such a large quantity of quality information that will either get you started or help you get further along on your road to success. This book is an investment in your future—your successful future!

—*David E. Wright*

TABLE OF CONTENTS

CHAPTER ONE

No one is coming...
Mark David

DAVID WRIGHT (WRIGHT)

Today I'm talking with Mark David. Mark is President of The Mark David Corporation, a boutique training company. He has provided customized training programs and coaching services to corporate America since 1987. Mark has inspired many Fortune 500–1000 companies with his practical and human approach to success. He specializes in three areas: 1) coaching individuals to grow and develop their overall skills and capabilities, 2) consulting organizations by providing solutions to tough business challenges. 3) developing customized training programs that drive immediate, positive results. Mark's strategies and unique productivity tools provide corporate citizens with the answers they need to thrive in challenging economic times and create increased balance and contentment throughout their organizations. After all, balanced and happy professionals are highly productive.

Mark's purpose is that of an adventurer. His exploration is with people, not land or water. His frontier is the human spirit. This aligns his energy with his passion and ultimate goals. Mark believes that success is an inside-outside game and there is unlimited potential in all of us waiting to be unlocked. He brings out the best in results by bringing out the best in people.

Mark welcome to *ROADMAP to Success*.

MARK DAVID (DAVID)

Thank you, David; it's an absolute honor and pleasure to be speaking with you today.

WRIGHT

How would you define "success" today?

DAVID

Success holds many different meanings for different people. I believe success means knowing that my personal and business life are in alignment with my vision. It means knowing who I am, including my feelings, my thoughts, my actions, and my purpose on this planet. As a result, this alignment creates a richer life of health, safety, security, and financial abundance. Success means that at the end of each day I can go to sleep and be in a state of contentment. What I mean by contentment is I have worked and lived each day generating the maximum amount of positive energy to meet and exceed my vision. The bottom line is I did the best I could, moving forward in the direction of my vision, my goals, and my objectives.

Success is living your purpose. A successful life should be simple and doable. Simple and doable means that no matter how much stress and uncertainty surrounds me, I know where I'm going and what I need to do to get there. If an adjustment is needed, make it and keep moving forward with clarity and integrity. When thinking about success or creating success, emotional maturity is critical. You must be in a state of acceptance of what is. Our lives were meant to be an adventure of learning from our experiences. Every experience *does* happen for a reason and that reason is personal growth. We have to be open to it, listen to it, and grow from it. This attitude is a magic formula for staying young in mind, body, and spirit. Success means knowing that you can only control the actions you perform in the present moment of now. When you are anxious about the future or stressed about the past, you are not performing from your highest, most truthful level. You must fight to stay present, as the current fast-paced world attempts to spin you like a top. Take a breath and stay in the now. By taking care of today you will automatically take care of your future.

Lastly, success is consciousness—being deliberately *awake*! When you are awake, you can unconditionally help others and help our planet be as healthy as possible. We're all connected. No one does anything without affecting the world they live in. Be conscious of your role and involvement in taking on the responsibility for the safety, security, health, and well-being of everyone. This consciousness manifests a richer, more meaningful life.

WRIGHT

So why do you feel we need a road map for success?

DAVID

It's been proven time after time—a well written plan is much more productive than "winging it." It's very similar to going to the grocery store without a list. You get distracted, forget items, buy items you don't need, and spend more money and time than needed. Life without a plan is the same. We get distracted and waste time, make the wrong decisions, and waste resources, especially time and money. The plan you build to achieve the outcomes you desire becomes the platform launching you into a successful life.

WRIGHT

You are a business and life coach and author of customized training programs. You are out in the field every day coaching and consulting with business professionals. What challenges are individuals facing in the corporate world today?

DAVID

That's a great question. Here are few challenges that immediately come to mind.

1. Individuals are finding it very difficult to create a work/life balance today. Evenings and weekends are filled with wall-to-wall activities. At the same time, it's difficult to unplug from work. It's like being on a conveyor belt with one activity after another. Because everything is so costly these days, the average couple feels as though they are always falling behind.

   Women today are taking on even more responsibility for their entire family's security, safety, and success. They truly never have a moment to safely shut down. They are always on. These women are incredible, silent warriors. They rarely complain and always find a way to continue and unconditionally give to others. These women are amazing!

2. Retirement is another issue. Retirement is being pushed out to later and later in life. When, if at all, will it happen? How do you truly prepare financially with all of the current uncertainty? How are you creating that future security today? What do you do when you retire when all you know what to do is work? It's a scary, anxious place for many people who are facing this reality.

3. Corporate interference is on the rise. Leadership is simply not supporting the front line in a manner that maximizes and inspires increased results. More work is being created based on bureaucracy and silos. Justified mistakes are made for the front lines to clean up and fix. Everything is extremely political and so much time is wasted on being politically correct. Many leaders ask for the truth to be told, yet the truth may have negative consequences. In many cases, if you do speak the truth, you're at risk of being let go. This creates a culture where you have to look over your shoulder, even when it isn't crowded. This reality slows productivity down under the camouflage of "everything is fine."

4. With workforces running lean, it's more important than ever to run your own business within your company. You have to take on the responsibility and mentality of owning your own business. It's truly up to you because, *No one is coming* to save the day! Managing your emotions is key. Please understand—business is *just* business. Know right from wrong; expect people to bend the truth and data to be distorted. Accept what is and make the correct decisions and move on. Don't get stuck in self-made negativity and become a victim of reality. It just won't serve you well. You can only control *you* and *your actions* in the present moment of now. Keep your eyes looking straight ahead and perform the actions that will pull your goals to you. Your job is the vehicle to achieve your personal life goals.

5. In order to get promoted today, you need to do more than an excellent job. Being recognized for your efforts and goal achievement is one thing, but it won't get you promoted. It's important to internally and externally brand yourself for the future position you would like to acquire. Short, medium, and long-range plans of action are needed to successfully put yourself in the career you desire or the next position you want. Remember, *No one is coming* to do what your family needs you to do. Self-marketing and branding is a key responsibility that many forget.

6. Through my many hours of infield coaching and consulting I see a very strong trend. Customers want the following from all of us: unconditional caring, focused attention, and disciplined determination. They also seek trust, respect, solutions that become the language of your long-term partnership, commitment, being a true subject matter expert, and imagination. The key is to proactively provide answers to questions and issues they are unaware of. Go beyond great customer service. Be a provider of true value. Lastly, authentically make customers feel good about themselves when you're around. To deliver these qualities to your customers, it requires an endless supply of positive energy within yourself. Manufacturing energy comes from executing the correct plan. Your customers will welcome you into their business life and be very happy that you are their partner.

WRIGHT

What is the key for individuals to create a road map to their success?

DAVID

I believe the first step is the inside game—get your mind right. Create the mind-set of a franchise player, taking 100 percent responsibility and ownership for your performance. Don't wait for others to tell you how to be successful. Assume the mind-set of self-coaching and self-accountability. Again, I say *No one is coming*—it's all up to you and you can do it! Accept that the key to success is structure and discipline. In all areas of success, it always starts with an internal vision and a plan. The plan will manifest your vision into reality. The bottom line is focus, discipline, and determination. Learn to give up control to gain control.

Lastly, write and review daily affirmations of what you want to achieve. Program your conscious and subconscious thoughts to deliver the actions to achieve your desired future state, which is your vision. By doing so, you will pull success to you like a magnet.

WRIGHT

Do you see any trends within this area of goal achievement?

DAVID

I do. I have studied high performers for more than twenty-five years and the same holds true in good times and bad. The key to success is doing the basics brilliantly. High performers in any area of life possess the keen sense of structure and discipline, which is the most difficult part of achieving any goal. It's just like going to the gym. You can want to work out, talk about working out, and think about working out all day long and all night. But if you don't pack your bag the night before and go to the gym three to five times a week, the goals you desire to achieve will not manifest. It's the structure, discipline, and consistency that are most difficult in regard to achieving the goals you desire. Once again, a plan or road map helps you stay on track.

My career has been dedicated to helping people build a road map to achieve their dreams. That's why I've designed productivity tools that make structure, discipline, and consistency much easier. I designed them so individuals can easily fill in the blanks, review, and modify on a monthly basis.

I see the same old ways of accomplishing more by working harder isn't effective. People are trying to outwork their work and it can't be done. There is just too much work as a byproduct of the last economic hit we all took in 2008. Now, most organizations are running flatter than ever. There are new basics that must be performed brilliantly for goal achievement, such as less is more, get rid of the mind clutter, increased imagination is mandatory, performing in the present moment of now, taking time to build your internal security/confidence, and belief/knowing. The key is using less of your academic brain and more of your heart brain to feel your way to success.

WRIGHT

You said the mind-set is the first step to building a road map. What's the next critical step to take?

DAVID

As I mentioned before, high performers execute the basics brilliantly, day in and day out. When you think of creating a road map for success, it boils down to the basics of goal planning.

7 Basic Steps to Goal Planning

1. **Define Your Life Goals**—Understand and identify what you want to achieve in your lifetime. You must know and define your life's purpose.

2. **Create a Vision for the Year**—Define what you would like to achieve by year-end. What is your desired future state? Describe your vision with as much detail as possible. Imagine it has already happened and you feel it within yourself (access your heart brain).

3. **Identify Goals**—Identify your Personal and Business Goals for the year that will lead to achieving your vision.

4. **Top 20 Percent Areas of Focus**—Use your Top 20 percent areas of focus to guide you and keep you on track. Define the areas where you need to focus the majority of your time to generate maximum results and avoid activity traps.

5. **Create a *Real* Job Description**—Include daily activities that keep you on track to achieving your vision. This is where the rubber meets the road. These are specific actions you need to take on a daily basis to ensure your success.

6. **Map out Monthly Goals and Milestones**—Map out the key milestones in your plan over a revolving twelve-month period.

7. **Monthly self-coaching**—Be your own coach and keep sharpening the saw. Consider yourself a constant work in progress. Just like painting a bridge, once you complete it, you have to start all over again.

These seven steps will create the blueprint for your road map to building a successful life, no matter what your goal is. Let your life unfold in front of you. Just relax and proactively create a plan. By being a control freak, you will only achieve a certain height of success. By trying to control everything in your life, you create blind spots you swear do not exist. Yet, your life will severely lack in these areas and the sad part is you just won't know it. Because you are blind to it, you simply go through the motions of living a successful life.

Within these seven steps of planning, successful people have learned to quiet their mind, their body, and their spirit. They have learned to slow down to get ahead. It only takes moments. They have learned to listen to the internal messages being sent to them regarding the correct actions to take each moment. This is where one's belief in self is so important. The seven steps must be in alignment with your belief in yourself. This will make your life fulfilling, happy, and abundant. These seven steps help you stay in touch with releasing your total human potential that has no limits. Your full-time job is to bring out more of you every day. From what I have seen, the world will reward you for this act of self-respect. The world is waiting to receive your many unique gifts.

Implement these seven basic steps to help you achieve your life goals and yearly goals. So how do you stay on track every day? Most people write out a plan for the year and they file it in their desk drawer and review it quarterly, if they're really good. Here's a system to maximize each day in connection with your overall goals. I say this to my clients every day: "Your today is your future." It's true—you have to align today with your future every day. This system will definitely make anyone's life robust, rich, and filled with abundance. Here is how it works:

4 Steps to Connecting Your Today to Your Future

Step One: Each night, review your life goals, your vision, your goals for the year, your Top 20 percent areas of focus, your job description, and your monthly milestones.

Step Two: Review your schedule for the next day. Ask yourself, "What do I expect to accomplish tomorrow?" Write a series of affirmations that align with these outcomes and goals you desire. Affirmations help you claim what you desire and pull these outcomes to you like a magnet.

Step Three: Identify what prep work needs to be accomplished to achieve these items. Preparation always increases your confidence and strengthens your belief system.

Step Four: Create an Achieve List. Write down your number one most important outcome that must be accomplished for the next day. Once this is accomplished, you can then move on to your next four and five daily goals.

This Achieve List replaces cumbersome to-do lists. Now you are ready for tomorrow. You are focused and aligned with your goals. You are also filled with confidence because you are prepared!

Once tomorrow is here, I want you to imagine and implement the following:

- Imagine that you are surrounded by a bubble, the *Bubble of Now*. You are living and performing in the now with all of this focused attention that is critical to your success. The bubble is keeping you highly conscious and present all day long. It's like having a shadow. It's with you all the time, you just can't see it.
- Bring your plan of execution into the *Bubble of Now*.
- Be awake in the now tapping into your five senses. See your success, hear your success, smell your success, taste your success, and touch your success. This accelerates the manifestation process of your goals.
- At the same time, accept what is the truth of the moment.
- As you are awake in the now, using your five senses in a state of acceptance you will understand the truth of any given situation
- Now listen to your IVOR—Internal Voice of Reason. It acts as an internal compass that identifies your feelings, attitudes, and actions

This information in the present moment of now will allow you to have the correct reaction to the environment you are in, which means your decision-making capabilities will be heightened. Your *Bubble of Now* will act as a magnet to pull to you all that you claimed the night before in your affirmations. By using all this structure and discipline in the moment of now, you *will* create a successful life.

Life is energy in motion. Your job is to produce the highest proactive energy for each moment of your life. That's why you must be 100 percent present and effortlessly be in a fluid, high energy state. When you're in the past or the future, you will most likely be producing negative energy. Live and perform in the now. It will produce positive energy. Life is also an energy boomerang—whatever energy you are sending out from within your *Bubble of Now* you will bring the same back into your life. Positive energy out, positive life back. Negative energy out, negative life back. Therefore, success doesn't just happen—you pull it to you. I'll say it again, *No one is coming* to make your life a success. Yes, you will have support along the way, but the ultimate responsibility is yours. This is the exciting part! It's all in your hands. It's all up to you to use this information to manifest the life you want. I hope individuals are empowered to implement this information. It really works!

WRIGHT

Mark, dive deeper into your seven steps to create a road map for success. I'd like to understand further why you feel these seven elements are needed when creating a road map for success.

DAVID

As I mentioned before, it's the structure and discipline that is the difficult part of achieving any goal. For many years, my clients have been implementing my productivity tool called the Personal Business Plan to help them create a road map to their success. Successful people use their well-defined plans to create greater energy levels. Energy is the key resource you need to be successful. The greater the energy you produce, the greater your success will be. The second benefit that the plan will give you is the capacity to see the truth of your life clearly and accurately.

All of our lives are the sum total of the decisions we make. We make decisions based on data we comprehend. Therefore, understanding the truth is directly connected to your decision-making ability. Seeing the truth of the matter sky rockets your decision-making effectiveness.

The third benefit of having a correct plan in place is that it will help you develop your value of who you are, what you do, and how you do it. Your worth to the world is equal to what you are contributing to this world. Your job is to keep increasing your value in the form of your capabilities, habits, and disciplines. I promise that the world will reflect back to you with abundance.

The first part of the road map is important because people do things for their reasons, not yours. The first part of the plan is creating a vision. Visioning includes defining your life goals. *What do you want to accomplish in the next five to ten to twenty years?* It should include both personal and business goals. Examples would include career achievements, family vacations, college for the children, retirement, homes, cars, family activities, weddings, graduations, and most importantly, defining and living your life purpose. These goals represent great energy reserves for you because your job/career funds your dreams. Tap into this energy by simply reviewing your life goals. These goals are the specific reasons why you work so hard. They will fuel your desire to succeed every day. It is very easy to lose sight of your goals and get lost in the weeds if you don't review them on a consistent basis.

Yearly goals and vision—I recommend you think and plan one year in advance. Define what you want to achieve by December 31 of each year in both your personal and business life. List your top five personal and business goals. Be specific and assign deadlines. Then develop your vision statement based on these goals. Your vision statement describes your desired future state using your five senses. Make it alive within you. By the end of the year, what does your world look like? What do you see, hear, taste, smell, and touch by year end? The key is to feel it—just like you feel the love of your family, dear friends, or your pets! Without any doubt, you feel it! This will act as a catalyst to manifest your vision and yearly goals into becoming your reality. Truly get your emotions working overtime for the manifestation process.

The second part of the plan is all about focus, execution, and self-coaching. Your Top 20 percent areas of focus are founded upon Pareto's 80/20 rule—twenty percent of what you do produces 80 percent of your results. Your Top 20 percent is your strategy to stay focused on your plan to achieve your vision and yearly goals. It defines the most important responsibilities and actions that are in direct alignment to achieving your goals in the quickest, most efficient time possible. You need to identify these areas of focus so that you minimize the amount of time you are pulled off track. A mental alarm should ring when you are not executing your Top 20 Percent. It should keep you *awake* and conscious throughout your day. Discipline! Discipline! Discipline!

For example, if you spend the majority of your time in the following areas you will remain focused and on track to achieving your goals. Some Top 20 percent examples are:

1. Family Time
2. Personal time
3. Strategic thinking and planning
4. Leadership
5. Coaching
6. Work out time
7. Key administrative duties, such as mandatory reports that have to get done to maintain your position
8. Customer meetings
9. Research
10. Client meetings
11. Growing and developing your team

Remember: what gets written gets done. If you don't plan it and write it into your schedule, you most likely will not accomplish it. The world is moving so fast it will pull you off track quickly and unexpectedly. You need to have a touchstone.

Next is your job description that must be in alignment with your Top 20 percent. Once you establish your Top 20 percent areas of focus, take each one and create a list of activities you need to execute on a daily basis to stay focused in these areas that bring you the greatest results. Your job description is where the rubber meets the road. You have taken your vision and narrowed it down to areas of focus and now daily activities that will ensure your success. Everything is in alignment. It's as simple as actions equaling results.

Mapping out your monthly goals and milestones is next. Look at the year as a twelve-month revolving process. If you do so, you can move yourself into a completely proactive state of planning and strategizing to dictate the outcomes you desire. Map out your milestones for the year by doing the following: Look at your next month and identify the single most important outcome you need to accomplish. Once you accomplish this item, identify the next four outcomes you need to accomplish. If you accomplish these items, identify the next five outcomes you need to accomplish. Don't go into each month with an unrealistic list of twenty items that will never be accomplished. Be fanatically focused on your most important outcomes. Once accomplished, you can always add more. This is the exact same concept we discussed for your preplanning the night before. Create an Achieve List for each month as well.

Most of the time I go into each month with a list of five or less outcomes that must be accomplished because they're in direct alignment with accomplishing my vision and life goals. At the same time, I'm looking out over the next twelve months, putting milestones down that need to be accomplished by specific dates. I also map out my vacations, educational workshops, specific report deadlines, and very important upcoming meetings. By writing them down every month, it gives me a quick idea of what I need to accomplish and what I need to proactively prepare for. This type of "futuring" process allows me to stay ahead of my work. It also shows me what my life will look like throughout the next twelve months. This provides me with a sense of control, confidence, and belief that I can do it because I've mapped it out.

Lastly, self-coaching on a monthly basis is critical. Remember *No one is coming*. No one is coming to help you, coach you, lead you, or manage you. Don't wait for someone else to tell you how to improve or what adjustments you need to make to achieve your goals. Take on the responsibility of self-accountability. Successful individuals self-coach in the following areas of their behavior on a consistent monthly basis: adjustments needed, their strengths, their opportunities for growth, and big ideas. A successful life is filled with many timely adjustments to be made. Your ability to self-coach by reviewing your vision, your goals, your Top 20 percent areas of focus, and your job description will move you closer to your desired future state quickly and efficiently. You have to know yourself well enough to make the correct adjustments. If you were your own boss, what would you tell yourself to do to stay on track?

I recommend that you take a few moments each month to self-coach. Simply analyze your behavior and performance before moving into the next month. You can do so by asking yourself the following five questions.

5 Monthly Self-Coaching Questions

1. **What activities, behaviors, do I need to stop performing?** These behaviors are like eating white bread—they have very little value. Examples include: Meetings that don't belong in your day-to-day activities because they are a waste of time. Individual relationships that are holding you back. Relationships that drain your time or where you shouldn't be investing time. Habits that are wasting your energy reserves. What should you stop doing now?

2. **What behavioral strengths stand out?** What behaviors did I execute really well last month that had a great impact on my success? How can I leverage that behavior?

3. **What opportunities for growth would I like to improve?** These behaviors keep you in a constant state of professional development and increase your value month after month.

4. **What behavioral adjustments do I need to make going into next month?** This is a huge lever for success. Making the correct adjustments to your behavior on a monthly basis will move you into the top 1 percent of high performers. Again, to do this right you have to slow down to get ahead. Take a few moments each month to see the truth of your performance. Therefore, you must accept what is, then

unemotionally decide whether you will leverage a strength or shore up an opportunity for growth. Making the correct adjustments month in and month out is the key for creating higher energy levels. The correct adjustments help you perform the correct actions with fluidity versus running into obstacle after obstacle that you have created or are facing.

5. **What is my big idea for the month?** What idea will increase your overall success? This question will help you tap into your imagination, creativity, and innovation. When you recognize a big idea each month you once again increase your energy levels, your confidence level, your belief in yourself, and your overall sense of value to the organization. Sometimes the simplest idea makes the biggest impact on your overall success. This question gets you in the habit of coming up with ideas to make each month more and more spectacular.

As you come up with new ideas and execute them month in and month out, your life keeps on getting better. Let these self-coaching questions help you manifest the life you desire; by doing so I promise many good things will come your way.

WRIGHT

So this type of road map does seem simple for any type of professional to use. How else can this approach benefit an individual or company?

DAVID

Great question. As I said, *"No one is coming..."* to save the day. Everyone must take ownership of their success. This type of road map will make it simple. Individuals can use this type of road map, whether they are managers, call center professionals, customer service agents, sales professionals, administrative assistants, CEOs, or engineers. The basics hold true for everyone. The beauty of this type of road map, from a management perspective, is that it makes coaching easy. As a manager I can see how my team players are thinking and going about their day. This process brings forth real-time data to coach in a more effective and meaningful manner. It becomes a communication tool.

As an employee, you can easily communicate your approach to achieve your desired outcomes. You can easily communicate where you are according to plan. It builds a proactive culture and language to achieve your goals. If everyone is running on the same page achieving what is important to him or her and is in alignment with what the company needs, the road map becomes the vehicle to his or her success. You then create loyal, hardworking individuals who want to do well for the company because you've taught them how to achieve their dreams.

By having a long-range plan that is implemented in the present moment of now, you have an excellent opportunity to create and live the life you want. All the structure and discipline of planning and being in the present moment of now will allow you to be more of you each day. That's the key to living a successful life. First, knowing who you are and the essence of why you're on this planet, then bringing your authentic self into this three-dimensional world and sharing your many gifts. By connecting a lifetime of moments together in alignment with who you are creates success. To say I was born and I lived the life I was supposed to live is something that most people cannot say. The majority of people live a life of quiet desperation, feeling unfulfilled, stressed, fearful, empty, and anxious. They can't shake the feeling that something is missing.

This is what I especially see in workaholics. They think they can bury themselves in their work, yet their work is creating a barrier that prevents them from looking inside themselves and truly connecting with their families.

Therefore, to help individuals to avoid this, I created a tool called *The Personal Business Plan ~ Your Roadmap for Success*. It leads you inside yourself and guides you through, creating a set of life goals, defining business and personal goals for the year, creating a vision of your desired future state, and identifying your Top 20 percent areas of focus. It helps you create a real job description, outlining daily actions you need to take to make your vision a reality. It then helps you develop a twelve-month revolving plan that proactively outlines your priorities and milestones, with self-coaching each month to stay on track. This creates an easy road map to follow to manifest a balanced and successful life.

This road map aligns your inner world with your outer world and they work in concert to maximize your success. The road map I described will give you the plan of action you need to make your dreams come true. Please, if you have read this chapter and it makes sense, then hear this battle cry: *Wake Up!* For those of you who want to live life to its fullest versus simply going through the motions, move out of your comfort zone and fight to live a highly proactive and energetic life; it can be done with a very simple process of deliberate consciousness. Since *No one is coming* and your results are completely in your hands, I encourage you to create a road map leading you to your success; you are worth it!

WRIGHT

Mark, this has been an outstanding conversation. Thank you for your time discussing this important topic with me today. I have learned a lot from what you said and I know our readers will also.

DAVID

Well, David, I appreciate your time so much. Everything we talked about today is a matter of making an internal decision regarding what you want in life. So many of my clients come to me and they know something's missing. Everything I've talked about today helps individuals get in touch with the internal essence of who they are, providing them with a feeling of expanding abundance, joy, and daily contentment. I know the readers who have been searching for answers are smiling now. Best of times to everyone.

WRIGHT

Today I have been talking with Mark David. Mark combines his talent as a successful turnaround expert and his passion for releasing total human potential to create a boutique training company. He specializes in providing field-tested strategies to help today's professionals thrive in challenging economic times. Mark is the author of *Coaching Illustrated, The Self-Manager's Success Journal, The Personal Business Plan ~ Your Roadmap to Success,* and other unique productivity tools in the areas of sales, goal planning, self-coaching, and leadership.

Mark, thank you so much for being with us today on *ROADMAP to Success.*

DAVID

Thank you, David, for having me.

Mark David founded *The Mark David Corporation* in 1987. Mark combined his talent as a successful turn-around expert and his passion for releasing total human potential to create a boutique training company. With his keen ability to uncover productivity road blocks and build high-performing teams, Mark develops customized training programs targeting specific business challenges.

As a natural born coach, Mark has guided front-line employees to entrepreneurs to CEOs to increased performance and profit through his practical and human approach to success. Mark specializes in providing field-tested strategies to help today's professionals thrive in challenging economic times. Mark spends most of his time as a performance coach inspiring individuals to move through challenges to not only achieve but exceed their goals.

Mark is the author of *Coaching Illustrated*, *The Self-Manager Success Journal*, *The Personal Business Plan ~ Your Roadmap to Success*, and other unique productivity tools in the areas of sales, goal planning, self-coaching, and leadership.

Mark David

The Mark David Corporation
23 Kelton Court
San Mateo, CA 94403
650-341-6504
mark@markdavid.com
www.markdavid.com

CHAPTER TWO

Discover Your Inner Resource
Dr. Deepak Chopra

DAVID E. WRIGHT (WRIGHT)

Today I am talking to Dr. Deepak Chopra, founder of the Chopra Center for Wellbeing in Carlsbad, California. Dr. Chopra is the foremost pioneer in integrated medicine. His insights have redefined our definition of health to embrace body, mind, and spirit. His books, which include, *Quantum Healing, Perfect Health, Ageless Body Timeless Mind*, and *The Seven Spiritual Laws of Success*, have become international bestsellers and are established classics.

Dr. Chopra, welcome to *Roadmap to Success*.

DR. DEEPAK CHOPRA (CHOPRA)

Thank you. How are you?

WRIGHT

I am doing just fine. It's great weather here in Tennessee.

CHOPRA

Great.

WRIGHT

Dr. Chopra, you stated in your book, *Grow Younger, Live Longer: 10 Steps to Reverse Aging,* that it is possible to reset your biostats up to fifteen years younger than your chronological age. Is that really possible?

CHOPRA

Yes. There are several examples of this. The literature on aging really began to become interesting in the 1980s when people showed that it was possible to reverse the biological marks of aging. This included things like blood pressure, bone density, body temperature, regulation of the metabolic rate, and other things like cardiovascular conditioning, cholesterol levels, muscle mass and strength of muscles, and even things like hearing, vision, sex hormone levels, and immune function.

One of the things that came out of those studies was that psychological age had a great influence on biological age. So you have three kinds of aging: chronological age is when you were born, biological age is what your biomarker shows, and psychological age is what your biostat says.

WRIGHT

You call our prior conditioning a prison. What do you mean?

CHOPRA

We have certain expectations about the aging process. Women expect to become menopausal in their early forties. People think they should retire at the age of sixty-five and then go Florida and spend the rest of their life in so-called retirement. These expectations actually influence the very biology of aging. What we call normal aging is actually the hypnosis of our social conditioning. If you can bypass that social conditioning, then you're free to reset your own biological clock.

WRIGHT

Everyone told me that I was supposed to retire at sixty-five. I'm somewhat older than that and as a matter of fact, today is my birthday.

CHOPRA

Well happy birthday. You know, the fact is that you should be having fun all the time and always feel youthful. You should always feel that you are contributing to society. It's not the retirement, but it's the passion with which you're involved in the wellbeing of your society, your community, or the world at large.

WRIGHT

Great things keep happening to me. I have two daughters; one was born when I was fifty. It has changed my life quite a bit. I feel a lot younger than my chronological age.

CHOPRA

The more you associate with young people, the more you will respond to that biological expression.

WRIGHT

Dr. Chopra, you suggest viewing our bodies from the perspective of quantum physics. That seems somewhat technical. Will you tell us a little bit more about that?

CHOPRA

You see, on one level, your body is made up of flesh and bone. That's the material level, but we know today that everything we consider matter is born of energy and information. By starting to think of our bodies as networks of energy information and even intelligence, we begin to shift our perspective. We don't think of our bodies so much as dense matter, but as vibrations of consciousness. Even though it sounds technical, everyone has had an experience with this so-called quantum body. After, for example, you do an intense workout, you feel a sense of energy in your body—a tingling sensation. You're actually experiencing what ancient wisdom traditions call the "vital force." The more you pay attention to this vital force inside your body, the more you will experience it as energy, information, and intelligence, and the more control you will have of its expressions.

WRIGHT

Does DNA have anything to do with that?

CHOPRA

DNA is the source of everything in our body. DNA is like the language that creates the molecules of our body. DNA is like a protein-making factory, but DNA doesn't give us the blueprint. When I build a house, I have to go to the factory to find the bricks, but having the bricks is not enough. I need to get an architect who, in his or her consciousness can create that blueprint. And that blueprint exists only in your spirit and consciousness—in your soul.

WRIGHT

I was interested in another statement from your book. You said that perceptions create reality. What perceptions must we change in order to reverse our biological image?

CHOPRA

You have to change three perceptions. First you have to get rid of the perceptions of aging itself. Most people believe that aging means disease and infirmities. You have to change that. You have to regard aging as an opportunity for personal growth and spiritual growth. You also have to regard it as an opportunity to express the wisdom of your experience and an opportunity to help others and lift them from ordinary and mundane experience to the kind of experiences you are capable of because you have much more experience than they do.

The second thing you have to change your perception of is your physical body. You have to start to experience it as information and energy—as a network of information and intelligence.

The third thing you have to change your perception of is the experience of dying. If you are the kind of person who is constantly running out of time, you will continue to run out of time. On the other hand, if you have a lot of time, and if you do everything with gusto and love and passion, then you will lose track of time. When you lose track of time, your body does not metabolize that experience.

WRIGHT

That is interesting. People who teach time management don't really teach the passion.

CHOPRA

No, no. Time management is such a restriction of time. Your biological clock starts to age much more rapidly. I think what you have to really do is live your life with passion so that time doesn't mean anything to you.

WRIGHT

That's a concept I've never heard.

CHOPRA

Well, there you are.

WRIGHT

You spend an entire chapter of your book on deep rest as an important part of the reversal of the aging process. What is "deep rest"?

CHOPRA

One of the most important mechanisms for renewal and survival is sleep. If you deprive an animal of sleep, then it ages very fast and dies prematurely. We live in a culture where most of our population has to resort to sleeping pills and tranquilizers in order to sleep. That doesn't bring natural rejuvenation and renewal. You know that you have had a good night's sleep when you wake up in the morning, feeling renewed, invigorated, and refreshed—like a baby does. So that's one kind of deep rest. That comes from deep sleep and from natural sleep. In the book I talk about how you go about making sure you get that.

The second deep rest comes from the experience of meditation, which is the ability to quiet your mind so you still your internal dialogue. When your internal dialogue is still, then you enter into a stage of deep rest. When your mind is agitated, your body is unable to rest.

WRIGHT

I have always heard of people who had bad eyesight and didn't realize it until they went to the doctor and were fitted for lenses. I had that same experience some years ago. For several years I had not really enjoyed the deep sleep you're talking about. The doctor diagnosed me with sleep apnea. Now I sleep like a baby, and it makes a tremendous difference.

CHOPRA

Of course it does. You now have energy and the ability to concentrate and do things.

WRIGHT

Dr. Chopra, how much do eating habits have to do with aging? Can we change and reverse our biological age by what we eat?

CHOPRA

Yes, you can. One of the most important things to remember is that certain types of foods actually contain anti-aging compounds. There are many chemicals that are contained in certain foods that have an anti-aging effect. Most of these chemicals are derived from light. There's no way to bottle them—there are no pills you can take that will give you these chemicals. But they're contained in plants that are rich in color and derived from photosynthesis. Anything that is yellow, green, and red or has a lot of color, such as fruits and vegetables, contain a lot of these very powerful anti-aging chemicals.

In addition, you have to be careful not to put food in your body that is dead or has no life energy. So anything that comes in a can or has a label, qualifies for that. You have to expose your body to six tastes: sweet, sour, salt, bitter, pungent, and astringent because those are the codes of intelligence that allow us to access the deep intelligence of nature. Nature and what she gives to us in bounty is actually experienced through the sense of taste. In fact, the light chemicals—the anti-aging substances in food—create the six tastes.

WRIGHT

Some time ago, I was talking to one of the ladies in your office and she sent me an invitation to a symposium that you had in California. I was really interested. The title was *Exploring the Reality of Soul.*

CHOPRA

Well, I conducted the symposium, but we had some of the world's scientists, physicists, and biologists who were doing research in what is called, non-local intelligence—the intelligence of soul or spirit. You could say it is the intelligence that orchestrates the activity of the universe—God, for example. Science and spirituality are now meeting together because by understanding how nature works and how the laws of nature work, we're beginning to get a glimpse of a deeper intelligence that people in spiritual traditions call divine, or God. I think this is a wonderful time to explore spirituality through science.

WRIGHT

She also sent me biographical information of the seven scientists who were with you. I have never read a list of seven more noted people in their industry.

CHOPRA

They are. The director of the Max Planck Institute in Berlin, Germany, where quantum physics was discovered was there. Dr. Grossam was a professor of physics at the University of Oregon, and he talked about the quantum creativity of death and the survival of consciousness after death. It was an extraordinary group of people.

WRIGHT

Dr. Chopra, with this book we're trying to encourage people to be better, live better, and be more fulfilled by reading the examples given by our guest authors.

Is there anything or anyone in your life who has made a difference for you and has helped you to become a better person?

CHOPRA

The most important person in my life was my father. Every day he asked himself, "What can I do in thought, word, and deed to nurture every relationship I encounter just for today?" That has lived with me for my entire life.

WRIGHT

What do you think makes up a great mentor? Are there characteristics mentors seem to have in common?

CHOPRA

I think the most important attribute of a great mentor is that he or she teaches by example and not necessarily through words.

WRIGHT

When you consider the choices you've made down through the years, has faith played an important role?

CHOPRA

I think more than faith, curiosity, wonder, a sense of reference, and humility have. Now, if you want to call that faith, then, yes it has.

WRIGHT

In a divine being?

CHOPRA

In a greater intelligence—intelligence that is supreme, infinite, unbounded, and too mysterious for the finite mind to comprehend.

WRIGHT

If you could have a platform and tell our audience something you feel would help them and encourage them, what would you say?

CHOPRA

I would say that there are many techniques that come to us from ancient wisdom and tradition that allow us to tap into our inner resources and allow us to become beings who have intuition, creativity, vision, and a connection to that which is sacred. Finding that within ourselves, we have the means to enhance our wellbeing. Whether it's physical, emotional, or environmental, we have the means to resolve conflicts and get rid of war. We have the means to be really healthy. We have the means for being economically uplifted. That knowledge is the most important knowledge that exists.

WRIGHT

I have seen you on several primetime television shows down through the years where you have had the time to explain your theories and beliefs. How does someone like me experience this? Do we get it out of books?

CHOPRA

Books are tools that offer you a road map. Sit down every day, close your eyes, put your attention in your heart, and ask yourself two questions: who am I and what do I want? Then maintain a short period of stillness in body and mind as in prayer or meditation, and the door will open.

WRIGHT

So, you think that the intelligence comes from within. Do all of us have that capacity?

CHOPRA

Every child born has that capacity.

WRIGHT

That's fascinating. So, it doesn't take trickery or anything like that?

CHOPRA

No, it says in the Bible in the book of Psalms, *"Be still and know that I am God"*—Psalm 46:10.

WRIGHT

That's great advice.

I really do appreciate your being with us today. What you say is fascinating. I wish I could talk with you for the rest of the afternoon. I'm certain I am one of millions who would like to do that!

CHOPRA

Thank you, sir. It was a pleasure to talk with you!

WRIGHT

Today I have been talking with Dr. Deepak Chopra, founder of The Chopra Center for Wellbeing. He has become the foremost pioneer in integrated medicine. We have found today that he really knows what he's talking about. After reading his book, *Grow Younger, Live Longer: 10 Steps to Reverse Aging,* I can tell you that I highly recommend looking into what he has to say. I certainly hope you'll go out to your favorite book store and buy a copy of that book.

Dr. Chopra, thank you so much for being with us today.

CHOPRA

Thank you for having me, David.

Deepak Chopra, M.D is the author of more than sixty-five books, including many *New York Times* bestsellers. His medical training is in internal medicine and endocrinology, and he is a Fellow of the American College of Physicians, a member of the American Association of Clinical Endocrinologists, and an adjunct professor of Executive Programs at the Kellogg School of Management at Northwestern University. He is also a Distinguished Executive Scholar at Columbia Business School, Columbia University, and a Senior Scientist at the Gallup organization. For more than a decade, he has participated as a lecturer at the Update in Internal Medicine, an annual event sponsored by Harvard Medical School's Department of Continuing Education and the Department of Medicine, Beth Israel Deaconess Medical Center.

Dr. Deepak Chopra

The Chopra Center
2013 Costa del Mar Rd.
Carlsbad, CA 92009
info@chopra.com
www.chopra.com

CHAPTER THREE

The Entrepreneurial Way to Leverage ADHD to Your ADDvantage...
Dr. Billi Bittan

DAVID WRIGHT (WRIGHT)

Today I am talking with Dr. Billi Bittan. Dr. Billi is a Neuro-Cognitive Behavioral Therapist and Coach specializing in ADHD, learning disabilities, and memory disorders. She developed the AttentionB™ Method using a rare combination of expressive art therapy, co-active coaching, and pedagogy. Dr. Billi holds a PhD in Education, MA in Expressive Art Therapy, and BA in Physical Education and Teaching. A certified Co-active Life/ADHD Coach, she is licensed in Mediation/Conflict Resolution and Academic Management, and she has lectured all over the world at conferences, seminars, and universities. With more than thirty-five years of experience, she has worked hands-on with entrepreneurs, executives, creative business people, and their teams/employees, connecting with them individually, understanding their distinct needs, and customizing a strategy that transforms their unique ADHD impairments into valuable assets that they can leverage to their ADDvantage.

Dr. Billi, welcome to *ROADMAP to Success*.

Will you give a brief overview of what ADHD and executive functions are?

DR. BILLI BITTAN (BITTAN)

ADHD is a neurobiological condition that affects executive functions in the brain. Executive functions are brain processes—they can essentially be considered the brain's management system. They help you make decisions, have a sense of time, recall past or foresee future events, regulate emotions, inhibit responses, and stay motivated. These functions are interconnected—they work in conjunction with each other to help you choose goals and sustain action toward reaching those goals. If one executive function is off balance, it can throw the other executive functions off.

I really like how Dr. Thomas Brown, a notable expert on ADHD, explains it. He suggests thinking of executive functions like an orchestra. All of the musicians are great performers with individual parts, but they also have to play a concert together as a group. If one instrument is out of tune, or one note is played out of key, the entire harmony is affected. It's the same principle with executive functions.

If you have ADHD, the chemicals in your brain function differently than most people. Here is a *very brief* overview of what's happening in the brain. Dopamine, a key neurotransmitter in the frontal lobe that regulates mood and generates a sense of reward and motivation, is found in reduced levels. As well, norepinephrine, another key neurotransmitter in the brain that helps you focus, is found in lowered levels. Due to these reduced amounts of dopamine and norepinephrine, the transporters and receptors in the pre-frontal cortex fire slower than usual, resulting in inadequate stimulation, which in turn impairs your executive function processes.

Because your executive functions are impaired, you may struggle with issues like impulsivity, hyperactivity, inattention, disorganization, procrastination, and poor time management. For entrepreneurs, these executive function impairments can affect areas of your business in the form of poor money management, chronic lateness, strained professional relationships, and falling behind in tasks, just to name a few.

It is important to understand, however, that ADHD affects individuals differently—it is not a generalized, cookie-cutter condition. Symptoms are specific to the individual. For example, one person may struggle with inattention but have no problems with hyperactivity, whereas another person may struggle with hyperactivity but not impulsivity. That is why it is crucial for professionals who have ADHD, and perhaps even more so for all of you entrepreneurs, to understand the nuance and unique combination of your executive function impairments, in addition to your positive ADHD traits, so you can devise a system and choose strategies that work for you personally.

Once you understand how you are affected by ADHD as an individual and develop a personalized road map to success, you can begin to work toward successfully managing ADHD.

One last thing: so much material is focused on the negative aspects of ADHD, but I believe that a positive outlook is one of the keys to living successfully with it and finding success as an entrepreneur. That's why this chapter will focus on the various attributes that ADHD can bestow upon entrepreneurs and how ADHD can be leveraged to your ADDvantage.

WRIGHT

What are some of the common executive function impairments?

BITTAN

Many entrepreneurs with ADHD struggle with issues like poor time management, procrastination, staying on task, impulsive decision-making, lack of organization, and hyper-focus. For this reason, working in corporate jobs can be challenging—there is a lot of pressure to conform to the workflows of others.

Because of this, many of you may have experienced falling behind in your work, getting written up for being late or missing deadlines, receiving poor performance evaluations, or even worse, being fired. This is why it's no surprise that *Fortune* magazine stated people with ADHD are three hundred times more likely to start their own business. Working for yourself offers you greater latitude to set your own pace and create your own personal workflow.

This is why I developed the LEVERAGE ADHD system. I want to help you be proactive in creating a personal system that addresses your individual needs and allows you to leverage your ADHD attributes to your fullest advantage.

WRIGHT

What is the LEVERAGE ADHD system, and how can entrepreneurs with ADHD leverage it to their ADDvantage?

BITTAN

My knowledge and experience shows that ADHD can be a tremendous asset to entrepreneurs, once you learn how to leverage it. Leveraging your ADHD is an individualized system that emphasizes eight key stages. The eight stages in the LEVERAGE ADHD system are: *Learn, Evaluate, Validate, Express, Reframe, Act, Grow, Explore.*

In order to work successfully with ADHD, you must develop a workflow that's personally tailored to suit your needs—one that enhances your strengths and interests and compensates for your weaknesses so they will be less impairing. Even the sky is not the limit—thanks to innovator Richard Branson, there really are no limits for entrepreneurs with ADHD. However, you need to remember that leveraging ADHD is a *process*, and it takes work and dedication. What I created in my own work with the AttentionB Method was so interesting and fun to me that it didn't feel like work at all. I continue to approach my business with a sense of joy and play, which really motivates me. By loving what I do, I am inspired to work hard. And by using my unique interests (my urge to help and teach others how to get results that change their lives) and channeling my ADHD strengths (my energy and creativity), I can leverage ADHD to work in my advantage.

This is what the LEVERAGE ADHD system is all about—understanding the neurological, cognitive, and emotional aspects of ADHD that affect your performance and behavior as an entrepreneur, and embracing your unique set of assets to get the results you want. This is how you can create your own personalized, individual-specific, and magnificent road map to success.

The road map below illustrates this *process* of successfully leveraging your ADHD. You'll notice that it's intentionally left open and flexible, as it's not meant to be an exact plan for everyone to follow the same way. It's meant to be tailored by you, depending on your personal ADHD strengths and impairments, and also on your own individual goals. It's also open so you can revisit the system anytime you need it, or want to re-examine or deepen your learning, reentering it at any one of the stages, to address any areas with which you're struggling or want to grow, be it work, home, school, relationships, or anything else.

Overall, the system is meant to shift your attitude about ADHD, get you to understand how uniquely your brain works, empower you to embrace your strengths, boost your self-confidence and self-efficacy, overcome your distorted self-image, and help you find your own motivation, sustain it, and take action so that you and your business can grow and prosper.

The LEVERAGE ADHD System: Learn, Evaluate, Validate, Express, Reframe, Act, Grow, Explore

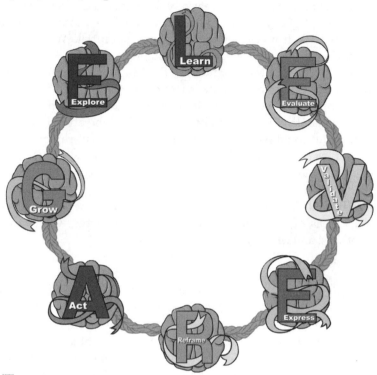

WRIGHT

Will you talk more in depth about each stage in the system?

BITTAN

Sure, here is a summary of each stage in the LEVERAGE ADHD system:

L: Learn

Learn about yourself and the unique combination of your ADHD. Know how your brain works and look at it from a positive perspective. Understand how ADHD affects the various realms of your life. How does it affect the way you work? How does the way you work affect others?

Educate yourself about the various types of ADHD. Get a formal assessment if you feel that you need it. Attend classes, support groups, training, and so on. Read books or listen to audio books about ADHD. Share your experiences in an online ADHD community, and listen to others who have shared similar struggles.

Knowledge is power. By learning more about ADHD and understanding how your brain works, you will be more equipped to take charge of your ADHD, instead of letting it take charge of your life or business. You will be in control.

E: Evaluate

Evaluate your own unique ADHD traits. Take an inventory of your personal strengths and weaknesses. In what areas of your business do you excel? What are your passions? What gets you excited and motivated? You also need to evaluate what holds you back from achieving your peak potential. What do you find frustrating, boring, or tedious? What makes you procrastinate?

This step is known as Metacognition—thinking about your own thinking. Essentially, it's like taking a bird's eye view of yourself—seeing yourself as an outside observer. Think of your ADHD in terms of cooking a recipe. If you already have all the ingredients at hand to make a carrot cake, why attempt to make a red velvet cake when it would require you to make a grocery list, run out to the store, and buy a lot of items you don't already have? It's the same with ADHD—you are the "carrot cake." Know what you already have to work with and learn how to use it.

By honestly and thoroughly evaluating yourself and the way you work, you can see what areas of your business need to be readjusted, what you need to delegate to others, and where you can focus on shining.

V: Validate

Validate yourself every day. How are you already successful? In what areas do you shine? People often get bogged down by the negative side of ADHD, feeling ashamed or inadequate because of it. So much energy is wasted by these negative emotions. Instead, embrace your attributes. See how valuable you really are. Practice daily affirmations or find a mantra that helps you keep a positive outlook. Hang up visual reminders like quotes or lyrics or an inspiring poem. Surround yourself and your workspace with uplifting material that makes you feel good about yourself. And be kind to yourself, too. When you succeed in reaching goals, big or small, reward yourself.

E: Express.

Express your emotions. How do you feel about yourself? What does having ADHD mean to you? Release your emotions in healthy ways. By this, I don't only mean unleashing your feelings without any brakes. There are creative techniques that can help you regulate your emotions and set emotional goals for yourself. One of the most effective emotional exercises that I use with my clients is expressive arts therapy. Dance out your frustration, paint away your pain, write down your thoughts in a poem or story, sing aloud how you feel, or create a metaphor for yourself. All of these are examples of how expressive arts can heal emotions, release negativity, or generate inspiration. I also incorporate a lot of goal-setting exercises into my expressive arts therapy, such as rewriting your life story in a positive way or visualizing your future. The key is to envision the happiest, healthiest version of yourself, and then map out the steps you need to take to get there.

Feeling inspired and confident about who you are is so important to getting and staying motivated about your business. Emotional expression and regulation through the arts serves as a healthy means of finding motivation. So don't hold in your emotions; express them—they are the motor for motivation.

R: Reframe

Reframe your attitude about ADHD; rephrase and restructure the way you see yourself. If you're constantly looking at ADHD as a prison sentence, it's going to feel like one. The only way to successfully leverage ADHD is to look at how you can work with it; that means looking on the bright side of it.

As an entrepreneur, there are many attributes of ADHD that can help you succeed. For example, hyper-focus (the intense concentration on one task) can be a tremendous asset to someone like a computer programmer. The key is to understand what your strengths are and to realize that you can make them work for your business.

A: Act

Act now. Set goals and take action, even if your goals are micro-goals. You have to start somewhere, so start small. Build up your confidence and accountability by rewarding yourself. Don't put off tasks because you don't like them, instead, hire others whose strengths complement your weaknesses.

Going back to the cooking metaphor, carrot cake and red velvet cake are two very different things, though some of their ingredients overlap such as butter, flour, and eggs. If you have everything to make a carrot cake, but want to make a red velvet cake, then you're going to need to gather the missing ingredients. It's the same principle with hiring others to fill in areas of your business where you're missing important ingredients.

Know that you must work your way, and not the way others think you should work. Be free to be yourself, even if that means making phone calls at the beach or at the park while riding a bike. As an entrepreneur, there is no rulebook for how you should work. If it works for you, it works. In the LEVERAGE ADHD system, you create your own rules and personal workflow for success.

G: Grow

Grow your business by growing yourself. By working through the previous stages, you will have an idea of your personal strengths and interests. These are areas of your business where you can blaze trails, such as brainstorming or sales, for example. You will also understand in what areas you need to delegate work to others, such as filing or invoicing. Many people with ADHD hesitate to delegate work because they don't have the patience to train others, or they need to control everything because they think they know best about how to do it all. By focusing on your areas of strength and hiring others to fill in for your weaknesses, you can build a successful and long-term business plan, which will help you grow your business successfully.

E: Explore

Explore your future and the future of your business. In what direction do you want to go? What is your vision? This is where you get to experiment, express, enjoy, energize, engage, and enhance your life and your business. You have completed all the groundwork to move toward the future with confidence. That means understanding your ADHD, knowing what your personal strengths and interests are, delegating tasks to others, embracing the positive side of ADHD, working the way you personally need to work, and setting goals for personal and professional growth. Remember, not even the sky is the limit, so don't let ADHD limit you; instead, leverage it.

WRIGHT

Part of the LEVERAGE ADHD system involves embracing the positive traits of ADHD. What are some of these positive traits that entrepreneurs with ADHD can leverage to their ADDvantage?

BITTAN

Though living with ADHD can certainly present individuals with its fair share of challenges, there are many positive traits associated with ADHD that are a natural fit for entrepreneurs that you can harness and use to your advantage.

For example, risk taking is one huge advantage for entrepreneurs. Many people never follow their dreams or take big risks because they are afraid of failing. People with ADHD, on the other hand, tend to not let fear hold them back as much. This stems from the executive function impairment of having a poor working memory. Some of you don't foresee the future or compare current events to the past before making big decisions. Because of this, you generally have a higher threshold for risk and take bigger leaps of faith, which is really what entrepreneurism is all about—risk big to win big.

Another positive trait ADHD offers entrepreneurs is having an independent spirit. Many of you tend to be renegades who march to the beat of your own drum. You aren't conformists by any means, but rather willing to explore creative paths and remain open to nontraditional ideas. A lot of you are visionaries. You aren't afraid of voicing original concepts, thinking outside of the box, or blazing trails. This is what gives you the dopamine rush and stimulates your enthusiasm. You'd get bored walking on the well-worn path and would much rather take the road less traveled, or even create a new road.

Creativity is yet another attribute of ADHD. This is why so many of you are artists, inventors, and pioneers. You tend to come up with original ideas and concepts, invent unforeseen products, and see things differently than most people. This trait is extremely advantageous for entrepreneurs who have ADHD, since the key to any successful entrepreneurial endeavor is innovation and originality.

Having a lot of energy is another great attribute that individuals with ADHD possess. When most people run out of gas, you are able to forge ahead and keep working until the job is done. This is a great asset for those of you who tend to wear many different hats within your business and have to shoulder the workload that most corporations could hire several people to do.

Hyper-focus can also be considered an asset for entrepreneurs. Some of you get hyper-focused on something that is interesting to you, so that it becomes more like fun and play than actual work. When this happens, you don't shift from one task to the next, but instead hone in on one single activity with great passion. If you are hyper-focused on something beneficial for your business, then it can result in great attention to detail and excellent quality of work.

As you can see, there are many aspects of ADHD that can be beneficial to you as an entrepreneur. Again, I want to emphasize that not every person with ADHD possesses all of these attributes, just as they don't all have the same exact impairments. Each person has a unique combination of ADHD traits. The key with the LEVERAGE ADHD system is to celebrate the unique combination of traits that make you great. For every negative trait you've been criticized about your entire life, there is a positive side to it. For example, perhaps you've been told that you're stubborn. The upside to being stubborn is that you are persistent and determined to achieve your goal.

Follow in the footsteps of other trailblazers and creative geniuses like Walt Disney, Leonardo da Vinci, Thomas Edison, or Albert Einstein. Recognize the valuable contribution you can make to society as a fellow innovator, renegade, and pioneer. And go out there and leverage your ADHD.

WRIGHT

Will you give an example of how you use the LEVERAGE ADHD system with clients and apply some of the stages to specific executive function impairments?

BITTAN

Many of my clients are entrepreneurs who have ADHD. They have a lot of talent, intelligence, and enthusiasm, but somehow they feel stuck in their professions—as if they're not achieving their full potential. We often go through the LEVERAGE ADHD system together to help them better manage their ADHD impairments and leverage their assets.

Here's an example of a client I have who is an attorney. He struggles a lot with procrastination, and as a result he misses a lot of deadlines, meetings, and so on. When he came to me, I could tell how frustrated he was with himself, and yet he was stuck in this cycle of procrastination and could not break it, which only fed his frustration levels even more. To help him learn how to manage his procrastination, I guided him through the LEVERAGE ADHD system.

First, we started with the *Evaluate stage*, in which I asked him to think about the effects of his procrastination. Specifically, I asked him what is the direct result of missing deadlines or client meetings? I told him to draw two circles and write inside one of them how procrastination affected his business, and inside the other how procrastination affected his personal life. Then we looked at his drawing together. His answer was that he lost money and respect whenever he missed client meetings, and he lost confidence whenever he missed deadlines. Because he evaluated and made a simple drawing of his procrastination, he had a measurable and relatable outcome of it. He understood what the direct consequences were of putting things off—it cost his business money and respect, and it cost him personally his confidence. I had him tape this drawing up where he could see it at work, as a visual reminder of the consequences of procrastinating.

As part of the *Evaluate stage*, we also considered what made him procrastinate. What generally distracted him from getting to a meeting on time or making a deadline? I asked him to close his eyes, visualize his day, and then take me through it with him. He was able to determine that his biggest distraction was surfing on the Internet, particularly on social media sites. He said he could spend hours on these sites without realizing it. So we made it a rule for him to log out of his social media sites on his computer and smart phone so he couldn't easily access them with the touch of a button throughout the day. We set a specific time at the end of the day for him to log into his social media accounts and browse for one hour.

We then turned to the *Express stage* to look at how his procrastination made him feel. He said it made him feel ashamed whenever he put things off for so long that he ended up missing deadlines or meetings. It also felt shameful to let others down. This shame then translated into frustration. We also considered how his procrastination affected others with whom he worked. He pointed out that they were constantly disappointed in him and frustrated as well. He realized that because others did not see him as an accountable person, he did not see himself as one either, and this is why he had stopped holding himself accountable.

Next, we turned to the *Reframe stage* to see what positive traits he had that we could work with to help manage his procrastination. He said that he was an auditory person and felt very motivated by music. So we looked at how we could apply music to his procrastination, a great example of how expressive arts can help people with ADHD. We chose his favorite song—the one that most motivated him to get up and move right away—and we set it as the ringtone for schedule reminders on his cell phone. Now, whenever he had a meeting to get to or a deadline to meet, that motivational song was set up (as a triple auditory reminder in increments of five minutes) to get him on his feet so that he wouldn't lose money, respect, or confidence, and so he wouldn't continue to feel ashamed and frustrated. The fact that it was a song that made him want to move really motivated him to take action rather than procrastinate.

You'll notice that we didn't follow the LEVERAGE ADHD stages in exact order, and we didn't have to work through every single one of them. For this particular situation, we only used what was necessary to address his specific impairment. This is why I intentionally leave the framework open for you to personalize so that you have the freedom to tailor it to your own needs. It's nonlinear on purpose, so you can start and stop at any point and re-enter it from any point whenever you need.

WRIGHT

The LEVERAGE ADHD system also highlights emotions as one area of importance in managing ADHD. How do emotions factor into successful ADHD management?

BITTAN

Building self-esteem and creating a positive emotional environment is an important step in the process of managing ADHD. There is a huge emotional impact on individuals who have ADHD. You have been told your whole life that you're doing things "the wrong way" and that you need to try harder. You've been pressured for so long to fit in, be more like everyone else, and do things "the right way." Since the time you were a child, it has been ingrained in you to not be your true self but to be more like others. As a result, you've resisted very real parts of yourself.

The emotional toll this negativity takes on you can be quite large, and in some cases, even paralyzing. It can leave many feeling inadequate, ashamed, or alienated. Even worse, it can hold you back from ever finding true success and happiness in your life.

In order to move forward in life, you have to feel good about yourself first. You must shift how you see and think about yourself. In order to do that, you must heal your wounded emotions and reframe your attitude about ADHD. Not only that, but you must also embrace your own personal strengths and interests. You need to realize that the same ADHD traits that held you back in your childhood can serve as huge assets in the entrepreneurial world.

These are the positive traits that I discussed earlier: creativity, energy, risk-taking, and independence. This is where the *Express* and *Reframe* stages of the LEVERAGE ADHD system come into play. By healing emotions and reframing your attitude about yourself and your ADHD, you can develop healthier and sustainable coping strategies.

One of the greatest emotional management tools I have used for more than twenty years with clients is expressive arts therapy. Expressive arts therapy is a well-established and thoroughly documented wing of psychology that naturally fits the traits of people with ADHD—visual, kinesthetic, and highly creative. The expressive arts give you a creative way to bypass all the excuses or explanations or apologies of your life circumstances and allow you to express hidden feelings and emotions.

Communicating your thoughts or feelings effectively can be frustrating if you have ADHD because sometimes your brain is racing too fast, or you simply can't find the right words or you don't have to the patience. This can end up with you feeling misunderstood and frustrated. Expressive arts therapy gives you a way to communicate in a language that's your own—one that's unbounded by rules or judgment, thereby bridging the communication gap. It can unlock the purest emotional states—ones you didn't even know were present. And these emotions act like an on/off switch for motivation.

Something simple like putting on an uplifting song can make you smile or even want to get up and conquer the world. Dancing and authentic movement can release stored up tension and energy. Drawing or creating a poem can inspire you and allow you to see yourself in a new light. Writing your own life narrative in a funny or touching story can be extremely therapeutic. I could go on and on about the benefits of expressive arts therapy for people with ADHD, as it is both my passion and area of expertise, but the most important thing to understand is that all of this is meant to heal emotions, build self-confidence, and boost motivation. And motivation, of course, is one of the keys to successfully managing ADHD.

Once you feel good about yourself, you start to value yourself more and develop a better self-esteem, thereby leading to greater self-efficacy. Self-efficacy is your belief that you are capable of performing an action toward attaining a goal. When your self-efficacy improves, you will be more motivated and inspired to make sustainable changes in your life that will lead to greater success and happiness. So emotions and the healing process factor very heavily into successful ADHD management, and one of the most effective tools that I have found for this is expressive arts therapy.

WRIGHT

How can a co-active ADHD coach help entrepreneurs with ADHD succeed?

BITTAN

Cognitive behavioral therapy, counseling, medication, and lifestyle changes are all viable solutions for managing ADHD, but I really believe that co-active coaching is one of the greatest resources available. Sometimes, despite the most sincere and earnest efforts, people with ADHD can still have difficulty with staying on task and managing their impairments.

For entrepreneurs, whose very success depends on themselves, co-active ADHD coaches can be invaluable in looking at issues objectively, giving constructive feedback, guiding you with difficult decisions and assisting with problem solving that is uniquely tailored to you. Co-active ADHD coaching generates external pressure (accountability) to help you stay on task and also generates internal pressure (motivation) that keeps you motivated to reach both long- and short-term goals for your business.

Since co-active coaching is a partnership, it is so important to find a co-active ADHD coach who utilizes strength and interest-based methods. The last thing you need is someone who is fixated on your impairments or constantly telling you how to overcome your weaknesses. You need to work with a co-active ADHD coach who can uplift and inspire you but also challenge you to work smarter, not harder. Avoid coaches who just prescribe a generalized list of steps or strategies to follow. Instead, find a coach who specializes in ADHD, who will listen to your unique needs, and who will tailor their coaching strategies according to your individual working style.

Coaching does not have to be in person either. If time or distance limits your ability to work with a coach face-to-face, there are many co-active ADHD coaches like myself who offer phone and online video conferencing sessions. Regardless of the medium, co-active coaches can help you make decisions, set goals, weigh potential outcomes, communicate more effectively with your team, manage your time more efficiently, and even assist you in developing your business plan.

WRIGHT

As a co-active ADHD coach, what tips do you have for entrepreneurs that can help them become the chief executive of their executive function impairments?

BITTAN

This question can be a bit tricky, since not all entrepreneurs share the same executive function impairments. Therefore, the strategies that each of you develop by going through the LEVERAGE ADHD system will be different and personalized. That said, here are a few generalized tips that some of you may find helpful in your daily tasks.

Procrastination: Many times people with ADHD put off tasks because they seem too boring or too stressful. To avoid feeling overwhelmed by mundane tasks, try to shift into seeing them from a positive or more fun angle.

For example, if you hate invoicing, think about what invoicing means: more money for your business. Pick your favorite color, like green, for example, and color code invoicing on your calendar with this color. Re-name the calendar entry for invoicing with something more motivating like "money in." Now, every time you look at your calendar and see the color green and the words "money in," it means more money for your company rather than just the boring job of invoicing. The task becomes more motivational if you associate it with the reward, and it's more positive if you associate it with a color you love, both of which stimulate you to not procrastinate.

Organization and planning: Very often individuals with ADHD feel plagued by disorganization. You're constantly misplacing things or forgetting to do things. One of the best solutions to getting and staying organized is to use a calendar and use it every day. This may seem obvious or cliché, but calendars are a powerful tool for people with ADHD.

I especially recommend online calendars in which you can set pop-up visual reminders and/or auditory reminders of your appointments, to-do items, and so on. Additionally, you can sync them with all of your devices so that you're never without a calendar. Be sure to not spend a lot of time being too detailed with your calendar, or the task itself of managing it could become too cumbersome. Be simple, simple, simple—the calendar needs to save your time, not spend your time.

In addition to using a calendar, hiring a personal assistant can also be of great help in getting organized or planning ahead. If it's not in your budget to hire full-time help, perhaps offer an internship to students, or hire a student to work just a few hours a week in your office.

Managing time: Missed deadlines, taking work home, or having to work overtime are all common problems that people with ADHD deal with frequently.

A strategy to avoid over-committing or developing unrealistic time frames is to write down all of your tasks and then rate them according to the level of importance. Once you've prioritized your tasks, write down how much time you need to complete each task. Only at this point, after you've listed, ranked, and estimated time frames, should you schedule them into your calendar. Another great tip is after you've completed the tasks, make a note in your calendar of how long it actually took to complete each of them. This will help you better estimate and plan your calendar next time.

Staying on task: A common impairment people with ADHD have is the inability to stay on task and sustain attention. Your brain needs constant stimulation, so very often you will be juggling many different things at once. The problem with this is that you end up not completing assignments or following through with responsibilities. And you end up feeling very tired and frustrated since you worked hard all day but did not accomplish everything you set out to do.

Some tips to help you stay on task include clearing away clutter or items from your workspace that may distract you from completing your tasks. Keep refreshments nearby to stimulate you when you need an energy boost. Get up and walk around, stretch, take deep breaths, and recharge throughout the day. This will keep your attention levels up.

Ensure that your workspace is efficient and suits your needs. For example, if you get distracted by things happening outside your window, turn your desk to face away from the window. If you need music in the background to keep you stimulated and focused, play music while you work or wear headphones. The idea is to set yourself up for success by making sure you have everything you need in your workspace that will keep you focused on the tasks at hand.

Keep a notepad or electronic tablet nearby, so you can write down or record your ideas as they come to you. You could also keep notepads in other places where ideas come to you, like near your bed or in the car. This way, the great ideas that suddenly come to you won't keep distracting you throughout the day.

You'd be amazed how many ideas actually come to you in one day, if you start recording them as they occur.

Working with others: Because of impulsivity and lack of emotional regulation, people with ADHD tend to say what's on their mind without thinking it through, or they interrupt others while they're speaking. Sometimes, this can be off-putting to coworkers or employees. A great way to prevent your colleagues from constantly getting upset with you is to be upfront and honest at the get-go. Explain to them that you don't intentionally mean to cut them off or interrupt them. Ask them to please not take offense if you do. This can mitigate their potential for constantly getting upset with you, if they know ahead of time how you function. Another option is to ask a trusted coworker to give you a look or a nudge when you start to say something you shouldn't.

Hyperactivity: For people with ADHD, a long sedentary workday can be counter-productive, especially for those who have desk jobs. Research shows that people with the hyperactive type of ADHD must fidget in order to focus. If you're a hyperactive person who needs to fidget in order to focus, then it's imperative that you create outlets during the workday for you to move around and expel some of that excess energy. Allow yourself the space to move around. Be proactive by setting an alarm to go off before you get to the point where you cannot focus any longer, reminding you to get up and move. If you get restless at work, take a walk on your lunch break or try working out, and then eat lunch at your desk afterward.

Be open with your coworkers about your needs to move in order to focus. If it helps you to be more productive at work to move around, chances are they won't mind.

Distractibility: Feeling distracted by myriad phone calls, e-mails, coworkers talking to you, office noise, and so on is a common situation among people with ADHD. Sometimes it's hard to focus on one thing because there are simply too many things competing for your attention.

For this very reason, it's important to reduce external stimuli in your work environment. For example, if you find yourself constantly distracted by the chime of your e-mail or social media notifications, log out of those accounts until you've completed your required tasks. If the phone is constantly ringing, turn the ringer off. You can check your voicemail at a designated time of day and return missed phone calls at that time. Turn your desk to face away from coworkers so they literally have to interrupt you if they need something in particular.

These are just some of the most common issues that people with ADHD struggle with at the workplace. The key is to embrace the idea that the way you need to work does not mirror the way most people work. Your work style requires creative solutions and personalized adjustments.

WRIGHT

As a final piece of advice, what are the most important items that entrepreneurs with ADHD need to consider in order to run a successful business?

BITTAN

One of the most important things you as an entrepreneur with ADHD should consider for your business is to make sure that you love what you do. You have to be passionate about your work; otherwise, you won't stay motivated or focused. So make sure you're doing something you have genuine passion for and that it is something you truly enjoy doing.

To run a sustainable business, entrepreneurs must have a vision and a clear business plan so that decisions aren't made on the spur of the moment. This business plan will essentially be your personal road map to success—without one, you'd be flying blind. The plan needs to outline your mission statement, finances, marketing and advertising strategies, and set specific goals for your business.

It's really important for you to set SMART goals (Specific, Measurable, Attainable, Relevant, and Timely) in your business plan because you have to be able to look ahead and know where you want to take your business. Anyone can set a goal. Simply stating you have a goal means nothing. You have to define the goal specifically, be able to measure your progress, know that it's attainable and realistic, and set a timeframe within which to achieve it.

For people with ADHD, there's another step in SMART goal-setting, and that is thinking about how your specific executive function impairments might affect your ability to reach your goals. In my work using the *Grow stage* of the LEVERAGE ADHD system, my clients must see the goals or else it's out of sight, out of mind. Using all of the senses, we create a unique plan that breaks down the goals into small, manageable stages. We also include in the goal-setting what the reward will be once the mini-goal is achieved. For example, the reward of returning e-mails by end of the day on Friday results in a care-free and leisurely weekend. I ask my clients to choose a motivational quote that expresses the reward or feeling of accomplishment and have them post it as inspiration throughout the week of how they will feel once they achieve their goal. The sense of reward and accomplishment is what activates the dopamine in the brain and pushes them to keep going. When these mini-goals are achieved, it generates a greater feeling of success and bolsters accountability. This helps improve self-efficacy, pushing them to trust themselves and believe they can go on to achieve more and more success. Goal-setting is a process, and it's a fascinating one at that. But for people with ADHD, this process must involve taking your neurobiological impairments into consideration and understanding how your ADHD affects your thinking and behavior. Looking again at the *Evaluate stage* of the LEVERAGE ADHD system, you should understand how your unique traits can enhance and hinder your ability to attain your goals.

Another thing that needs to be included in your business plan—and this is what will make all the difference for entrepreneurs with ADHD—is the team of professionals who will be responsible for various aspects of your business. A common theme among people who have ADHD is the tendency to want to do everything themselves. You tend to over-commit yourself or assume unrealistic timelines. However, as much as you want to do it all, you really should look at ways you can outsource some of your ADHD impairments to people whose strengths complement them.

In both the *Evaluate* and *Grow stages* of the LEVERAGE ADHD system, I like to guide my clients through a very effective method known as SWOT to determine where they should focus their energy and where they could outsource some areas of their business. It stands for Strengths, Weaknesses, Opportunities, and Threats. What SWOT analysis essentially does is identify the various factors within a business that will affect its ability to meet an objective.

I use a modified version of SWOT by tailoring it towards people with ADHD. Essentially, I have you ask yourself different questions that take into consideration your neurobiological traits. These include asking yourself what about my ADHD impairments represent a weakness to my business? What about my ADHD traits are strengths that benefit my business? With SWOT, I want you to be mindful of your unique ADHD characteristics so you can see how they can affect and benefit your business. We all have traits that we need to embrace, both good and bad, and everyone's SWOT analysis will look different. But being mindful of your ADHD traits will help you make wise, confident strategies in your business plan and help you trust yourself to lead your business forward.

A business plan for entrepreneurs with ADHD is not the usual business plan. I believe it needs to be visual and tangible. It also needs to include tools and techniques that will bypass your natural resistance to structure and free your mind of the personal limitations or bias that you've carried around all your life. In your business plan, you need to give yourself permission to think big and forget all of the past experiences when others told you to try harder or that you weren't doing it the right way.

When you work through the LEVERAGE ADHD system, especially in the *Grow* stage, you allow yourself to reach your full potential and to do it your way. I really love it when people embrace their ADHD traits and learn how to work effectively with them. It's not always easy, but I believe that if you work through the LEVERAGE ADHD system, you will understand yourself better, appreciate yourself more, feel emotionally healthier, and develop practical strategies that can lift your business to new heights. This is what motivates me every day—helping others stand up and be proud of who they are and letting them work the way they need to without judgment or comparison. This is what I call leveraging ADHD to your ADDvantage.

Dr. Billi Bittan, PhD, Neuro-Cognitive Behavioral Therapist and ADHD Coach, has more than thirty-five years of experience helping people of all ages manage ADHD. She specializes in innovative coaching and therapy intervention for ADHD, Asperger's, Learning Disabilities, and Memory Disorders. Combining her MA in expressive arts therapy, her experience in co-active coaching and her BA in teaching, Dr. Billi developed the AttentionB Method™ to empower others to take pride in their unique traits and transform their personal ADHD challenges into useful assets. Dr. Billi's commitment to a higher quality of life for people of all ages has been her primary source of motivation throughout her career.

Dr. Billi Bittan

AttentionB
15720 Ventura Blvd., Suite 503
Encino, CA 91436
855-DR-BILLI (372-4554)
DrBilli@AttentionB.com
www.AttentionB.com

CHAPTER FOUR

Women Driven To Success: Standing In Your Power
Dr. Jane S. Goldner

DAVID WRIGHT (WRIGHT)

Today I'm talking with Jane S. Goldner PhD. Dr. Goldner is a sought-after, highly-rated speaker, author, role integration coach, and talent strategy consultant. She has thirty years of internal and external corporate experience with Fortune 500 and mid-sized companies as well as the military. Jane has advanced degrees in counseling and human resource development.

Dr. Goldner's first book, *Driven to Success: A 10-Point Checkup for Achieving High Performance in Business,* is a toolkit for leaders to get everyone communicating across the company and focused on achieving corporate goals. Her upcoming book, *Women Driven to Success: Everything to Everybody,* provides women the understanding of how to integrate multiple roles without sacrificing their success, health, or peace of mind.

WRIGHT

Dr. Goldner, welcome to *ROADMAP to Success.*

JANE GOLDNER (GOLDNER)

Thank you David, I'm happy to be here.

WRIGHT

The title of this chapter is "Women Driven to Success: Standing in Your Power." What does it mean to stand in your power?

GOLDNER

Standing in your power is knowing who you are and what is important to you so you can make good choices and trade-offs—the decisions between "yeses" and "nos." In spite of what anyone may tell you, nobody has it all. Everybody has to make choices. The best ones come from clarifying your personal Core—mission, vision, and values.

Just like a company has a mission, vision, and set of values, so should an individual. And if your individual Core is aligned with the Core of your workplace, that is powerful. It allows you to bring passion and purpose to work.

For my upcoming book, I have interviewed fifteen fabulous female senior leaders. One of the women addressed choices and tradeoffs in a very interesting way. She said, "You can have it all, just not every day." The bottom line is that you have to really know your Core—what your center is—so you can make those good decisions.

WRIGHT

Why is it important for women to stand in their power in order to be successful?

GOLDNER

Women, especially women driven to success, need to stand in their power so they can live the right life and negotiate based on that right life. Many women are still trying to be everything to everybody. They are sacrificing their own needs, wants, and wishes, and often their health. We conduct a workshop titled "Women Driven to Success: Integrating Multiple Roles is the New Leadership Imperative." In one of these workshops, a woman told us that she had been recently divorced. Her son asked her what she wanted for dinner, did she like fish? She responded that she didn't know. All these years she had been catering to her family and never even thought about the basic answer to what foods she liked.

Furthermore, on a more global level, women need to stand in their power so they can change the statistics that indicate, for example, if women off-ramp for two years from their career, they have 18 percent less earning power and three or more years 37 percent less earning power. In many companies, Unilever was cited as one example, women are typically 50 percent of frontline management. What's incredible is that number drops to 6 percent at the senior level. If you read into the statistics about Fortune 500 top wage earners, only 6.7 percent are females. And put in the mix a survey of senior leaders indicated that two thirds of the male senior leaders have children and only one third of the senior level female leaders have children. Are women being forced to make a choice they wouldn't ordinarily make? Those women who have children are doing three times the amount of child rearing and, in general, women are doing two times the amount of housework.

There is much research that says women need to learn how to stand in their power. Women need to see the workplace circumstances, as they are not as they wish them to be. They need to change the dynamics from both an individual and corporate perspective. They need to ask: What can I control? What can I influence?

Another woman I interviewed is in a large CPA firm. She became partner when she had her first child. The male partner asked her, what kind of partner do you want to be? She responded, "I want to be the kind of partner who makes it easier for women to become partners."

WRIGHT

I would have thought that the glass ceiling would have been a little bit more cracked than what that. You're talking about the corporate world, so is it any better in the entrepreneurial arena?

GOLDNER

That's a very interesting question. What's happening is that as women are leaving the corporate world, usually when they have children, it is because they decide they can't juggle it all. They find ways to convert their skills outside of the formal corporate world. These women are, in fact, becoming entrepreneurs because they can then call the shots and juggle their multiple roles with control.

WRIGHT

What are the benefits to standing in your power?

GOLDNER

Standing in your power allows you to move from being reactive to being proactive. That translates into shifting from wishing things to happen to visioning and taking action on what you want to have happen. That allows you to be focused and not frustrated, that power moves you from staying in your comfort zone and avoiding risk to being comfortable with managing the risk. The bottom line is that rather than being a victim of others' expectations of you, you create the desirable and realistic expectations of yourself.

FROM	TO
Reactive	Proactive
Wishing	Visioning
Frustrated	Focused
Comfort Zone Avoiding Risk	Comfortable Managing Risk
Others' Expectations	Expectations of Yourself
Right Life?	Right Life!

WRIGHT

On the other hand, are there consequences of not standing in your power?

GOLDNER

Absolutely. The biggest consequence is not living the right life. I can't imagine at the end, wondering if I should have done my life differently. We all have things we would have done differently given the chance to do it over again, but I'm talking about major choices that impacted the life journey we took. So again, standing in our power is making the right choices, acknowledging the tradeoffs, and being okay about that.

More specifically, women who don't stand in their power tend to overextend their time and resources to accommodate and acquiesce to others' demands. Those others can be a boss, a significant other, a spouse, a child, a friend, other family members or people who want you to donate your time and services in community activities. The result is that these women live their lives according to others' expectations and not their own. They become everything to everybody except themselves.

WRIGHT

Are there differences in how women and men view power?

GOLDNER

There is a danger in generalization but I'm going to go for it. You can always find outliers and atypical gender differences within groups of people. The different views of power may go back to cave people. Way back, men hunted, they went for the kill; women were gatherers, a much more collaborative activity. Fast forward to today in business negotiations, men go for the win in full battle armor; I win as much as I can and you lose accordingly. Women tend to find more of the win-win result through identifying common interests and goals and particularly in building relationships. While the workplace norms may be changing, and I do think they are as more women get into significant roles, it is shifting toward collaboration as a way to do business. However, power and negotiations still lag behind, it's still very much a win-lose proposition.

There is an old adage that money is power. Women are becoming a financial powerhouse with their earnings and therefore spending ability. A Boston Consulting Group study indicated that by 2014 women are expected to have 15 trillion dollars in spending power. In view of that, perhaps women's view of that type of power may be shifting. I also think there is a prevailing view of power as control, specifically control of others. Women don't always warm to that definition. If they reframed their power as being influential and developing the right strategic relationships to accomplish goals and make a difference, then maybe they wouldn't perceive power quite as negatively as a lot of women perceive it now.

If women learn that real power comes from within, not from an official position, they can reframe how they think and feel about power. The road to success would be a great deal easier with that frame of reference.

WRIGHT

What do you think the common man and the common woman think about the entire subject of women and men in leadership? It seems to me that if a male leader is a tyrant, he's aggressive and if a woman is a tyrannical leader she's a . . . well, worse.

GOLDNER

There are many studies throughout the years indicating effective leadership is associated with male characteristics and people would rather work for a man than a woman. I believe much of this thinking is because the role models throughout the years have predominately been men. Men have created the norms of how to be successful in organizations.

We see that view slowly changing. For example, as I mentioned earlier, collaboration and developing relationships are becoming more important. Women do that particularly well. What I find that women don't do particularly well is becoming strategic about whom they develop relationships with in their organizations. This is a key skill that I help women develop in my coaching practice.

Getting back to your point, there is still a ways to go where if a woman gets angry, she's not considered as being . . . well, let's say overly aggressive.

WRIGHT

So in your opinion, how do women diffuse their power?

GOLDNER

Your question gets to the heart of what we're talking about. Women diffuse their power by trying to be everything to everybody and trying to do everything perfectly. Let me give you some examples that I've recently heard from women as I've done keynote speaking.

A woman diffuses her power by always saying "yes" when her plate is already overflowing and not going to her boss for help in putting things in a different priority order. One woman told me that her boss came and dumped an urgent task on her. She said that she already had all she could handle, but felt obligated to say "yes." I asked her why she had to say "yes" unconditionally. I asked her, "Couldn't you have asked your boss, 'If this is a high priority for me and if this is what you want me to focus my time on, tell me which of these things are not as important, so that I can put to the side for a while." Women don't negotiate well; they negotiate eight times less than men.

Another example is women tend not to delegate. When I ask why, some of the responses are: "It takes too long to explain to someone else how to do it so I'll just do it myself," "I don't want to bother someone else," or the belief that "I'm the only one who can do it exactly right." Women need to learn to let go, explain what needs to get done, realize that there are probably multiple ways of how to get it done, and accept that someone else can do it right. It might not be exactly the way she would do it but if it comes out right, then does it matter that it wasn't done her way.

Addressing the issue of doing everything perfectly, I need to relate a personal story. When I was in my thirties, I was working full-time, raising two young sons, and was in my doctoral program. When my housekeeper quit, I told my husband that I could clean the house. Weeks later, I had chest pains and a significant health scare. My husband asked me why I didn't ask for help. My response was that I thought I could do it all. I didn't want to bother him. He should have asked me if I needed help—become a mind-reader!

Another fabulous woman I interviewed lives by the 80/20 rule. She said when something is 80 percent good and she knows it is right, she goes with it. "Otherwise," she said, "I'll be spending 20 percent more time trying to make it more perfect and more perfect and it doesn't need to be more perfect and more perfect."

The other way women diffuse their power is at home, and some of those examples are, "I'm the wife it's my role, I'm the mother it's my role." I say, "Who says? Who says that there are such definitive roles that you have to take on all those pieces?"

Another example at home, and I've had this happen to me, a charity calls you to canvass the neighborhood for donations, my head is screaming, "No! I don't have the time, I'm already into overload!" but I feel guilty and I say "yes."

All of this, trying to be everything to everybody not only diffuses power but it creates unhealthy stress and that has health consequences attached to it as demonstrated by my story.

WRIGHT

So is this concept of standing in your power not just for the workplace but also applies outside work as well?

GOLDNER

It absolutely does. Standing in your power permeates all aspects of life. I just gave a few examples. Let's take a deeper dive with some personal examples.

I went back to work when each of my sons was eight weeks old. I had a full-time job outside of home. After my health scare, I made it very clear that home was not my other full-time job—it is a shared responsibility. That translated into the fact that my husband was and still is a better cook, so most of the time he cooked dinners. He doesn't like to stand at the sink and wash dishes so I do that. When my husband and my sons needed something ironed, they learned to iron; I didn't come out of the womb holding an iron. I don't know how to iron so they learned.

Women need to develop the skills of delegation for all parts of their life. I love this quote (I can't remember who the CEO was) but it was a female CEO who convinced her husband that when their young daughter called "mommy" in the middle of the night, the child really meant parent of either sex. I love that.

WRIGHT

What is the first step in the journey women need to take to stand in their power?

GOLDNER

A great exercise to begin the journey is defining your well-being. Martin Seligman is the father of authentic happiness and well-being. He has a Web site with some great assessments. It is www.authentichappiness .sas.upenn.edu. He talks about five categories of well-being: positive emotion, engagement, meaning, positive relationships, and achievement. He's moved from simple happiness to those five categories.

Happiness is positive emotion. Those are the things that evoke positive happy emotion such as when you hear an old song that reminds you of a happy time in your past.

He describes *engagement* as when we're so engaged in something time slips by us. It's what athletes call being in the zone.

The third category he describes is *meaning*. Interestingly, research indicates that this category gives us the most life satisfaction. It's the unselfish act, when we get outside ourselves, that provides real meaning.

The fourth category is *positive relationships* and the fifth is *accomplishments*. Seligman indicated that accomplishments don't always make us happy or create happiness, but we have the sense that we've done something that gives us a sense of achievement.

In our workshop, we ask the women to create a collage that demonstrates what defines each of these categories for them. The women love doing it and they love sharing it. The women start to identify what's really important to them. They also realize that they have a lot of commonalities and get positive support.

We then ask them to use their collages to begin to define their personal Cores—mission, vision, and values in life, not just in work. The biggest ah-ha moment, David, comes from using the Core to create a pie chart depicting a typical week of how they spend their time. It's amazing how many women have a misalignment between what is important to them and how they are actually spending their time. As a result, we spend a lot of time helping them realign their Core and their time so they can live the right life.

WRIGHT

I've produced a lot of books about happiness since I've had this publishing company. That's the first time I've ever heard about positive emotion as happiness. It makes more sense. It takes the nebulousness out of the word happiness.

GOLDNER

That's what Seligman was talking about. Happiness, as defined by positive emotion as I indicated before, is when you hear a song that came from a happy time in your life. For you, it would be a particular kind of jazz music that would make you smile. It would make you feel happy for the moment or for the duration of the song but that's not well-being, per se—that's a piece of it but not the sum total.

WRIGHT

Very interesting.

What are the crucial skills women should learn in order to stand in their power?

GOLDNER

That's the deep dive we take in the workshop. "I'm going to be powerful" is not something you can just read in a book or decide. It's a big piece of what I do when people ask me, "What is role integration coaching?" It's about identifying your multiple roles and figuring out how to integrate all them. I'm not a believer in work/life balance because I think that signifies you've got things 50/50 and that's not life. It's how you integrate all those roles you either have to play or want to play in a way that helps you live the right life.

The first thing you need to take a look at is who you are at your Core, which includes (not exclusively) what skills you want to use in the workplace and a career direction to use those skills. Then, it's important to self-assess and get feedback. You can do that through any number of self-assessment instruments like the Myers-Briggs Type Indicator, the FIRO-B, the Strong (a career-focused inventory), and the Strengths Finder. Once you're clear about your strengths, then it is getting clarity about your career goals and ambitions, not just what your organization wants you to do because that's other directed, but what you really want to do in your career. We all spend too much time at work not to bring passion and purpose to work.

For women particularly it's about developing strategic relationships with the right power people. Power people are the ones who have information and/or who can be sponsors.

Women need to learn the difference between mentors and sponsors. Mentors are people who can help guide you in your career by giving you advice. Sponsors are the people who can open the doors to challenging assignments and the right promotions.

I have recently been coaching a woman who is on a high potential list of an organization. She was running an international meeting. We strategized before the meeting about whom she needed to meet and spend time with in order to build those relationships to move to the right position. She was very excited after the first day and e-mailed me that she worked one of our strategies and that night one of the vice presidents called her because he liked the value she added to the meeting and the time he spent with her. It really does work when women learn how to be strategic about building those relationships and getting over the idea that "everybody has to like me and I have to like everybody." It is about speaking up, getting visibility, and developing those right relationships.

Men do that very well, by the way, and it may be from growing up playing team sports. Men don't have to like the guy who plays first base as long as he plays great first base. Women seem to have to like everybody they work with and want to take them home for dinner. They need to learn that it's okay if everyone doesn't like you and if you don't like everybody, when you're at work. It would be nice to like everyone, but it's more important that everybody is competent and working toward common goals.

Women need to build the kind of support system that enables them to get more resources. They need to learn how to call in chips when they have done favors for others.

Another skill is learning the "gracious no." Women must get over the feeling that if I say no they won't like me or they'll feel I'm not competent. The gracious no is that you can say no and graciously suggest an alternative or say to the boss, "I can't do this unless you help me re-prioritize."

Another skill we previously talked about is negotiation. Women need to learn to negotiate more, particularly with salary requirements. Women can lose up to a million dollars in their career by not learning how to negotiate.

Lastly, I believe one of the toughest skills for women to learn is constructive confrontation. We've been brought up to believe that if you don't have anything nice to say then don't say it. The truth is, the echoes of what your mother told you: it's not what you say, it's how you say it. Women need to learn that it is okay to confront somebody as long as it's done constructively.

Here is a list:

1. Clarify your Core and use it as the touchstone for all your decisions.
2. Complete self-assessments and get feedback.
3. Decide on what skills you want to use and a career direction.
4. Build a support network inside and outside of the workplace. Get more resources. Call in chips.
5. Develop strategic relationships with power people.
6. Learn the skills of the "gracious no," delegation, negotiation, and constructive confrontation.
7. Celebrate your accomplishments.

WRIGHT

Women can get away with saying anything to you as long as she's smiling, seems to me.

GOLDNER

Is that right? Actually, David, I had written an article on gender in the workplace a few years ago. One of the leaders I interviewed said that using the smile or the sexy type of dress was viewed as manipulation and a turnoff to him. Once again, it's tough to generalize—it's very individual-specific about what works and what doesn't.

WRIGHT

How can networking with other women who are driven to succeed help?

GOLDNER

Networking is a key skill as well. Women need to learn to network more. Unfortunately, when you look at women in their careers, particularly when they get to the stage when they have children, they start not doing the networking so they can go home to be with their family. They lose a lot of the support and a lot of the advantage in growing their careers.

First and foremost, networking with other women helps women to learn that they are not alone and they can do it. That's one of the reasons I included a chapter in my upcoming book that shares the success strategies of successful senior level female leaders who have done it. They are wonderful role models. These women are real women with multiple children. All are all senior leaders who have figured out what works. Networking creates a great support system for practical ideas.

Joining networking groups for support helps women keep their sanity so they can talk through issues. There are still some gender issues in the workplace that are specific to women. It's nice to be able to get some support and talk through those challenges, particularly the ability to reach out on a bad day.

Networking Benefits

1. Learn that you are not alone and that you can succeed.
2. Create a great support system for practical ideas about what works.
3. Have a group to help you keep your sanity on bad days, to be your cheerleaders.
4. Find mentors and sponsors.

I've been sharing a lot of these practical ideas and lessons born from these interviews through presentations. The women in the audiences have walked away with great practical ideas they may not have thought about before. For example, one woman said that she never allowed herself to have a light touch on herself—to not be perfect. In one of the last presentations, a woman said, "I do spend that extra 20 percent trying to be more perfect and more perfect, and at the end of the day it really didn't matter to my boss."

WRIGHT

Well, what a great a conversation. A lot of the things you have said apply to me as a male. I know you don't deal exclusively with women. Do you deal with them primarily and if so, why?

GOLDNER

Actually, the last thirty years of my career, which is the basis of my first book, I was dealing with senior leaders who, 99 percent of the time, were men. I was consulting on major change and transition interventions in organizations. We mentioned early on that I have also worked for fifteen years with the military, which is male dominated. Inside the context of a major change and transition, I was coaching the senior male leaders because a lot of them were technically competent but didn't necessarily have the interpersonal skills to pull off what we were trying to do to get their organizations to the next level.

You're absolutely right that a lot of what I'm talking about now is relevant for men as well. I am dealing predominately with women because that's where my passion is, but not exclusively. There was an article in the *Wall Street Journal* not too long ago that focused on how men are getting much more involved in parenting and that they are beginning to have the same issues around juggling the multiple roles.

I have a Generation X son who recently had twins and you talk about needing to get involved! It is a *group* effort! He's very involved in parenting and he's learning what it's like to juggle those roles. But, of course, he grew up in a house where we didn't have stereotypical roles, so he saw different role models. I think more and more of the next generation males want more involvement outside of work, so men are also looking for better role integration.

WRIGHT

This has really been an enlightening conversation, Jane. I really appreciate the time you've taken to participate in this project. It has been delightful for me. I've learned a lot and I'm sure our readers will.

GOLDNER

I hope so because when I talk about defining your own Core, I certainly have done mine. My mission is to help others learn as I continue my own learning. I'm passionate about sharing learning. I hope this benefits the readers and that they walk away with some practical advice.

WRIGHT

Today we have been talking to Jane S. Goldner PhD. Her company, the Goldner Group LLC, has great tagline—Driven to Success: Accelerating Business and Individual Achievement. She is a highly rated speaker, author, role integration coach, and talent strategy consultant.

Jane, thank you so much for being with us today on *ROADMAP to Success*.

GOLDNER

You're welcome, David. It was a pleasure.

Dr. Jane S. Goldner, author of *Driven to Success: A 10-Point Checkup for Achieving High Performance in Business,* has been quoted in the *New York Times, CNN Money,* and *GO,* the *Air*Tran magazine, among other publications. Jane has appeared several times on *11-Alive Television* and is a member of the USA Today CEO panel.

Throughout her thirty years in business and family life, she has learned the secrets of integrating multiple roles and great leadership for women, which she brings to companies and coaching clients. She is an adjunct professor at the Coles School of Business Kennesaw State University and in the PCOM Master's Degree program. Her new book, *Women Driven to Success,* is due out in 2013. Her greatest accomplishment is that her grown son still calls her for career advice!

Jane Goldner PhD

The Goldner Group, LLC
5555 Glenridge Connector, Suite 200
Atlanta, Georgia 30342
404-459-2860
www.thegoldnergroup.com
jane@thegoldnergroup.com
Follow me on Twitter:
jane@corporate_women
Jane@thegoldnergroup
Read my blogs:
thegoldnergroup.wordpress.com
Connect with me on LinkedIn: Jane Goldner

Chapter Five

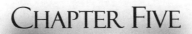

Know Thyself: A Success That Succeeds
Judith L. Harrison

DAVID WRIGHT (WRIGHT)

Today I'm talking with Judith L. Harrison. She offers an effective perspective and solution in the world of employee relations, and in general, human interactions. As a clinically trained and professionally accredited human behavior specialist and psychotherapist, Judith is equipped to find lasting solutions to the challenges faced by today's business leaders as well as those in small business enterprises.

Her process challenges organizations and individuals to break down the systemic mental barriers and obstacles that prevent people from working optimally—individually and collectively. This is achieved through customizing her approach, incorporating the particular techniques and workshops that are right for each organization.

Judith, welcome to *ROADMAP to Success*.

JUDITH L. HARRISON (HARRISON)

Thank you, David. It's great to be here.

WRIGHT

So how would you define success?

HARRISON

We could spend endless hours pontificating and reflecting upon this question, but we're not going to do that here. First of all, I think of us, as humans, as being verbs rather than the usual proclivity to treat ourselves and others as objects, nouns. By design, we are very fluid, therefore, meant to be fluid and our expression of ourselves—the life we're given to live. Success then becomes something that is very organic and contextual.

Let's look at context for a moment. Context is generic and intrinsic to all human behavior and what drives those behaviors. Examples include beliefs, expectations, and fears, as well as the nonspecific noise around us.

Also by context, I would include reference to cultural circumstances as well as time-oriented places along a continuum. What are the prevailing conditions or driving forces by which we inform our values, choices, and behaviors? Here I'm referring to a consideration of whether we're defining success for ourselves from our authentic Self—a territorial imperative—or from our socialized value base. There is a distinction between these two orientations in the way that I would look at and work with the individuals who are my clients.

Success is also conditional in that it will be the reflection of a process rather than being end-pointed. Roger Martin, who is deemed to be one of the great thinkers of our time, says we make the mistake of thinking that when we arrive at a solution it is iron-clad and fixed; it is not. Because we are designed to be fluid and flexible, we must not hold out for perfect solutions. The information we have at our fingertips at a point in time will inform the solution. But the information that will be available to us as time goes on will change. Such is the process of life and, therefore, so too will be the desired outcomes and defined positions as we move along in our process. And so it is that success, and our understanding thereof, is best served with mindfulness that regards both context and conditions working from the authentic Self.

Though success is fluid, I hasten to add it is not whimsical. It is a continuum. And as with any journey, a road map is useful.

WRIGHT

Would you say more about how it is that success must be personal rather than what is determined or dictated by society?

HARRISON

On the road to success, there must be sustainability and satisfaction to go the distance! Because success is a process, not an overnight phenomenon, we must have the energy to stay the course. Whether one is an employee inside of a corporation or an individual in a personal relationship, the ongoing journey will require personal staying power. Therefore, if the intention of the objective isn't deeply personal to the core Self, the question is will we have what it takes to stay he course and to do so with excellence?

In terms of satisfaction, if we're only pursuing a course of action according to our socialized selves or what the group wants, we're going to power out because the battery will run dry. I remember when I was doing my thesis for a master's program, my advisor said to me, "You'd better be very, very passionate about what your subject matter is or you won't see it through to the end." As I had a great deal of respect for him, I took his words at face value and found a subject matter for which I had that passion.

Through the course of doing my thesis, the process of this experience allowed me to own the significance of his advice and appreciate the deep truth of what he had said to me. Because my subject matter was deeply personal to me, even when the going got rough and I met adversity, and even when I really wanted to give up, I kept going. The deep intrinsic value my subject matter held for me would not let me give up.

WRIGHT

Would you say more as to why success should be a reflection of values?

HARRISON

Ah, thank you. That's such a great question, very near and dear to my heart. In the process of fitting in as we grow up, we've got to fit into our family and we've got to fit into maybe our church environment. We've got to fit into the requirements of the school classrooms we find ourselves in as we go along life's journey. In that process we are socialized to subscribe to some given norms that are held to be the right way to do something, and we will be given a sense of ourself and our worth according to how well we fit into those societal norms, regardless of how well they suit us.

What's unfortunate about this, David, is that these norms and the dictates of this socializing process are, as far as I'm concerned, quite archaic. If we go back to the time we lived in tribes, it was very important for everybody to fit into a particular norm for the survival and safety of the tribe, and that was right and good. However, we're not really tribal anymore. The idea is that we're to have evolved beyond these conditions, but we still live with these archaic ways of determining one's worth or value. Socialization obscures that which is deeply personal and that is the source of our profound passion—the energy that gives us our staying power.

So in reflecting on success, our values are something we have to look at and take ownership of for ourselves as we go along. Even if some of our values reflect societal norms, we have to accept them on our own terms through a process of our own experience rather than by somebody else's say so. This allows us to live our lives by design rather than by default.

There was a study done by Robert Ardrey in 1966 regarding territorial imperative. When I read that study, and though it was done on a biological species in their natural habitats, I saw the parallel to us as human beings. What he discovered in that research was that biological species in the central area of their natural domain are virtually indestructible. But the more they move away from the center of their natural habitat toward the periphery, and indeed if they go beyond the peripheral, it is virtually impossible for them to survive. The implication of this information, as it pertains to us as humans, made a stunning impact on me. In living our lives, are we not also a biological species? Therefore, if we are not living from what is deeply personal to the authentic Self, our natural domain, are we thriving or merely surviving?

I assert that if we are not living at the central core point of our authentic self, then it's virtually impossible to thrive. We exist, we don't thrive. George Bernard Shaw is known to have said that most people die at the age of twenty-seven. The problem is that they won't lie down and let us throw dirt on them until they're seventy-two. They exist rather than thrive. And so it is that our personal values become a very important reference point for how we define what we are and what has sustaining value for us. Therefore, inroads have to be constructed from the socialized self or external values toward the authentic Self, our internal value base—our territorial imperative. We can't have a road map unless there is a road.

WRIGHT

You make reference to building inroads. How do we build this inroad?

HARRISON

I think of the road less traveled as being the road of our authentic self. A lot of my work as a psychotherapist is based on marriage and family-systems-thinking that comes from a great pioneer in the field, Virginia Satir. She worked with the iceberg as a metaphor of who and what we are as human beings. The connection being that just as the part of the iceberg that is visible above the waterline is such a small representation of the overall mass of the iceberg, so too is the behavior of human beings a minuscule iteration of what is the sum total of being human.

The discernible behaviors of an individual cannot begin to span the overall magnitude of being human. Below the waterline are all of our hopes, our wishes, our dreams, our expectations, our unmet expectations, our desires, and our frustrations. Those things below the waterline are actually what drive the behavior above the waterline, but we don't stop to take note of that which drives our own behavior, let alone what's driving somebody else. So when I meet David on the street, and he ignores me with a scowl on his face perhaps, do I jump to conclusions or do I stop to reflect? We don't stop to think about what's happening below the waterline and have engaging compassion for David as other. However, it could also be said that if we have no compassion for self, there can't be compassion for another. Therefore, extreme self-care and a sincere valuing of Self is the wellspring of being a good corporate citizen!

We're quick to write people off on first impressions. We are meaning-making machines—we make it all up. How often do we hear that our first impression is a lasting impression? We don't often get a second chance at making a first impression. What could our world be like if we were more circumspect from a place of curiosity rather than judgment?

There is a whole lot of compost going on below the waterline driving that behavior *and* below all of that compost is what Virginia Satir referred to as the core *I am*—the authentic self. Hemingway also developed an analogy working with the iceberg, alternatively known as the theory of omission. His approach is different and beautifully compliments with an edge of the nonspecific—the mystery of our lives, referring to the strength of the submerged or hidden.

So the inroad back to that Self, in order to have that road map for success, is first a deconstruction process. What is being broken up are the socialized norms that have conditioned our thought process. In so doing, the inroad or path to the authentic self is made known to us. "If you go as far as you can see, you will then see enough to go even farther"—John Wooden.

For me, Epictetus is a hero. I wish I would have known him personally, but I don't need to in the sense that his legacy lives on. In the time of his life (AD 55–AD 135), he was born into slavery. He was crippled by treatment he endured as a slave, and then eventually earned his way to freedom. When he was freed, he started a school of philosophy; how amazing is that? His philosophy is what we know as stoicism. It's just so remarkable that through his life of slavery, crippling ill treatment, and all else that he may have endured, that he came out of this with his core self intact. The integrity of self is never destroyed, however, access to it often is.

The dictates espoused by his philosophy were further translated more recently by another philosopher, Sharon Lebell. Through this translation found in *Epictetus: The Art of Living*, we learn that for Epictetus, our greatest challenge as humans is to live our lives with equanimity, therefore, he goes on to say, it behooves us to articulate a coherent set of values and then live by them. If this is in place, then when we hit the rough waters of life, we have a natural way of steering ourselves toward that which has meaning, value, and purpose for us intrinsically. In the absence thereof, when we hit the white water rapids of life, we are bereft of orientation, getting drowned in the swells. However, it is also true that breaking up that status quo of socialization will throw us into chaos. Nevertheless, it is chaos that makes conscious choice possible on our road to success.

WRIGHT

Are you suggesting that we make friends with chaos?

HARRISON

Whoohoo, you bet. I suggest to a listening audience that if they have chaos in their life, they may need to come and see me; but by the same token, if they don't have chaos in their life, they really need to come and see me. If you don't have chaos and you make a point of not having chaos, you're likely committing to a life of suboptimum struggle, victory, and the resulting joy of celebration and exhilaration that comes from the victory. There can be no victory without the struggle. Chaos is an integral part of our ongoing process of growth and development, personally and professionally. Because we are designed to grow and change, if we aren't growing, we are dying. We are existing and not thriving. So, yes, make friends with chaos; chaos is critical to our process of change and living a life of vitality. It's akin to a farmer's field that requires a process of plowing and tending, preparing the ground for new seeds.

WRIGHT

Farmers have their steps to achieve success. What would be our steps?

HARRISON

Farmers go out to their fields in the spring, surveying their "kingdom," seeing what is required for new crops. The dormant season has left the soil packed down, completely unready for any new growth. In order to have the prospect of a successful crop, the farmers begin a process of breaking up that soil; they'll plow it, till it, and harrow it. They get out in the field and they make a lot of dust. And only then can they plant the seeds for a new crop.

The equivalent of the farmer's packed fields is the conditioned status quo within which we live season to season, leaving us ill prepared for new possibilities. And so it is that we must break up the soil—our status quo. In so doing, we free up energy for new choices, and in this process of change, chaos ensues. The equivalent of the farmer's equipment would be the foreign elements we encounter in life, the things that come at us from out of "left field." Things like a new position within a company, a new life partner, or having already established a significant-other relationship, the patter of little feet that might come along, and the list goes on. This foreign element doesn't necessarily have to be something we perceive to be bad. Nevertheless, it is an agent for change in the pre-existing status quo.

When that soil is broken up, we may find ourselves in a maelstrom of feelings and emotions—a sense of being out of control. This plethora of emotions such as shock, anxiety, anger, depression, frustration is what I refer to as chaos in this process of seeding new possibilities. These new seeds, in our case, are the choices and the energy with which to practice and implement new behaviors. These behaviors, having made them by choice, give us a life by design rather than by default. These are the pared-down steps in constructing the inroads to the authentic Self. Sounds simple, but it's not easy. And there is precious little in socialization that encourages us to live with such a personal accountability to Self. With the iceberg as a metaphor, we can begin to have a working knowledge of some of the necessary plowing required to break up the socialization process— a process that will have programmed veils over the core essence of the *I am*.

To move through chaos, there are critical C's that can assist us. They are Clarity, Courage, Connecting through Communication—Crucial Conversations with nonviolent communication—Commitment, and Consistency. Clarity comes through asking questions that bring us through the confusion.

This process of being congruent with the discomfort and stress of *I don't know what I'm doing; I don't know where I'm going; I don't know who or what I am* requires courage. Courage is being authentic, whereas stress will typically cause us to default to our coping stances, which are distracting and likely divisive. The divisiveness disconnects us from our emotional body and the authentic connect with other.

The healthy, constructive way of responding to stress is to be congruent with what's really going on, owning those feelings, naming them, and taking responsibility for them. This requires courage. This process also requires an unrelenting commitment to stay the course with consistency and response-ability. This consistency will be strengthened as we stay the course and grow to trust our process, both the struggles and the victories. This is a pattern that will oft repeat itself on our journey back to Self. We will not get there in a hurry; we will meet with adversity, but once begun, we can never go back to a pre-existing status quo or socialized way of being. In addition to the constructive C's, there is a P for patience. As my editor says of her mother's admonishment, "Rome wasn't built in a day." It is the willingness to stay the course that will build trust and confidence on the journey back to Self.

In *Smart Trust*, Stephen M. R. Covey talks about the invaluable component of trust to be successful in business. He cites a quote by Ralph Waldo Emerson, as follows: "Self-trust is the first secret of success . . . the essence of heroism. . . . In self-trust, all the virtues are comprehended." And I say that just as business has a life, so too do we need to treat our life as a business. The trust factor applies both in the business of our life and the life of a business. Trust is an issue if we are committed to live with integrity. The courage to be congruent is what helps us to live with our vulnerabilities and build an internal foundation of trust. Trust is, after all, an inside-out job. When we say we can or can't trust something or someone, it is actually more useful to consider: can I trust myself to discern what works for me? Thus trust is more about me and my willingness to take good care of what does or does not work for me. When I do this response-ably, then too others will know by my actions that I can be trusted.

In the winter of 2012, there was an interview in *The Globe and Mail* (January 21, 2012) with author Eva Stachniak. In this interview, she talks about having discovered, through one of her main characters, that it isn't power that creates violence, contrary to our popular belief. It's vulnerability. That just made my head spin. As a psychotherapist, I've always worked from the perspective and maintained that to be vulnerable is one of our greatest strengths, so to be vulnerable would not beget violence in my world. Thus her observation really jarred me. In this case she maintained that, through this main character, she has learned that it is vulnerability that begets violence. What I understand her to have meant is that if and when we are not comfortable with our vulnerability, we will use violent means in order to avoid that stress. In the end, I am back to a position that our true strength is in our capacity and our willingness to be vulnerable in the face of our experience of stress.

WRIGHT

Would you say more about connecting through communication for success?

HARRISON

True relationship requires communication that connects. Words are my passion, albeit sometimes much to the chagrin of others around me. And I feel that we use words far too frivolously, not realizing the impact of the words we speak, both the impact on ourselves as well as on the people around us. Whether these are the people with whom we work, other colleagues, or our friends and family, our words have power. They have the power to lift us up and the power to tear us down. And the body listens to these words, not knowing the difference between what is so and what we tell ourselves is so. However, not all words are understood by the listener in the manner they're being used by the speaker.

Connecting is more than just words, which represent less than 10 percent of all communication. Many people communicate; few people connect. Communication that connects depends, first of all, on our own authentic connection with ourselves as well as a commitment to be truly present with another. This requires the courage to be vulnerable. We must be willing to get real with ourselves and to trust this authentic being, without which connecting with another is impossible. Crucial conversations with nonviolent communication or active listening are essential to true relationship.

Whatever we're working at, whatever we're dealing with, whatever we're talking about, can we stay present in crucial conversations, allowing for both parties to be seen and heard without it being a battle for win/lose? In so doing, we can discern and negotiate what is going to be most propitious for all concerned in any given moment. This is connecting through communication. This is relationship.

We can be right, but it doesn't mean everybody has to agree. Far better to first seek to understand than to be understood. Relationship or true connecting is through communication that allows both parties to have their needs met. And communication is the vehicle for connecting, first self with Self, and then self with another, such that everybody wins. This is not only a special way of speaking, it is also a distinct way of listening. If communication is to meet the needs of both parties, then a willingness and ability to listen for meaning (the intended meaning) is critical.

Listening is a highly dynamic process that involves not only hearing the words, but also a commitment to understand what those words mean to the one speaking. When we share a common mother tongue, we tend to err on the side of carelessness. We presume to know what the other person means and not take time to discern the true message. Often there is greater connection between two or more people who do not share a common mother tongue. These obvious differences predispose us and set us up for success, with a heightened conscious awareness and effort to connect. It is said that Eva (article noted above) refers to this process and commitment as decoding the secrets of a foreign culture. In keeping with Eva's position, it could be said that with committed listening, we aren't as likely to fall prey to our assumptions; we are more inclined to a commitment to truly understand than merely to hear.

Roger Martin, to whom I made reference earlier, has a book titled *The Opposable Mind*. In his book he talks about the ability of our mind to actually take two opposing thoughts and arrive at a third position—I call it a holy third— where you put the two together and arrive at something superior to either one position or the other. Yet, in choice making, we tend to think in duality, going one way or the other. With nonviolent communication, the challenge and the opportunity are: can I hear you without making it mean that I'm wrong or bad, even when your position doesn't agree with mine and vice versa? And so it is with connecting. We're all about relationship; if we can't form viable relationships through our communication, then what are we?

There is a quote by Joseph Hellel that fits in this context, "If I'm not for me, who will be, and if I'm only for me, what am I, and if not now, when?" I need to be able to really stand for myself and I also need to be willing to listen to you as you stand for yourself. If I can truly listen to you and you feel truly heard, you're going to feel safe and not combative, and then you'll be able to listen to me and so on and so forth. So it is that we could spiral upward and make room for both people on the page of conversation, remaining open to new possibilities even in the face of vulnerability. Indeed, it would be as a result of our courage to be vulnerable.

WRIGHT

Would you say more about relationship in our consideration of success?

HARRISON

First we must be aligned with our interior authority, standing fully in the ground of our core *I am* and refer again to our definition of success to answer this question. Too often success in the Western world is expressed through external values and endpoints; very often these values and endpoints are informed by what we have been socialized to believe is a measure of our success. But if I go back to the fact that I, and you, and all of us here are all about relationship, and if we don't work that out, well, then whatever we define as success will not be sustainable. Neither will it give us lasting satisfaction, vitality, or zest. All that comes from standing in alignment with those values that honor our authentic Self, and skill sets that dignify ourselves and another, celebrating our sameness and growing from our differences.

WRIGHT

Would it be fair to say that building relationships and communication supersede goal setting on the road to success?

HARRISON

No and yes, yes and no. Goal setting is important; I tell my clients when I'm working with them that "if you don't know where you want to go, how will you know when you've arrived?" So, yes, we need goals, David, but if those goals are only defined by external definitional properties dictated by socialized positions as to what's important, could this be why so many people miss the mark even though they've set a goal?

Also, humans have a weak connection with accountability. I don't mean we're lazy; we just have this inherent flaw in our mechanism. Example: we want to lose weight, we know how to lose weight, and yet we live in a continent marked by obesity. Goals are good and absolutely essential. If you want to cross America, you need to know your intended destination, otherwise there is no possible road map. Goal setting serves a purpose. But what might be more important is why you want to go across America. Questioning and being clear as to our "why" improves our chances of success that provides both sustainability and satisfaction.

Goals need to have a deep anchoring within the root core self in order to hold us to an endpoint where we can go: *Ah eureka, I've arrived, I'm there, I've made it.* However, it is also true that goals are not carved in stone and there is no final destination. The journey ensues as we continue to evolve. Goals simply provide an intentional direction for an ensuing journey. As we embark on a journey, our actions will lead us to new information and resources—personal or otherwise— that will further inform the next leg of the journey. So it's not about not setting goals; it's for what purpose are we choosing to pursue them. We have one life to live. Let us live it well by becoming what is required in order to achieve the success we set out to achieve.

WRIGHT

Who or what is it that we have to become to achieve these goals?

HARRISON

We have to become aligned with what is truly meaningful to our core Self— living a life worthy of the calling to which we are called. Thomas, in the Bible, gets a lot of bad press because he was a "doubting Thomas." I, however, like him. The reason I say I like Thomas is that he had the courage to question, he had the courage to look more closely and not simply accept it on blind faith. When we have the courage to look more closely from that sense of an authentic core self, living our purpose, at times it could still seem as though we are merely following the madding crowd. The difference, however, will be that because of our questioning process, enduring the ambiguities, we live our life by design with accountability, rather than by default.

WRIGHT

It is comforting to know that the person (Jesus) about whom Thomas was doing all the doubting, wasn't bothered at all; He just proved it.

HARRISON

Exactly! Isn't that wonderful? And why did it not bother Jesus at all? Because He knew who He was, knew His purpose, and was, is, and always will be, deeply rooted in that purpose. His roots were deep into the soil of the true and the ultimate *I am*.

WRIGHT

So do you think there is one road map that will serve everyone on the road to success?

HARRISON

I sure do, and that one road map would be to know that there is purpose in process, and to embrace the process to our purpose. If I think of success as a personal process, no matter what the end goal is, the road that we would be on—the road less traveled—is a process. This process does have a template, not a rigid formula or form; nevertheless, there are steps applicable to all. So we could say the road map is an understanding and embracing of a process, its directive being our purpose. Therefore, the one road map would be to know thyself and to thine own self be true. And in the words of Willis Harmon (1918–1997), "Because of the interconnectedness of all minds, affirming a positive vision [living our purpose] may be about the most sophisticated action any one of us can take."

WRIGHT

What an interesting conversation, Judith. I've learned a lot here today. I'm sure our readers are going to get a great deal out of this chapter, and I appreciate your taking so much time with me to answer these questions. It has been a delight.

HARRISON

It's been a privilege to be listened to so well, David. There is that listening key—the key to communication that connects. Thank you.

WRIGHT

Today I have been talking with Judith L. Harrison, an authoritative voice in the human behavior field. Through her private practice, she has spent the last thirty years helping many people discover how reframing their own experience and perceived or actual strengths and weaknesses can lead them to increased performance and overall job satisfaction. Judith uses these deeply personal insights to create a road map for her clients to best interact with others in personal and professional settings, achieving results they may have thought were never possible.

Judith, thank you so much for being with us today on our journey for *ROADMAP to Success*.

HARRISON

Thank you, David; it's been a pleasure. I look forward to meeting you on the road again.

Judith L. Harrison's well-rounded background includes several degrees, being clinically trained as a psychotherapist, and as a Master Trainer in Human Behavior. However, she counts her many years of living abroad and traveling through many different cultures to be one of the greatest experiences in her education and learning about what it takes to be fully human.

An authoritative voice in the Human Behavior field, Judith launched her career as a speaker and trainer in 1996 when she was invited to lead a workshop at the First World Conference of Combined Psychologists, Psychiatrists, and Psychotherapists, which was held in Vienna.

She also treasures her beginnings, being raised in rural Alberta, Canada, as one of nine children. She is married and lives with her husband in Southern Ontario. They have a fabulous daughter, son-in-law, and three amazing grandchildren who, she says, are the apple of her eye. She lives believing that life is a miracle, a blessing, and to be lived boldly.

Judith L. Harrison

Trumpeter's Choice Consulting, Inc.
Kitchener, Ontario
Judithlharrison@rogers.com
www.judithlharrison.com

CHAPTER SIX

An Extraordinary Life In An Ordinary Way
Segolene King

DAVID WRIGHT (WRIGHT)

Today I'm talking with Segolene King. Segolene awoke spiritually at an age when most are still asleep. She became disillusioned with the "successful" life expected of her. The high-paying job, nice house, husband and children scenario was not enough; she wanted more and went searching for it. Now a transformation coach, mentor, spiritual teacher, and author with students and clients worldwide, she is a director of the Cosmosis® Mentoring Centre, a school facilitating the ancient process of personal spiritual alchemy. She has also helped many women with her Feminine Source teachings. She was published in *Adventures in Manifesting* and is currently writing further books. She has a beautiful family in Australia.

Segolene, welcome to *ROADMAP to Success*.

SEGOLENE KING (KING)

Thank you.

WRIGHT

Let's start with the obvious question: what is your definition of success?

KING

To me, success is about realizing your highest calling or destiny. If you are successful materially or in terms of your status in society or your popularity, but you are not answering your true calling, then you are not really successful. No matter how it may look on the outside, if you are completely off track with your greater destiny, then you are not where you are meant to be.

I guess you could say that success is more about the bigger picture. I am more interested in eternal wealth than temporal wealth. I do feel that real success has to do with the discovering of the true self, being more than a little ego running around on the ground, pursuing selfishly motivated needs and wants. Realizing who you truly are goes hand-in-hand with realizing your destiny. Everything you do flows out of who you are.

You can have a big, lucrative business or many books published, have millions in the bank or lots of fans, but when this life is over, then what—be the richest man in the graveyard? Big deal! This life is just a bleep within eternity. All that matters at the end of any life is who you are and how much love or fear you brought into this world. This is what gets "weighed" at the end of any life; this is your karma.

Enjoy life, of course. But if you choose the way of ego, genuine fulfillment will have eluded you. This only comes to those who allow themselves to get sucked into place by the universe and those who find their true path.

Now, let me clarify my understanding of destiny. This is not something that is set in stone like an already-written book, stealing your right to make your own decisions along the way. However, all of us have a choice in each moment to either pander to our own little ego, or to step up to more of our potential, embracing a greater destiny unique to each. Take the easy way, or the higher road. There are different options available to us all in any given moment and different possible directions in life. Each moment, we choose who we can be and what kind of life we live. To me, pursuing that greater destiny of actualizing our highest potential, and fulfilling our soul's purpose, which we all carry within us like a road map to reclaiming who we really are, is real success.

Of course, being successful materially is not exclusive to fulfilling your calling. The two can be wonderful companions. But following your heart and higher destiny should not be compromised for the sake of money, fame, or status. The higher love and integrity need to need to come first and anything else is just a bonus. At the same time, embracing eternal success also means remaining real and grounded in your everyday life, enjoying it.

I know it's quite a grand definition of success, but at the same time your path may not be grand. Some people's calling is to be the best mother they can be, or be a strong leader of their community, or be the best cleaner this planet has ever seen. But whatever your calling, it will feel right in your heart and make you feel that you are in the right place, at the right time.

Embracing eternal success is not about floating off into the universe and becoming "holier than thou." It is living an extraordinary life in an ordinary way.

WRIGHT

How does one know if one is successful in that way?

KING

It can be tricky, as it is somewhat intangible compared to measuring success in terms of having your first million in the bank. But there are ways to know—if you really want to. And that is just why it can be tricky. How much do you really want to know if it meant that you had to drastically change how you live your life?

We need to understand that success in the eternal term is not a static goal. It's not a place you get to and once you are "there," that's it: "I'm the true self" or "I am fully realizing my destiny." You may have realized your destiny for now, but who says there is nowhere to go from there? It is eternal success because it links into eternity, and eternity doesn't stop. As long as you exist as a soul, traveling and experiencing life in one form or another through eternity, you never stop evolving and moving. That is simply the nature of the Universe. So as we grow, our potential grows with us and there is always more to learn, and always more to grow into. We need to redefine our sense away from the linear understanding of reaching a set point of success. At the same time we need to acknowledge and celebrate the successful steps and achievements on the way.

Another important understanding is that everyone is different and unique in achieving that particular mark of success. Depending on where you are in your journey of evolution and your growth on your spiritual journey, success will mean a different thing. It is just like a successful achievement for a child who is five years old might be to make a beautiful drawing or learn to count up to thirty. It is a very different kind of scale of success for a full-grown man with a qualification and big business. It's the same for being at different stages of spiritual growth.

So gauging how you are being successful is based on getting in touch with the feeling and knowing that it is deep within your heart. This is the only place where you will find Truth within yourself. It goes beyond what you think, or trying to figure it out by ticking boxes in a mental checklist. The logic of the mind can prove just about anything, including that $2 = 0$ (I have seen a mathematician friend of mine do it). Gauging this is about getting to know yourself at a deeper level, and being drastically honest about whether you are being true to yourself and to your own unique path. Are you really doing your best, and being your best at that? Everyone is unique and the more you do your best, the more you are able to do even more. It is a self-feeding process. It is something you need to learn, an ability you need to develop by working on opening the heart, and living from the heart's knowing more than the head. Then there are certain self-monitoring practices that can assist.

Learn to be able to face the truth of whether you are actually being in your integrity, being in your truth, and doing your best. There are people who teach this, as I do.

WRIGHT

Will you tell us about your journey to get where you are today?

KING

I was quite a sweet, shy, and insecure child—a "good little girl." In my teens I became deeply unhappy when I started to feel the weight of expectations placed on me by my parents, my teachers at school, and by society. I feel most teenagers to some degree feel this as they struggle to find their own identity. It can be a challenge, as there is so much pressure in our world to fit in, to go along with the crowd. On top of that, there often are expectations parents have for their children because they want the best for them as *they* see it, not necessarily as the child sees it. I felt the weight of all that and began to wonder where I was going in my life. I actually became quite depressed for a while, feeling despondent and directionless. I even entertained suicidal thoughts.

One day, at about fifteen or sixteen, I had an epiphany. I realized that as much as dark thoughts haunted me, I was not going to kill myself. There was something in me that just wasn't ready to give up. That day I decided that if I was going to live my life, then I was going to make it worth living. So I started seeking a sense of meaning and find something more that would make it all worthwhile.

I experienced a phase of wanting to be a rock star. This was because at that time in my life, music was a great comfort and inspiration to me. I wanted to bring that same comfort and inspiration to others, and so that was where I started to realize that having meaning for me came not only from doing something that made my heart sing, but also from giving back and doing something for the benefit of others or the world—to do something in service somehow.

Although born and grown in France, I eventually traveled to London at the end of my first year at university, as I felt it could take me closer to my dream. It just felt right, even though it was scary to do on my own in a foreign country speaking a foreign language. I met my first husband there and as I continued my studies and completed my degree, I traveled a lot between England and France. I even lived in Spain for a while.

At some point, I had to face the reality that I was not going to become a rock star, simply because I was way too shy to sing in front of anyone—I had too much fear. I saw how desperately attached I had become to that dream. Eventually I grew out of it as I continued my search. I began wanting to find the meaning of everything, not just for my own life, but everything. I turned to ancient history and archeology for a time. Then one day I realized that what actually appealed to me there was to find the answers about what greater truth ancient civilizations knew that has been forgotten.

This is how I started on the spiritual path. I read books, attended workshops, and classes. I traveled, learned, researched and eventually found this path, which is my work now—the path of personal spiritual alchemy. This has been the most rewarding journey in terms of transformation in my life. It has turned me around from being that confused, messed up gypsy girl, traveling around looking for answers, to being in a place where I have now realized everything I used to dream of when I was in my early 20s, and more.

I dreamed of work that would give me a sense of meaning, I wanted to find a way to contribute positively to the world, I wanted to live in a beautiful place, close to nature, find true love, have a wonderful family, work from home, be really free with my time. I have all of that! I feel very blessed and very grateful for this. At the same time I feel so different about myself that my motives for living this way are no longer about filling an emptiness within, or giving myself meaning. I am simply doing it because I love it and it feels right. I feel that I've been sucked into place.

It has not always been an easy path. It has taken much courage to confront my demons and let go of my safety blankets. Fortunately, I have the alchemical teachings and processes to clear and transform issues and limitations toward eternal success. And the journey continues. I have new dreams, new pursuits, and new success that I'm heading toward now. It is always unfolding.

WRIGHT

Will you explain a bit more about the relationship between this more eternal success and material success?

KING

Often spirituality has been associated with deprivation and sacrifice. To me this is far from the only way. Material deprivation can be a formative lesson for those who have tended to be greedy, so they can overcome their greed and selfishness. But this is a whole new age of rediscovering, or remembering, that

God/Goddess is Love, which is a teaching found in many spiritual traditions. Love can be many things, tough love or gentle healing love. Embracing spirit, God, or the Universe—however you want to call it—is about love, not being miserable. But it is about love of spirit, not love of indulging the selfish ego.

For eternal success, you do have to sacrifice the selfish ego. You have to sacrifice fear, you have to sacrifice your commitment to mediocrity, hedonism, and laziness. So, yes of course there are required sacrifices but they are not necessarily exclusive of material wealth—not unless the material things you consider part of your success actually hold you back spiritually.

Everything is possible. An example would be holding on to your big house, which is preventing you from moving somewhere to challenge some of your fears and self-imposed limitations, or meet a teacher. Another example is staying in a particular job for the financial security, or a dysfunctional relationship, even though it might mean betraying your own integrity and killing something precious inside of you. There are ways that material success and eternal success can go against each other, but it is not necessarily so.

The other side of that coin is that someone amazing and successful in eternal terms is also someone who is very real, grounded, and authentic—one who embraces the everyday life from a perspective of wisdom and integrity.

Sometimes I meet spiritual people who seem to be floating three feet above the ground. They are lofty and full of "love and light" talk but there is something disconnected and aloof in them, as though they are not really present in the nitty-gritty humanness of it. While these people may connect with a sense of spirituality, they do not integrate their spirituality in a wholesome way. There is a split in their being. That is not eternal success either, and these people are often challenged to manifest material success.

Appreciate the opportunity to be on planet Earth. You need to develop skills that demonstrate your ability to understand how things work, mastering the art of living in human form. Manifesting some degree of material success can be a nice side benefit, but it should not be the primary motivation because this would be a selfish motivation. If you are embracing spirituality to achieve fame, riches, or power, then your alignment is off. There is only so far you can go in terms of eternal success when coming from such a place.

WRIGHT

You talked earlier about the notion of karma. Will you expand on this?

KING

In my experience, when I start speaking of karma, students or clients often start to worry. They equate karma with a sense of being punished for past perceived mistakes, or rewarded for their good actions—"what goes around comes around" and all that. Karma is not about punishment or revenge, or even reward. In essence, it is about choices and consequences and learning our lessons to become better at living in love and wisdom. Every choice you make has a consequence. Karma is designed to help us take responsibility for the consequences of our choices—on any level—and learn to make wiser, more loving choices. Whether it is our words, our actions, or our thoughts, everything we do has an impact. The Law of Karma affects everyone on the planet, there is no escaping it.

Karma is not even about good or bad, it is about assisting us to grow into becoming the best we can be, to embrace more of our potential by helping us see the consequences of our actions so that we learn to make better choices and evolve into better versions of ourselves. If you make a choice of love, you will generally get consequences of love; if you make a choice of fear, the consequences of that choice will be of fear. This is where the adage "life is your mirror" comes in. The things that happen in your life and the phenomena you manifest around you are not random. They are all the consequences of choices you have made, or energy that you have projected out into the world, all coming back at you as an opportunity to be better. No matter what you think you are doing or choosing, if what you are manifesting comes back all wrong, chances are you are not facing the truth about your choices and motives.

At the end of any one life, the karma from that life boils down to one balance: how much love you have brought into this world versus how much fear you have produced during that life. It's not just what you do, but who you are and the energy you hold.

Wherever you still come from a place of fear and ego, therefore producing fear, so there is still room for learning and improvement. That sets up the karmic flows, events, and necessary experiences for your future in this life or another, so you can learn and embrace a better, wiser, more loving way.

WRIGHT

What are your main tips to readers about achieving this eternal success?

KING

Okay. Remember that eternal success means embracing more of the greater potential of whom and what you can be as part of this wonderful Creation. So firstly, you must realize that life is a lot more than running around "doing stuff" in order to "get" stuff—"stuff" being the operative term here. You need to awaken to the fact that there is a life beyond what the eyes can see and what the ears can hear, beyond the comfort zone, beyond the recognition of other egos or your place in the pecking order of the "tribe." You need to make space for the richness of your inner life and the presence of an all-pervading force just behind the veil and make it a part of your everyday reality.

If you really want to be successful in that eternal sense, you have to commit to making it a way of life. It does not necessarily mean leaving your job or family to lead a spiritual life. Do what you do, but in a spiritual way.

This is not a hobby that you can do part-time and then forget about it for the rest of the day. You can't just engage in the process of growing and looking at yourself once or twice a week and then during the rest of the week indulge your fears, selfishness, and ego. This is something that needs to transpire into every moment and aspect of your life. That's why it is called *integrated spirituality* or *integrated mastery*, because it is about integrating it into your everyday life. This is a big key to being successful here—making the commitment and prioritizing that aspect of your life as it pervades everything you do, everything you are.

Secondly, being eternally successful requires wanting to know and realize the truth—the truth of who you are, how your life really is, the truth about the universe, and everything. You have to want the truth more than you want the comfort of your familiar life, or the self-imposed limitations that you have carried or the glamour of living a materially focused life. If you don't have the truth, all you have is lies and illusions. Prioritizing the truth above all things goes a long way to help you see where you carry illusions, faulty beliefs, and self-imposed limitations. It realigns your perception so that you can, in contrast, notice more of where you are not embracing the truth or trying to make your life and yourself so much smaller than it truly is. Once you see that, it is important to be willing to let go in order to embrace more of what is possible in love and wisdom.

Much of this process of embracing the greater potential has more to do with undoing rather than doing. It's a bit like uncovering the diamond in the rough, buried under many layers. It is a process of unraveling all the false identities, all the illusions and self-imposed limitations to make room for your greater self. It takes courage and it takes commitment; it also takes surrendering and allowing. I guess these are some of the main key elements.

WRIGHT

So what are the main pitfalls to watch out for on this road to success?

KING

To excel in any field of endeavor requires a certain amount of navigating through challenges and pitfalls in order to master that particular skill or art. If it was so easy to be a master of spiritual evolution, everybody would be a great spiritual master but that is not the case. This path of spiritual mastery is always about a fine balance between two extremes. It takes awareness, wisdom, and a certain amount of attention to walking that razor edge path between the extremes to remain in humility, integrity, and equanimity.

Here are some common pitfalls I'd like to point out. I mentioned before about becoming ungrounded. Some people actually use spirituality almost like an addiction; they use it to escape their lives and escape themselves. As you begin to experience spirituality in a deeper way, it can be quite intoxicating—so much energy, so much love, so much light. It can become a way to get away from what they judge and struggle with, rather than to embrace and resolve it in order to grow into more wholeness of being.

The process of spiritual realization is not about floating off to go somewhere else, it's about being really here and making room for spirit to fill you up and illuminate your whole life. It is about bringing that light and love into the world where it is really needed, and to be and share this with wisdom. It is actually quite selfish to use spirituality to escape life rather than bring a spiritual presence into this world in service of the greater good. Spirituality is about wholeness, not separation. So it is important to stay grounded, and constantly work on facing what you judge about yourself, your life, and the world in order to harmonize it all and bring the love and clarity of spirit into every area of your experience.

Another common pitfall is spiritual pride and a sense of important work. Once some people begin to feel that they've achieved a certain amount of growth—perhaps cleared a load of issues, experienced certain states of being in meditation or otherwise, or a sense of oneness—they can develop a feeling of superiority. They begin to take themselves too seriously; perhaps they feel they have an important mission to "save" others. Consciously or not they believe they are better than people who are not spiritual and that they are special. Often enough they then proceed to do spiritual work such as teaching, healing, or writing, but they do it with unclear motives. They forget that spiritual work is about being a vessel or a channel for certain energies to work through you, that it is not about becoming a spiritual groupie magnet. It has nothing to do with this "you," which is just the ego. This is not spirituality. Spirituality is about grounding and expressing love. You are just a channel, a messenger.

And here is another very important thing: The higher on the ladder you are, the harder you can fall. On this path, the more you achieve in terms of mastery and integration of being, the more you have to remain very thorough with your practices, self-monitoring, and your level of integrity and clarity. The more you grow spiritually, the more there is no room for fear, doubt, or indulging egocentric habits in your life. The clearer you become, the more sensitive you become to energies and choices of fear and the more you can be affected by it. As in any discipline, such as a virtuoso musician for instance, when you reach high levels of mastery you need to practice all the time and maintain ever higher standards for yourself in order to remain at such level of proficiency. You must also keep growing and evolving. So it is with spiritual mastery. This journey doesn't just end, it's always unfolding.

Sadly, spirituality is not something that is greatly supported in our societies. We live in a world where there is still much fear, selfishness, and cruelty and we all carry our own baggage of unresolved issues. Individuals are not encouraged to wake up to themselves and embrace their greater wholeness as spiritual beings in human form. So we need to some degree to go against the tide, to be a bit of a maverick of wisdom, and to uphold high standards of clarity in order to not get caught up in our own negative ego or the collective ego surrounding us.

WRIGHT

Your teaching work is rooted in the ancient tradition of personal and spiritual alchemy. What is it and how can it help achieve success?

KING

Alchemy is often associated with early chemistry, dusty laboratories, and white-bearded old men boiling strange potions. But alchemy is one of the most ancient traditions of mankind. It is usually associated with the transformation or transmutation of lead into gold, base metals into noble metals, or even the creation of the philosopher's stone, or the elixir of eternal life. In fact, alchemy was born in ancient Egypt, well before recorded history. It was born out of a desire to reach eternal life, yes, but in more than one way. The Egyptians, as you know, have a strong belief in life after death and so this sparked the impetus for the tradition of ancient alchemy to be born.

Alchemy was in part the early stages of chemistry, looking for a way to create substances that would help the body live longer and achieve eternal life. But the basis of alchemy was about the theory that by refining our body and the human vessel as a whole—the emotions, the mind, and the soul—we could achieve eternal life. What is often forgotten is that a big section of alchemy was about refining the human vessel through the practice of transformational spirituality.

Now, these days science, especially quantum physics and such more recent branches of physics, has established that everything is made of energy, every single object, every atom, every particle; everything is energy at various levels of vibration. This is where science meets alchemy. We know that not only is everything made of energy, but that the human will and the human intention has an effect on this energy and can change it. We all affect everything around us.

Personal spiritual alchemy works with this fact of the energetic and interconnected nature of all Creation in order to refine ourselves so we can become the clearest possible vessel for our greater spirit self, to ground that eternal loving presence into our body. It's not about transmuting lead into gold, it's about transmuting fear into love. Fear and love are not opposites. Fear is not "bad" and love "good." They are actually the same energy, which is the same energy of creation that runs through everything, but vibrating at different degrees of vibration. Fear is a lower vibration of love. So you can actually raise the vibration of fear into all kinds of energies and then take it into the levels of unconditional love and beyond. We actually teach how to do this.

The tradition of alchemy has been often persecuted throughout history, and eventually near stamped out, because it's a very self-empowering tradition. It refuses to place an intermediary between you and the universe/Source/God. It's not about worshiping anyone; it's about empowering you to develop your own connection with Source. It makes it harder to indoctrinate and control people.

And so the teachings have mostly been forgotten, or remembered only in fragments. I haven't met many people who actually demonstrate that they have in-depth knowledge of the old mechanism of spiritual alchemy.

However, being empowering does not mean that you won't need a teacher at some point. In any area in life, if you really wish to excel, you need to receive mentoring from someone who is an expert or master at that craft. If you want to learn an instrument and you are really gifted (which is rare), you can do quite well teaching yourself for a while. But if you really want to get to virtuoso level, you have to take teaching from a master musician in that particular instrument. In the same way, if you really want to excel in alchemy, you need to find a teacher who demonstrates that he or she actually knows and understand those teachings, and that the person actually applies them in his or her life, walking the talk of it every day, even when no one is watching.

No one is perfect, but be discerning in choosing a teacher who really demonstrates embodying the truth of those teachings and is an example of those teachings at work.

WRIGHT

Your work also includes teaching healing and empowerment of women. What do you have to share about the road map to success for women in particular?

KING

We are at a very interesting stage in history for women in the aftermath of the whole feminist movement. After so many centuries of repression, we have now really achieved—in the West at least—some degree of economic and political equality. However, women in general still carry the scars and the unconscious influences of our past.

You may not be familiar with this notion, which Carl Jung also wrote about, but there actually is a collective psyche of women throughout the world, just as there is a collective psyche for men, for each nation and for humanity as a whole.

We all have our individual psyche and we have a collective one that carries strong forces. This gives us common qualities and concepts because we can all be motivated by similar archetypal forces and can relate to each other—we all share a certain collective reality.

The collective female consciousness still feels the weight of past repression, anger and shame. So for women to be successful, we need to work on clearing the burden of our past so prevalent in the collective. We need to live our life not trying to *prove* that we are equal. I have met a number of outwardly successful women who, after some years of the high-powered life, come to that realization for themselves. While they're trying to become equal to men, they have to some degree lost the unique qualities and presence of being women. Women fought to be equal to men, to be taken seriously in a man's world, being tough and competitive. This has sometimes led to the detriment of their femininity and being in touch with themselves as women. I have had many students comment that they still feel they're not always taken as seriously as men in the workplace unless they act that way.

Women can achieve so much more of the greater potential of "being woman" in the outer world and in the eternal sense. For this, we need to let go of the past and heal the old wounds and limiting history. We must let go of our mistrust and anger against men, and of our sense of being less than or the need to prove something. We need to simply realize the unique wondrousness of what women can bring to this world, to their work, to their family and to themselves. Women are generally naturally more receptive to feeling, intuition, spirit's whispers, and nature. This actually gives women a natural ease in terms of their journey toward eternal success.

WRIGHT

Very interesting.

Finally, if there was one key piece of wisdom that readers should take away from this chapter to use in everyday life, what would that be?

KING

To wake up to the fact that there is a lot more to life than meets the eye. If you live life just by going along with what you are told, what you see on television, what everybody else does, or what you've been taught at school, then you are merely going through the motions. That is not really living. Life is a co-creative process, and for this you need to uncover who you truly are, explore and embrace that truth, and contribute to life in your own unique way, in harmony with your heart's unique "song."

Staying within the comfort of your rational little world means you miss out on so much experience, so much learning, and so much life!

Even though it can be confrontational and can seem a little surreal if you're not familiar with this understanding of success, simply consider that there may something beyond what your eyes can see and your mind's boxes can quantify. Living out of the box may seem like jumping into the void, but it's also one of them most enriching things you'll ever do.

WRIGHT

This has been a great conversation. I have learned a lot here today. In your spirituality I hear a lot of pragmatism as well.

KING

Well, yes. It is all about being real and authentic in the deepest possible way. There is so much more that I could share and explain but I don't have the time within this chapter to really go in depth—the subject is vast and far-reaching.

WRIGHT

I think you approached the subject well and I think you've given us—men and women alike—much to think about and work on.

I deeply appreciate all the time you've taken with me to answer these questions; it's been a delightful conversation.

KING

Likewise. Thank you very much.

WRIGHT

Today I have been talking with Segolene King. Segolene is a transformation coach, a mentor, a spiritual teacher, and author who has students and clients worldwide. She is a director of the Cosmosis® Mentoring Centre, a school facilitating the ancient process of Personal Spiritual Alchemy. She has also helped many women with her feminine source teachings.

Segolene, thank you so much for being with us today on *ROADMAP to Success*.

KING

It has been a pleasure, thank you.

Born and bred in France, Segolene King has always been thirsty for travel and exploration, both within and without. Graduating in International Business and Languages, she lived in England, Scotland, Spain, Northern Ireland, and is now based in Australia with her husband and daughter. She and her husband are the directors of the Cosmosis® Mentoring Centre, which offers mentoring programs in the ancient art of Personal Spiritual Alchemy to students worldwide. This is facilitated online with regular teleclasses, face-to-face intensives, and workshops. Segolene also offers Feminine Source courses to empower women to reclaim the wondrousness of the Sacred Feminine within.

Segolene King

Cosmosis® Mentoring Centre
PO Box 2350
Clarkson, WA 6032, AUSTRALIA
+61 (0)8 9407 4310
segolene@mysteryschool.org.au
http://mysteryschool.org.au
http://segolene.com.au

CHAPTER SEVEN

It's About The Journey AND The Destination
Patrina Clark SPHR, HCS

DAVID WRIGHT (WRIGHT)

I'm speaking today with Patrina Clark, founder and president of Pivotal Practices Consulting LLC. Patrina has more than twenty-five years of experience in optimizing individual and organizational performance. She is certified as a Human Capital Strategist (HCS), a Senior Professional in Human Resources (SPHR), and an Infinite Possibilities Coach. She is pursuing certification as a Results Coach with the NueroLeadership Group.

Patrina has held executive and senior leadership positions at the United States Government Accountability Office (GAO), the Federal Election Commission (FEC), Department of the Navy, and Internal Revenue Service (IRS). She serves on the Board of Experts for the United States Women's Chamber of Commerce (USWCC).

The Department of the Navy awarded her the Meritorious Civilian Service Medal for Outstanding Meritorious Service as the Region's highest ranking civilian. She is also the recipient of a Hammer Award from the National Partnership for Reinventing Government for her exemplary contributions to the IRS's modernization efforts.

WRIGHT

Patrina, welcome to *ROADMAP to Success*.

PATRINA M. CLARK (CLARK)

Thank you very much, David. It's my great pleasure to be here.

WRIGHT

It's really great to talk to you again. I always enjoy it.

You were featured in another of our success series books just a few years ago. So, tell me, what have you been up to since we spoke last?

CLARK

Wow, quite a bit! I actually ended up deferring the launch of my consulting practice for a few years to take another executive position in the federal government.

I'm very glad I made that decision because I gained invaluable perspective about organizations, organizational dynamics, change leadership, and authentic leadership. I also forged some great relationships and learned quite a bit more about myself—both personally and professionally.

Perhaps one of the most significant benefits of waiting to launch, though, was allowing the concept of my own practice to mature and evolve a bit more so that when I finally did launch, I was definitely clearer about what I wanted to do.

WRIGHT

I understand there are three main pillars for your consulting practice: *Coaching, Organizational Consulting and Training,* and *Public Speaking.*

Will you share a bit more about your specific areas of focus with our audience?

CLARK

I'm happy to! As you mentioned, there are three main focus areas or pillars. I've actually refined them a bit as follows:

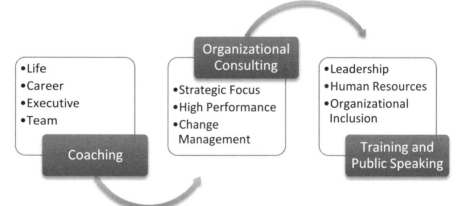

These three pillars encapsulate what I believe to be one of my competitive advantages as a coach and consultant: bringing order to chaos, whether it is a slightly chaotic situation or one in complete disarray. I work with individuals and groups to help identify ways to enhance performance, get them started on their transformative journey, and support them along the way.

Coaching

As you mentioned in the introduction, I am a certified Infinite Possibilities Coach and working on my coaching certification with the NeuroLeadership Group. Both of these programs have very special meaning to me.

The Infinite Possibilities framework provides a spiritual, non-religious program for living deliberately, or with intention. And, in our intentional living, we are endowed with the power to create our own greatest happiness.

The Results Coaching System is a program based on neuro—brain—science, with an emphasis on supporting clients while they develop their own insights about how to live their greatest lives.

Because we are both physical and spiritual beings, I have a great appreciation for the importance of integrating the whole person into the coaching process. And, I very much appreciate the tools and perspectives these two frameworks offer. Both have certainly made a difference in how I think about and live my own life. And, in my opinion, there are few things more rewarding than helping others see their own brilliant light illuminating their individual path to greatness.

Consulting

My consulting practice is focused more at the strategic rather than tactical level. This means that I help my clients see the forest made up by the trees. And, while I can certainly help an organization very effectively resolve their tactical issues, my greater satisfaction comes from helping them identify what is causing the issue. This ensures that when we develop a solution, it's a solution that is going to address the root cause rather than merely treat a symptom of the problem.

That having been said, there are absolutely times when treating a symptom is critical. Sometimes you have to stop the pain to be able to focus on the deeper issue. Eventually, though, I believe the greatest value in a consulting engagement is realized when client and consultant take the time to identify and resolve those deeper issues.

Public Speaking and Training

I am often asked to deliver speeches or facilitate sessions on:
- "soft" skills (e.g., effective communication, effective networking)
- diversity and inclusion
- human resources issues (particularly HR issues in the federal government)
- leadership

I have had the privilege of addressing many wonderful audiences, and public speaking is another of my passions. Because of the depth and breath of my experience, I bring great insights to my audiences, and my presentations are highly relatable.

I was recently added to the U.S. Women's Chamber of Commerce's Board of Experts. As part of my responsibilities, I have the opportunity to address global groups and organizations. Most recently, I was asked to serve on a panel with Dr. Mae Jemison (the first African American female astronaut) to deliver a speech at the South African Embassy, commemorating their National Women's Day, for approximately 125 invited guests.

My remarks were focused on women entrepreneurs and their vital role in the American economy. As part of those remarks, I shared information about the Chamber's Women-Led Economy initiative. This initiative is aimed at maximizing the economic power of American women and women across the globe. American women control an estimated $4.3 trillion of the $5.9 trillion in annual consumer spending— making American women the largest single economic force in the world. And, globally, women control $20 trillion in spending—truly an economic powerhouse capable of dramatically reshaping the economic future of women around the world.

WRIGHT

Well, congratulations on officially launching your practice. I'm guessing that must have taken quite a bit of courage, given the state of the economy.

CLARK

It was actually pretty terrifying. And, I wish I could say that I courageously stared my fear in the face and did what I knew I had to do. While taking the leap was an act of great courage and faith, I actually had a forcing function that made leaving federal service the lesser of evils.

I was diagnosed with scleroderma approximately ten years ago. Scleroderma is a connective tissue disease that involves changes in the skin, blood vessels, muscles, and internal organs. It's a type of autoimmune disorder that occurs when the immune system mistakenly attacks and destroys healthy body tissue.

Fortunately, I have the less severe form of the disease so it's not life-threatening. However, it has created some physical limitations for me. These limitations and the risks of my condition worsening were what ultimately led to my decision to leave.

What I can now tell you on the other side of my decision is that the idea of a thing is oftentimes so much scarier than the thing itself. It was absolutely terrifying to walk away from a reliable, dependable, federal position and go into this completely unknown arena.

One of the analogies I use for the experience is zip-lining, but you could use any experience. I used to be very afraid of heights and imagined that I would never be able to do anything like zip-lining. Now, it's actually one of my favorite things to do on vacation.

So if you equip yourself, get trustworthy coaching or instruction, and take the necessary safety precautions, an otherwise scary experience can turn out to be a truly exhilarating one.

WRIGHT

Do you feel okay about the timing of your decision, given the economy?

CLARK

I am amazed by how much better my life is in so many ways. We see what we choose to see and believe what we choose to believe. There were and continue to be some absolutely horrific stories about the impact the economy has had on so many lives. At the same, though, there were and continue to be lots of stories about abundance and wealth and increase.

While you could see scarcity or risk in a particular situation, there is usually an equal opportunity to see abundance or great opportunity in the same situation. We each get to choose our focus and perspective and that fuels our emotions and actions.

Henry Ford is famously quoted as saying "If you think you can, if you think you can't, you're right." I finally decided to think that I could—so, I did.

WRIGHT

When we last spoke—and it's been a while—you defined success as being at peace with every aspect of your life and fully present in the here and now, while continuing to move confidently, even boldly, toward tomorrow. Does that still hold true for you?

CLARK

I have to be honest and say when I read that I just thought "Really?" While it sounded pretty good at the time in an academic sort of way, it now sounds to me to be incredibly absolute and naïve about the human experience.

I don't think it's necessary to be totally at peace with everything. In fact, given that most of us will grapple with the physical and emotional aspects of being human, I think that definition set an unrealistically high bar.

I'm more comfortable saying success is a very individual experience. Each of us has to figure out for ourselves what it means for us to be successful and not rely so much on others or external indicators of what success is supposed to be. By aligning our purpose and passion and focusing more on the journey than the destination, I think we make great progress in living a life well lived, which to me is the ultimate definition of success.

WRIGHT

Your résumé is quite impressive, and you're clearly quite accomplished. But, I understand that you would not personally describe yourself as a success. Why is that?

CLARK

Well, first thank you very much for the compliments and acknowledgement of my résumé. I used to look it over and think "Wow! I did all that stuff?" So, without question I've had some phenomenal experiences.

I truly think success is more of a journey than a destination. And, while I have absolutely done some really cool things, I still feel that I have so much more to do.

I think a part of my reluctance to give myself the "success" label is it might make it too easy to say, "Okay, I've arrived. I've done enough." And, I don't think that any of us ever really fully arrives because as long as we are on the planet, we should be evolving—gaining new experiences, new perspectives.

I am very appreciative of the opportunities and the experiences I've had. But, in terms of calling myself a success, I'm hesitant to do that.

WRIGHT

So, tell me about the interrelationship between passion and purpose as they relate to success.

CLARK

It's a very close relationship—at least, I think that it should be. Too often I think we end up doing what we think we're *supposed* to do rather than what we're really excited and enthusiastic about doing. We sometimes move through life with most of our days looking very much the same.

We can amass accomplishments, accolades, and awards, but those can be hollow if we're not really aligned with our passion—those things that really thrill us, excite us.

Our passion gives us clues about our purpose. Cultivating the ability to consistently live a passion-filled life is its own reward. And, your passion may not make a bit of sense to someone else. That's okay—it only needs to make sense or feel good to you. When we live a passion-filled life, it may or may not yield what others would view as external benchmarks of success (e.g., cars, houses, bling). So what! Who cares?

Your life isn't about what someone else thinks it ought to be about. Make your life about what you feel it ought to be about. If you're living a life that thrills you and doesn't harm anyone else, then in my book, that makes you wildly successful.

WRIGHT

Discovering our purpose can be very challenging; at least, I have found it that way. Have you figured out your purpose yet, and what advice do you have for helping others discover theirs?

CLARK

You're definitely right about it being a challenge, for some more than others.

I enjoy biographies, especially those about people I admire and respect. One thing I've noted that is almost always true among them is clarity of purpose and persistence in living out that purpose, no matter the challenges or obstacles.

For many of us, part of the challenge with connecting with our purpose is not having had our natural talents nurtured in a way that provides that kind of clarity. For so many of us, our existence becomes shaped by the attitudes and beliefs of those around us about what our greatest life looks like or should be. And, it can take some time to cut through all of that and rediscover our truest selves.

I have to rely more on myself to define what my purpose is rather than to have my purpose defined by people or situations outside of myself. So, I am much more often these days doing what thrills me rather than what people think I should be doing. And, I am feeling better and better about the alignment of my passion and my purpose.

In terms of advice, follow your own internal compass. I believe that there is a voice inside of us with all of the guidance and wisdom we need. The key is learning how to hear it above all of the other noise we fill our lives with.

One of the things that has worked well for me is being willing to take a risk every now and then—do something outside of my comfort zone.

While some of my friends see me as a trailblazer, I feel as though I have typically played it fairly safe, coloring inside the lines. Admittedly, I probably have broader lines than many, but I generally did what was comfortable. And, that helps underscore my point about each of us needing to be the judge of our own actions because only we have the complete picture.

I think it's important to take risk or color outside of the lines every now and then. Always playing it safe or doing what's familiar is not necessarily going to yield the kind of energy and excitement you get from living a passionate life.

I think it's also important to spend time being quiet and still. That can be really hard for someone who has a high energy level like me, but it doesn't take a lot of time to be quiet and still. Just every now and then, slow yourself down long enough to hear your internal compass guide you in the direction of your passion. Not taking this time is a lot like trying to listen to multiple songs at the same time—you may be listening, but it's difficult to truly hear.

When something speaks to your soul, you should answer the call. Some of us make the call ring quite a few times before answering, and that's okay—as long as we answer. We should not be afraid to answer when something from deep inside calls us. Discovering what's on the other side of that answered call is what this journey is really all about. We have to travel or move in a way that feels authentic or true. Toward that end, we just have to get more comfortable worrying less about other people's opinions. Sure, we are social beings and we are part of a broader society. The greater truth, though, is that our individual purpose is unique to us.

Our ultimate responsibility to the greater society is to be the greatest individual contributor to that society that we can possibly be. And, I believe we do that by living passion-filled lives.

WRIGHT

I've always been a little suspicious of people who tell you to find your purpose before you do anything. I'm an old guy and I've done a lot of things; I've always found purpose in what I was doing.

CLARK

That's an excellent point and the truth is that if we waited to find our purpose before we did anything, many of us would be sitting idle for a long time. It is in the very doing that we develop clarity. That's certainly been true for me.

WRIGHT

What has been your most significant challenge and what were your lessons learned from that situation?

CLARK

That's a great question. I think most of my greatest challenges fit very nicely in this bucket labeled "worrying too much about what someone else thinks." I think I have spent entirely too much time caring more about someone else's opinion about what I needed to be doing than trusting myself to do what was ultimately best for me. And, that's been true for me both personally and professionally. So, my big takeaway is that I can and must love and trust myself enough to listen to my inner voice, spending quiet time, and deliberately focusing on what I want and need to be happy. This has provided amazing insight and clarity on living my own personal best life.

That doesn't mean my life is without challenges. It just means I have a greater peace about moving through those challenges. And, while I absolutely have friends and family who support me through those challenges, I know that ultimately it is up to me to save myself.

WRIGHT

So, who have been the most influential people in your life?

CLARK

Well, that's another great question. It's also a dangerous one to answer because once you start naming names, you run the risk of leaving someone out. Fortunately, I anticipated your asking me this.

Rather than naming specific people, I'd like to describe three categories, or groups, of people who have been most influential in my life. And, these are listed in no particular order.

The first group includes the people who have loved and supported me deeply and faithfully—those folks who have nurtured my soul and facilitated my being the person I am today.

The second group includes those who have dreamed bigger dreams for me than I could have dreamed for myself. They have and continue to be great sources of inspiration for me.

And, the third group includes those who have adored me. Being totally honest, that feeling of adoration can be intoxicating! It absolutely makes my spirit soar. And, I'm looking forward to having more of these people in my life.

I'd like to just make a quick note about so called "haters." A hater is someone who focuses on a person's so-called flaws as a way of taking away from that person's success. As a counter to the negativity, some people say things like, "My haters are my motivators." For me, though, that is still giving the negativity too much energy. So, while it is unavoidable to have people who will be judgmental and even mean-spirited, I think it's possible to not succumb to that negativity.

While competition can be a great energizer, too often there is an unhealthy or negative competitive dynamic, seemingly more so among women. I try to give this dynamic as little energy as humanly possible and instead, focus on the people who nurture and fuel me. This helps me to have a more rewarding, light-spirited experience as I strive to be the best me I can be.

WRIGHT

It's been my experience that most people are harder on themselves than they are on other people. So, when you find someone who dreams bigger dreams than you do, that's great. You get to take off your judicial robes and go for it.

CLARK

That's exactly right! And, I think that's another great insight from you. That insight is exactly what led me to identifying the three types of most influential people in my life.

I have a long history of being very hard on myself. I am truly my absolute worst critic—sometimes to the point of getting in my own way.

So the people I want to give the most energy to are those people who take me out of that space and move me into the space of infinite possibilities. In that way, I can move more in the direction of passionate living rather than focusing on all these things that aren't necessarily truly constructive and helpful.

WRIGHT

What would you most like to be remembered for? You're not going to die tomorrow or anything, but have you thought about your legacy?

CLARK

I was going to say maybe we can have another interview in about twenty years, and you can ask me that. I'm sure I'll have greater clarity then.

I don't know. If I have to give an answer right now, I would like to be remembered as someone who understood what it means to be human and who radiated humanity.

WRIGHT

That would be good.

CLARK

It's actually my daily mantra, so I'm hopeful that I'm showing up this way every day—or, at least most days.

And, I like the simplicity of my answer. I think that when you answer those kinds of questions, it's good to keep it simple. I still cringe a bit when I think about that definition of success from my first chat with you a few years ago. So, I'm definitely learning to keep it simple.

WRIGHT

And, more realistic it sounds like to me.

CLARK

Thank you, David. Yes, absolutely. And, more relatable.

WRIGHT

Well, Patrina, what a great conversation. As I said before, I always enjoy talking with you. I really do appreciate your spending all this time with me this afternoon answering all these questions. It's just been delightful. I have learned a lot, as I always do.

CLARK

Well, David, thank you so much for taking the time. You're always such a gracious host, and I equally appreciate chatting with you and your willingness to share your own insights about these things.

WRIGHT

Today I've been talking with Patrina Clark. She is the founder and president of Pivotal Practices Consulting, LLC. She has twenty-five years of experience in effective change management, performance improvement, strategy development, and organizational development. It sounds like she knows what she's talking about, at least *I'm* listening.

Patrina, thank you so much for being with me today on *ROADMAP to Success*.

CLARK

Thank you, David.

Patrina Clark, founder and president of Pivotal Practices Consulting LLC, has more than twenty-five years of executive and organizational leadership experience. As a coach and consultant, one of her greatest joys is using her life's experiences to help others make the most of theirs. Patrina is a well-decorated former government executive, and she holds several professional certifications. She is available for public speaking engagements and as an individual coach or organizational consultant.

Patrina M. Clark, HCS, SPHR

Pivotal Practices Consulting LLC
"practice really does make perfect"
301-927-2389 land
443-481-8511 cell
855-85-PIVOT (855-857-4868) toll-free
and fax
patrina@pivotalpractices.com
www.pivotalpractices.com

CHAPTER EIGHT

Bounce Forward to Business and Team Success
Charmaine Hammond

DAVID WRIGHT (WRIGHT)

Today I'm talking with Charmaine Hammond, known internationally as the Bounce Forward Expert. Charmaine Hammond MA, BA, is a transformational speaker, team-building expert, international bestselling/award-winning author, and radio host helping people live inspired resilient lives and transforming workplaces. She is also an award-winning businesswoman, and best-selling author of *On Toby's Terms: Toby the Pet Therapy Dog and His Hospital friends*, *Bounce Forward, Building Resilient and Inspired Teams,* and co-author of *GPS Your Best Life- Charting Your Destination and Getting There in Style.* Her wildly popular book, *On Toby's Terms,* is currently in development to become a major motion picture. She is a sought-after guest in all forms of media and is host of three popular radio shows.

Charmaine welcome to *ROADMAP to Success.*

CHARMAINE HAMMOND (HAMMOND)

Thank you; it's great to be here with you today.

WRIGHT

You have had an interesting career as a correctional officer, crisis intervention worker, contract specialist for government, a corporate mediator, and trainer. How have these past careers helped you now as an international transformational speaker, leader, and successful business owner?

HAMMOND

There has been a common thread woven through each of these careers, even though on the surface they appear quite different. These professional experiences have taught me about communication, interpersonal relationships, leadership, and resilience. I also discovered how easy it is for people to get stuck in patterns of behavior, relationships, communication, and situations that don't serve them well.

These careers also taught me a great deal about communication, "difficult conversations," and conflict resolution; they inspired me to become a dispute resolution expert and mediator. Returning to University, I obtained a master's degree in Conflict Analysis and Management and was a mediator in the corporate world for a number of years.

Now, as an international transformational speaker and consultant, I work with business owners and corporate leaders to develop the skills necessary to achieve team and business success and build inspired, resilient, and productive teams.

Leaders and business owners frequently tell me that managing the talent and human capital aspect of the business is the most challenging responsibility and, for many, the most stressful.

WRIGHT

You're known and respected as the Bounce Forward and collaboration expert. What exactly does it mean to Bounce Forward and how is this tied into business success?

HAMMOND

Resilience is commonly defined as the ability to bounce back after change, challenge, crisis, and adversity. For many years I subscribed to that definition; however, I noticed one common difficulty—the multitude of professionals were (and are still) stuck. Every day I was meeting with professionals and business owners who were not bouncing back after business challenges, which of course made it difficult for their teams to bounce back. It became evident that many were stuck in relationships, situations of the past, unresolved drama, and habits or behaviors that do not serve them well. I thought, "There must be another path to resilience."

Studying resilience, and the traits and qualities of resilient people resulted in me creating my own working definition of resilience, and that is to Bounce Forward not back. Essentially, I view resilience as the ability to stand tall, brush off your knees, move forward, and learn after experiencing life and business challenges. I now know that this is what ignites transformation and professional growth.

Leaders and teams that are resilient work through challenges with less drama, they forgive one another and themselves and move forward, they can find hope in a situation that appears dismal, they collaborate and support one another, ask for help, and they often thrive in times when other businesses are failing.

One government department I consulted with had a team that grew from five to sixteen in less than a year. This rapid growth and constantly evolving and changing expectations were just some of the many difficulties this team dealt with on a daily basis. Their leader, John, was experienced and resilient. He invested in his team, ensured that he communicated clearly and consistently, and took time weekly to build the team while managing change. While there were many growing pains, the business of this department was not impacted. Deadlines were met, services were of high quality and, most importantly, the team bounced forward. There was high collaboration, a clear vision to work toward, respectful communication, and trust. All great benefits of a resilient leader helping the team navigate through changing times.

After presenting to thousands of people around the world, consulting with hundreds of leaders and just as many business owners, I know firsthand the need for collaboration and resilience.

WRIGHT

What specific life or business experiences shaped your beliefs about resilience and bouncing forward?

HAMMOND

I love this question because many years ago I used to think I was the pro at being resilient. I remember the very day that this definition of bouncing forward (not back) became clear to me. I was sitting on our sixteen-foot Hobie Cat Caterman sailboat, on the grass in the back yard experiencing one of many fearful moments of getting back on the boat.

Years earlier, my husband and I were out sailing and capsized. We swam for our lives and barely survived the ordeal before being rescued. The following day, my husband, Christopher, got back on the boat. I froze, decided I no longer liked sailing, and remained fearful of the sport for years.

Christopher was ready to sell the sailboat since he was the only one sailing. I finally convinced myself to give sailing another try, but my fear of experiencing a similar ordeal again created intense stress and nervousness. This was tough to deal with, as I am typically a confident person and have been able to work through fear. In fact, I remember thinking "I thought I was the resilient one" then realized I needed to Bounce Forward instead of bouncing back into the drama and fear that kept me from doing what I once enjoyed. We both experienced the same situation, yet we dealt differently with it. The same holds true in the workplace. Team members can all experience the same event (e.g., a workplace change, downsizing, cut back, conflict); however, the responses to the change or crisis may be very different. When my husband and I sold the sailboat that we capsized on, and purchased a different catamaran—one that was bigger and more stable—I was able to move through my fear and I now very much enjoy sailing.

Life and business will always be accompanied by challenges and storms such crisis, conflict, change, and adversity. To Bounce Forward means that we lean into the situation, even if it's uncomfortable, stand tall, and brush off our knees if we fall down. Ultimately we learn and grow through the challenges so that we Bounce Forward resulting in a more resilient and, of course, healthier outcome.

The connection between this sailing accident, resilience and business, is that life-changing or catastrophic events may happen in the workplace. There will be some team members who work through these challenges with ease, grace, and skill, as my husband did with the sailing accident. There will be other team members who become paralyzed by fear, as I did. When a team is strong, healthy, and resilient, there is a strong foundation to keep hope afloat and the team bouncing forward.

Now, this sailboat accident has actually become the basis of one of the keynotes that I speak about around the world in corporations and businesses to help people to understand the importance of developing solid skills to be able to Bounce Forward and be resilient in business and personally so they can adapt and adjust to any situation that comes their way.

WRIGHT

As an international speaker and facilitator, you have worked with hundreds of teams and thousands of people. What gets in the way of bouncing forward?

HAMMOND

This list is long one. The most frequent barriers to bouncing forward that I hear from my corporate clients and leaders are:

- Time. We are in an era where professionals are doing a great deal more with less time (and sometimes fewer resources). Lack of time and resources becomes a barrier, but the good news is we can manage time and resources differently to be able to Bounce Forward.

- History impacts a business or team's overall resilience. Many organizations and corporations are plagued by unresolved issues and conflicts and individuals who compare how things used to be to how things are now, and who get stuck in the past.
- Relationships, believe it or not, are something else that can get in the way of resilience. A lot of relationships come with a certain set of behaviors, values, and assumptions. Healthy relationships help build healthy people (and teams).
- Technology definitely impacts resilience. We live in a time of urgency and immediacy. Many professionals feel overwhelmed by the amount of information they receive and are exposed to on a daily basis through cell calls, e-mail, texting, and so on.
- Unhealthy coping patterns and lifestyles. Many people are on the run, keeping up a fast pace, not taking breaks, eating while working (or not eating at all). The body needs proper sleep, exercise, hydration, and healthy food.

These are a few of the many issues that get in the way of resilience.

We must not forget the importance of continually investing in the team. Taking time to build the team is an essential foundation of success, and strengthens trust, communication, and relationships. With the organizations I have worked with that have invested time and resources into building and sustaining trust and by developing strong effective relationships, they are able to cope with the challenges that come their way. Even if it's tough, they get through it and the relationships aren't harmed.

WRIGHT

When you talk about your Bounce Forward Model, you explain there are four key elements, each contributing to personal and professional success. Would you tell our readers what these four components are and how they impact success?

HAMMOND

The Bounce Forward Model I developed has four key areas that, when understood and practiced, contribute to high levels of workplace resilience and business success.

The first is what I refer to as Courageous Dialogue—having the conversations that matter most but are mostly avoided. Consider Sue, a leader for twelve years with strong technical skills but lacking in leadership skills. She was consistent in avoiding difficult conversations with her peers and those she supervised. When conflict surfaced, she was more likely to drop hints, speak in innuendos, and hope that the dispute would work itself out. Many of her team members were exasperated by her discomfort in addressing performance issues, setting clear expectations around communication and professional relationships, managing differences and conflict, and giving sensitive feedback. In short order, the team followed her lead, avoiding conversations, and gossiping about issues instead of resolving them. The result? Diminishing trust, unnecessary drama, unresolved issues, and limited resilience.

One of the first steps in helping this team build resilience was to facilitate the development of a Team Charter. This charter was built with the team for the team. It offered guidance around providing and receiving feedback, dealing with sensitive issues, addressing and resolving conflict, how the team would hold one another accountable and, essentially, how the team would work together. This charter gave the team permission to move toward resilience and to communicate courageously. In time, trust improved, old conflicts were put aside, and communication was more direct and respectful.

The second component of the Bounce Forward Model is the aspect of work/life balance (or harmony), wellness, and stress management. Managing our stress on a day-to-day basis is essential. This includes taking care of our bodies physically by getting enough rest, regular activity and exercise, eating healthy, and drinking enough water. It also involves taking care of ourselves emotionally and being able to manage our time and our energy.

One team I worked with implemented some highly effective wellness activities including a lunch time walking club, healthy snacks and meals at meetings, water coolers in various hallways (not just the coffee room), corporate wellness challenges and activities, wellness awards, and fitness equipment in the staff lounge. The underlying message (as told to me by the employees) was that the health of the employees mattered.

The third component is what I call teamwork by design, not default. It is not uncommon to see businesses that establish their teams out of necessity, without really having the time to plan the team or build the team. Leaders who build the team by design take into consideration the skill sets and working styles of the team members. When leaders build the team and work from standards, guidelines, or a set of values (I like to call it a team charter) by which the team agrees to operate, the result is not only individual resilience but team resilience. Teams are like vehicles—they require ongoing maintenance, repair, monitoring, and care. Building a team by design is not a destination, but rather a journey that is ongoing. Karen is a great example of a business owner who builds her team by design. As a small business owner, Karen learned that hiring smart contributed to overall business success and profit. She does not rush into hiring decisions, she hired staff who had a passion for the work, exhibited strong work ethics, and who were a good fit with her existing team. Karen told me that hiring smart was better for business than hiring to simply fill the position vacancy. She discovered that careful hiring led to less frequent hiring. There was less turnover, and overall a stronger team.

And lastly, the fourth component is what I refer to as the Ask—asking for what one needs. Asking for help is very difficult for many leaders and business owners; in fact, it's very difficult for many people in general. When you master the skill of asking for help as well as the skill of receiving the help, you build your resilience. Additionally, there are organizational benefits in that when leaders model the ability to ask for help, it actually sets a culture in the team that perfectionism is not required. Instead, excellence is the goal. Leaders who demonstrate these skills encourage their team to ask for help rather than sticking with something that turns into a catastrophe because no one asked for help. Modeling these skills challenges the myth that asking for help is a sign of weaknesses—it's actually a sign of strength, good judgement, and collaboration.

These four components: courageous dialogue, stress management, resilience, teamwork by design, and the Ask are what create a Bounce Forward response in the workplace.

WRIGHT

So what are practical and tactical strategies that leaders and business owners can implement to bounce forward?

HAMMOND

I'm all about simplifying tactical approaches and practical approaches so that we can actually apply them. Some very basic actions to be able promote more resilience, or a higher Bounce Forward response rate in the organization, is first of all to help team members be extremely clear on the team's vision and values. When the team members understand what they're striving for, they can go in the direction they need to go.

I love to see these organizations and companies that are replacing junk food in their vending machines with healthier snacks. This and having lots of water in the workplace are very basic, but they help maintain a strong degree of health. In fact, one of the companies I was working for created a great lunchtime program. Every lunchtime they had a different activity going on. There was a walking club on Mondays, on Tuesdays they had a staff member who did yoga, so she would run a yoga class, on Wednesdays they would do another activity. They were optional participation programs but very effective for those who participated.

One company I worked with bought pedometers for every single staff member in the organization. They had, I think, several thousand people working for them. They created monthly challenges that helped built the team and got people stepping into action, literally, to improve their health and Bounce Forward.

I think the last part of the practical/tactical tips to being resilient and bouncing forward is about managing conflict. We are often under stress because we're not dealing with things that are upsetting us or that need to get put on the table for the team to resolve. So we have to be able to have those courageous dialogs and not spend so much time worrying about what's going on. Spend that time resolving what's going on.

WRIGHT

You've mentioned that you have very little stress in your life, despite the fact that you're playing a bigger game in business and life and the demands are higher on you now than ever. You said that the only stress you have is that which you create yourself or decide to breathe life into. Many people would welcome having little to no stress, so what's your secret?

HAMMOND

It took me years to figure this out but one of the most powerful lesson I learned is that much of the stress people experience is not from the event itself, but rather by the way they perceive the event—the meaning that they assign to it.

For example, Mary accepted a leadership position in a team that was falling apart at the seams. Conflict was high, trust was low, and turnover was at an all-time high. Mary's fellow leaders made comments to her such as "Wow! Could it get any worse?" and "Sometimes a team has to hit rock bottom before they crawl their way out of the mess," and "This team is going to destroy itself before it gets any better. They are like a walking time bomb!"

As you can see, her colleagues chose to see the situation as hopeless, extremely negative, and without much hope for improvement. Instead, Mary described her team as, "A team that needs leadership now more than ever," and her team's situation as, "the situation has hope, and we begin where we are with what we have," and "the situation is a symptom of issues needing immediate attention and correction." Mary chose to see the situation through a different lens, one of hope and where the issues could be resolved and improved. Her colleagues frequently made comments such as, "You must be so stressed," "I'll bet you have a few more grey hairs than yesterday," and "Are you wishing that you never took this post?" These comments all focused on the stress, but Mary chose to focus on and tap into people's resilience, therefore her stress was greatly reduced. Had she chosen to see the situation as her colleagues did, it is safe to say that her stress and frustration level would have been much higher.

I've spent a lot of time training myself and teaching people to look at situations differently. Going back to the sailboat accident I referred to earlier on, I remember thinking that day in the lake could be fatal and that I could be swimming for my life. When I allowed my thoughts to come from fear, hopelessness, and doubt, my ability to swim, and my physical strength were reduced drastically. When my thoughts were focused on hope, courage, strength, and the shoreline, my strength improved, time passed quickly, and I believed I was getting closer to shore.

Another approach is to focus on what is within your control to fix, change, or influence, instead of worrying about things you can not directly impact. This practice alone can dramatically improve your focus and reduce worry and stress.

The other essential ingredient is self-care. When you are not taking care of yourself in terms of sleep, exercise, fresh air, and health, your ability to manage stress decreases. The more you do every day to be resilient, the better prepared you are to handle the big challenges that surface in life and in business.

WRIGHT

Some people say that 95 percent of the things one worries about never come to fruition and the 5 percent is inevitable.

HAMMOND

That statement really makes me smile because it is so true. This statement reminds us to be careful where we put our thoughts and our attention. Our outcomes are impacted by what we think. What we think impacts how we show up in life and in business. Thoughts impact our words and how we are in relationship with others. A great way to improve resilience is to carefully choose your thoughts, be present to know when your thoughts are not supportive to a resilient mind-set, and then have the focus and ability to change them.

WRIGHT

So what does it mean to you to be successful and how do you measure success?

HAMMOND

What a great question! My definition of success has changed over the years as I've faced different challenges. I measure my success by how I show up in life. By being true to my values and beliefs such as integrity, kindness, authenticity, and being a champion for others in their journey to success. I also measure success by my ability to Bounce Forward.

I do know that success is easier to achieve when you are working in your passion and knowing that you are on purpose. Success breeds success. I am a firm believer that when you are a champion for others and their success, it comes back to you tenfold, therefore, I enjoy sharing my learning, paying it forward to other people.

Success isn't really about status, money, or fame; it's more about being able to say yes to these questions:

Am I completing the goals that I set for myself?

Am I keeping commitments to myself as well as to others?

Am I achieving the dreams I created?

Am I taking steps to Bounce Forward?

Am I playing full out being in service to others?

And, am I helping enough people along the way?

WRIGHT

On the way to success there are often defining moments, obstacles to overcome, and learning. What stands out for you as the most important, meaningful lessons you have learned along the way?

HAMMOND

There is a long list of lessons and defining moments, but the most profound and game-changing was discovering that I was a perfectionist. My all-or-nothing thinking was problematic. Being a perfectionist created incongruence in my life, personally and professionally, and it created a great deal of stress. The biggest disappointment was admitting that that when you're a perfectionist, you often miss tremendous opportunities.

At the same time this discovery of perfectionism came to light, we adopted a dog who had behavioral issues, in fact he was a master at turning our life upside down. This challenging dog, Toby, was costing us thousands of dollars in property damage to the house, vet bills, and doggie daycare. I discovered that you can't be perfect and live with a dog like Toby. I was in love with the dog—he wasn't going anywhere—and I thought that maybe it would be easier to change myself than to change him. This mind-set and expectation led to reduced stress, less behavioral challenges with Toby, and new opportunities opened up. We discovered that Toby was a dog who needed a job—a purpose. When we rechanneled his destructive behaviors in a positive way, by getting him trained to be an animal assisted therapy dog, his behavior improved dramatically. He went on to impact thousands of people around the world.

Toby connected me with my passion for writing, and he became the star of my books, and an upcoming movie.

WRIGHT

Success usually does not come from working in isolation. I remember a wise man told me one time that if I were ever walking down a country road and saw a turtle sitting on top of a fence post I could bet he didn't get up there by himself. So who has impacted your success and growth and in what way?

HAMMOND

Oh there are so many people who have impacted my growth, on a personal and a professional level. I've always had coaches and mentors, right back to my first career in the correctional system. Deepak Chopra taught me how to relax and be present.

Masterminds have also been an important part of my success. Collaborating with and masterminding with other professionals, sharing influence, and learning from those who were where I wanted to be has been a very important ingredient.

Then, of course, I have people in my world who just love me dearly—my family, my friends, and my husband who has supported me in taking risks and stretching outside my comfort zone.

On our path to success, whether that be personal, business, or both, there is a lot of risk. There are times when you will feel very vulnerable. Having strong family and collegial relations to support you in those times will help immensely.

A stranger impacted my success. I was at a conference and was returning the car to the Hertz car rental place. The gentleman, Glen, who was helping me, explained that he was retired and he was missing working with people so much that he came back to work. He observed the binder title page and made a comment that it looked like I had attended an event for speakers. I nodded my head and said, "Yes, the course provided great knowledge about how to deliver powerful presentations and facilitate transformation." Glen's questions intrigued me; he seemed to know a great deal about the speaking industry. Glen gave me some incredible advice. I was curious how he knew all this advice about the speaking industry and then he shared that he had worked with all the greats. Glen had spent his first career working for some incredible speakers like Anthony Robbins. It was a chance meeting that a stranger impacted my life and my career. As I was walking away, he called "Charmaine! There is one thing I want you to always remember. It's a quote from Oscar Wilde, "Be yourself—everyone else is taken!" That quote became my foundation of how I showed up in life and in business!

WRIGHT

If you could summarize five takeaway actions that you think are critical for business and professional resilience what would they be?

HAMMOND

The first would be to build your team, then put time, care, and energy into building your team. Pay attention to team relationships, trust, and communication.

Two more takeaway actions are the importance of building resilience and to take time away from business and work. Many leaders and business owners work extremely long hours and because they are in their passion and working on purpose, the work doesn't feel like work. I can relate to that because what I love what I do; it gives me energy. Speaking and writing do not feel like work for me, I have to ensure I take time away from it to reflect, recharge, and disengage from the business.

The third takeaway is the importance of having goals (and focus). It is my hope that resilience and the ability to Bounce Forward become the two top goals for our readers.

The fourth takeaways are to take time and care to build professional and business relationships, and resolve issues. Business owners and leaders get caught up in the day-to-day tasks of running the business or leading the team and it doesn't take long before the small issues grow into big, complicated issues. It is very important to take time to resolve the issues that are getting in the way; they usually don't go away or improve with age. If something is irritating you, causing you to lose sleep, or it continually runs through your mind, it probably requires your attention to either deal with it or have a conversation with someone who can help you solve it.

I would say the fifth and final tip to help business and professionals stay resilient is to have fun. Try and find time every single day to connect with what gives you purpose or what gives you joy. Think about what puts a bounce in your step and where you can use your talents.

Those are five ways we can boost our business resilience.

WRIGHT

What a great conversation.

HAMMOND

Thank you. Talking about bouncing forward and working with purpose gives me great joy.

WRIGHT

I have learned a lot here today this has been great. Not only have I learned a lot but I am positive that our readers will as well.

I appreciate your taking all this time with me to answer these questions.

HAMMOND

It's been my pleasure; I really appreciate the opportunity.

WRIGHT

Today I've been talking with Charmaine Hammond. Charmaine is a transformational speaker, team building expert, best-selling and award-winning author, and radio host. She helps people live inspired, resilient lives and she transforms workplaces.

Charmaine, thank you so much for being with us today on *ROADMAP to Success*.

HAMMOND

Thank you.

Charmaine Hammond, MA, BA, is an international transformational speaker, helping people live inspired, resilient lives. She is a leading trainer in corporate North America helping transform workplaces.

Charmaine is also an award-winning and best-selling author of *On Toby's Terms*, and *Bounce Forward Building Resilient and Inspired Teams*. She is co-author of *GPS Your Best Life: Charting Your Destination and Getting There in Style*. She has been published in *Chicken Soup for the Soul: What I learned from the Dog*. Her book, *On Toby's Terms*, is currently in development to become a major motion picture! She has been featured on CBC, CTV, Global TV, 820 CHAM, *Alberta Prime Time News*, many major newspapers, and in various magazines.

Charmaine Hammond

Hammond International Inc.
Box 418 Plamondon
Alberta Canada T0A 2T0
780-798-2426
charmaine@hammondgroup.biz
www.hammondgroup.biz

CHAPTER NINE

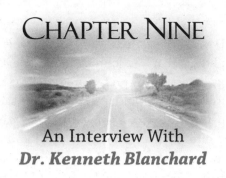

An Interview With
Dr. Kenneth Blanchard

DAVID WRIGHT (WRIGHT)

Few people have created a positive impact on the day-to-day management of people and companies more than Dr. Kenneth Blanchard, who is known around the world simply as Ken, a prominent, gregarious, sought-after author, speaker, and business consultant. Ken is universally characterized by friends, colleagues, and clients as one of the most insightful, powerful, and compassionate men in business today. Ken's impact as a writer is far-reaching. His phenomenal best-selling book, *The One Minute Manager*®, coauthored with Spencer Johnson, has sold more than thirteen million copies worldwide and has been translated into more than twenty-five languages. Ken is Chairman and "Chief Spiritual Officer" of the Ken Blanchard Companies. The organization's focus is to energize organizations around the world with customized training in bottom line business strategies based on the simple yet powerful principles inspired by Ken's best-selling books.

Dr. Blanchard, welcome to *ROADMAP to Success*.

DR. KEN BLANCHARD (BLANCHARD)

Well, it's nice to talk with you, David. It's good to be here.

WRIGHT

I must tell you that preparing for your interview took quite a bit more time than usual. The scope of your life's work and your business, the Ken Blanchard Companies, would make for a dozen fascinating interviews. Before we dive into the specifics of some of your projects and strategies, will you give our readers a brief synopsis of your life—how you came to be the Ken Blanchard we all know and respect?

BLANCHARD

Well, I'll tell you, David, I think life is what you do when you are planning on doing something else. I think that was John Lennon's line. I never intended to do what I have been doing. In fact, all my professors in college told me that I couldn't write. I wanted to do college work, which I did, and they said, "You had better be an administrator." So I decided I was going to be a Dean of Students. I was provisionally accepted into my master's degree program and then provisionally accepted at Cornell because I never could take any of those standardized tests.

I took the college boards four times and finally got 502 in English. I don't have a test-taking mind. I ended up in a university in Athens, Ohio, in 1966 as an Administrative Assistant to the Dean of the Business School. When I got there, he said, "Ken, I want you to teach a course. I want all my deans to teach." I had never thought about teaching because they said I couldn't write, and teachers had to publish.

He put me in the manager's department. I've taken enough bad courses in my day and I wasn't going to teach one. I really prepared and had a wonderful time with the students. I was chosen as one of the top ten teachers on the campus coming out of the chute. I just had a marvelous time.

A colleague by the name of Paul Hersey was chairman of the Management Department. He wasn't real friendly to me initially because the Dean had led me into his department, but I heard he was a great teacher. He taught organizational behavior and leadership. So I said, "Can I sit in on your course next semester?"

"Nobody audits my courses," he replied. "If you want to take it for credit, you're welcome."

I couldn't believe it. I had a doctoral degree and he wanted me to take his course for credit, so I signed up. The registrar didn't know what to do with me because I already had a doctorate, but I wrote the papers and took the course, and it was great.

In June 1967, Hersey came into my office and said, "Ken, I've been teaching in this field for ten years. I think I'm better than anybody, but I can't write. I'm a nervous wreck, and I'd love to write a textbook with somebody. Would you write one with me?"

I said, "We ought to be a great team. You can't write and I'm not supposed to be able to, so let's do it!"

Thus began this great career of writing and teaching. We wrote a textbook called *Management of Organizational Behavior: Utilizing Human Resources*. It just came out in its eighth edition last year and has sold more than any other textbook in that area over the years. It's been nearly thirty-five years since that book came out. I quit my administrative job, became a professor, and ended up working my way up the ranks.

I obtained a sabbatical leave and went to California for one year twenty-five years ago. I ended up meeting Spencer Johnson at a cocktail party. He wrote children's books—a wonderful series called *Value Tales for Kids* including, *The Value of Courage: The Story of Jackie Robinson,* and *The Value of Believing In Yourself: The Story Louis Pasteur.* My wife, Margie, met him first and said, "You guys ought to write a children's book for managers because they won't read anything else."

That was my introduction to Spencer. So, *The One Minute Manager* was really a kid's book for big people. That is a long way from saying that my career was well planned.

WRIGHT

Ken, what and/or who were your early influences in the areas of business, leadership, and success? In other words, who shaped you in your early years?

BLANCHARD

My father had a great effect on me. He was retired as an admiral in the Navy and had a wonderful philosophy. I remember when I was elected to president of the seventh grade, and I came home all pumped up. My father said, "Son, it's great that you're the president of the seventh grade, but now that you have that leadership position, don't ever use it. Great leaders are followed because people respect them and like them, not because they have power." That was a wonderful lesson for me early on. He was just a great model for me. I got a lot from him.

Then I had this wonderful opportunity in the mid 1980s to write a book with Norman Vincent Peale. He wrote *The Power of Positive Thinking.* I met him when he was eighty-six years old when we were asked to write a book on ethics together, *The Power of Ethical Management: Integrity Pays, You Don't Have to Cheat to Win.* It didn't matter what we were writing together, I learned so much from him, and he just built the positive stuff I learned from my mother.

When I was born, my mother said that I laughed before I cried, I danced before I walked, and I smiled before I frowned. So that, on top of Norman Vincent Peale's influence, really affected me as I focused on what I could do to train leaders. How do you make them positive? How do you make them realize that it's not about them, it's about whom they are serving? It's not about their position, it's about what they can do to help other people win.

So, I'd say my mother and father, then Norman Vincent Peale, had a tremendous effect on me.

WRIGHT

I can imagine. I read a summary of your undergraduate and graduate degrees. I had assumed you studied Business Administration, Marketing Management, and related courses. Instead, at Cornell you studied Government and Philosophy. You received your master's from Colgate in Sociology and Counseling and your PhD from Cornell in Educational Administration and Leadership. Why did you choose this course of study? How has it affected your writing and consulting?

BLANCHARD

Well, again, it wasn't really well planned out. I originally went to Colgate to get a master's degree in Education because I was going to be a Dean of Students over men. I had been a government major because it was the best department at Cornell in the Liberal Arts School. It was exciting. We would study what the people were doing at the league governments. And then, the Philosophy Department was great. I just loved the philosophical arguments. I wasn't a great student in terms of getting grades, but I'm a total learner. I would sit there and listen, and I would really soak it in.

When I went over to Colgate and took some education courses; they were awful. They were boring. The second week, I was sitting at the bar at the Colgate Inn saying, "I can't believe I've been here two years for this." This is just the way the Lord works—sitting next to me in the bar was a young sociology professor who had just gotten his PhD at Illinois. He was staying at the Inn. I was moaning and groaning about what I was doing, and he said, "Why don't you come and major with me in Sociology? It's really exciting."

"I can do that?" I asked.

He said, "Yes."

I knew they would probably let me do whatever I wanted the first week. Suddenly, I switched out of Education and went with Warren Ramshaw. He had a tremendous affect on me. He retired a few years ago as the leading professor at Colgate in the Arts and Sciences, and got me interested in leadership and organizations. That's why I got a master's in Sociology.

The reason I went into Educational Administration and Leadership? It was a doctoral program I could get into because I knew the guy heading up the program. He said, "The greatest thing about Cornell is that you will be in a School of Education. It's not very big, so you don't have to take many Education courses, and you can take stuff all over the place."

There was a marvelous man by the name of Don McCarty who ended up going on to be the Dean of the School of Education, Wisconsin. He had an effect on my life, but I was always just searching around. My mission statement is: to be a loving teacher and example of simple truths that help myself and others to awaken the presence of God in our lives. The reason I mention "God" is that I believe the biggest addiction in the world is the human ego, but I'm really into simple truth. I used to tell people I was trying to get the B.S. out of the Behavioral Sciences.

WRIGHT

I can't help but think when you mentioned your father, and how he just bottomed-lined it for you about leadership.

BLANCHARD

Yes.

WRIGHT

Years and years ago when I went to a conference in Texas, a man I met, Paul Myers, told me, "David, if you think you're a leader, and you look around and no one is following you, you're just out for a walk."

BLANCHARD

Well, you'd get a kick—I'm just reaching over to pick up a picture of Paul Myers on my desk. He's a good friend, and he's a part of our Center for FaithWalk Leadership, where we're trying to challenge and equip people to lead like Jesus. It's non-profit. I tell people I'm not an evangelist because we've got enough trouble with the Christians we have, we don't need any more new ones. But, this is a picture of Paul on top of a mountain, and there's another picture below of him under the sea with stingrays. It says, "Attitude is Everything. Whether you're on the top of the mountain or the bottom of the sea, true happiness is achieved by accepting God's promises, and by having a biblically positive frame of mind. Your attitude is everything." Isn't that something?

WRIGHT

He's a fine, fine man. He helped me tremendously.

I want to get a sense from you about your success journey. Many people know you best from *The One Minute Manager* books you coauthored with Spencer

Johnson. Would you consider these books as a high water mark for you, or have you defined success for yourself in different terms?

BLANCHARD

Well, *The One Minute Manager* was an absurdly successful book, so quickly that I found I couldn't take credit for it. It was published around the time when I really got on my own spiritual journey and started to try to find out what the real meaning of life and success was. That's been a wonderful journey for me.

The problem with most people is they think their self-worth is a function of their performance plus the opinion of others. The minute you think that is what your self-worth is, your self-worth is up for grabs every day because your performance is going to fluctuate on a day-to-day basis. People are fickle. Their opinions are going to go up and down. You need to ground your self-worth in the unconditional love that God has ready for us, and that really grew out of the unbelievable success of *The One Minute Manager*. When I started to realize where all that came from, that's how I got involved in the ministry I mentioned. Paul Myers is a part of it. As I started to read the Bible, I realized that everything I've ever written about or taught, Jesus did. You know, He did it with twelve incompetent guys that he hired. The only guy with much education was Judas, and he was His only turnover problem.

WRIGHT

Right.

BLANCHARD

It was a really interesting thing. What I see in people is not only do they think their self-worth is a function of their performance plus the opinion of others, but they measure their success on the amount of accumulation of wealth, on recognition, power, and status. I think those are nice success items. There's nothing wrong with those, as long as you don't define your life by that. What I think you need to focus on rather than success is what Bob Buford, in his book *Halftime,* calls significance—you know, moving from success to significance.

I think the opposite of accumulation of wealth is generosity. I wrote a book called *The Generosity Factor* with Truett Cathy, who is the founder of Chick-fil-A, one of the most generous men I've ever met in my life. I thought we needed to have a model of generosity. It's not only your treasure, but it's time and talent. Truett and I added *touch* as a fourth one.

The opposite of recognition is service. I think you become an adult when you realize you're here to serve rather than to be served. Finally, the opposite of power and status is loving relationships. Take Mother Teresa, as an example. She couldn't have cared less about recognition, power, and status because she was focused on generosity, service, and loving relationships, but she got all of that earthly stuff. If you focus on the earthly, such as money, recognition, and power, you're never going to get to significance. But if you focus on significance, you'll be amazed at how much success can come your way.

WRIGHT

I spoke with Truett Cathy recently and was impressed by what a down-to-earth good man he seems to be. When my friends found out that I had talked to him they said, "Boy, he must be a great Christian man, but he's rich." I said, "Well, to put his faith into perspective, by closing on Sunday it cost him $500 million a year." He lives his faith, doesn't he?

BLANCHARD

Absolutely, but he still outsells everybody else.

WRIGHT

That's right.

BLANCHARD

Chick-fil-A was chosen as the number one quick service restaurant in Los Angeles. They only have five restaurants here and they've only been here for a year.

WRIGHT

The simplest market scheme, I told him, tripped me up. I walked by the first Chick-fil-A I had ever seen, and some girl came out with chicken stuck on toothpicks and handed me one; I just grabbed it and ate it, it's history from there on.

BLANCHARD

Yes, I think so. It's really special. It is so important that people understand generosity, service, and loving relationships because too many people are running around like a bunch of peacocks. You even see pastors who say, how many in your congregation? Authors, how many books have you sold? Business, what's your profit margin? What's your sales? The reality is that's all well and good, but I think what you need to focus on is relationships. I think if business did that more and we got Wall Street off our backs with all the short-term evaluation, we'd be a lot better off.

WRIGHT

Absolutely. There seems to be a clear theme that winds through many of your books that have to do with success in business and organizations. It is how people are treated by management and how they feel about their value to a company. Is this an accurate observation? If so, can you elaborate on it?

BLANCHARD

Yes, it's a very accurate observation. See, I think the profit is the applause you get for taking care of your customers and creating a motivating environment for your people. Very often people think that business is only about your bottom line. But no, that happens to be the result of creating raving fan customers, which I've described with Sheldon Bowles in our book, *Raving Fans*. Customers want to brag about you, if you create an environment where people can be gung-ho and committed. You've got to take care of your customers and your people, and then your cash register is going to go ka-ching! and you can make some big bucks.

WRIGHT

I noticed that your professional title with the Ken Blanchard Companies is somewhat unique—Chairman and Chief Spiritual Officer. What does your title mean to you personally and to your company? How does it affect the books you choose to write?

BLANCHARD

I remember having lunch with Max DuPree one time. He is the legendary Chairman of Herman Miller. Max wrote a wonderful book called *Leadership Is An Art*. I asked him, "What's your job?"

"I basically work in the vision area," he replied.

"Well, what do you do?" I asked.

He said, "I'm like a third grade teacher. I say our vision and values over, and over, and over again until people get it right, right, right."

I decided from that, I was going to become the Chief Spiritual Officer, which means I would be working in the vision, values, and energy part of our business.

I ended up leaving a morning message every day for everybody in our company. We have about 275 to 300 around the country, in Canada, and the U.K. Then we have partners in about thirty nations.

I leave a voice mail every morning, and I do three things on that as Chief Spiritual Officer. One, people tell me who we need to pray for. Two, people tell me who we need to praise—our unsung heroes and people like that. And then three, I leave an inspirational morning message. I really am the cheerleader—the energy bunny—in our company, and the reminder of why we're here and what we're trying to do.

We think that our business in the Ken Blanchard Companies is to help people to lead at a higher level, and help individuals and organizations. Our mission statement is to unleash the power and potential of people and organizations for the common good. So if we are going to do that, we've really got to believe in that. I'm working on getting more Chief Spiritual Officers around the country. I think it's a great title and we should get more of them.

WRIGHT

So those people for whom you pray, where do you get the names?

BLANCHARD

The people in the company tell me who needs help—whether it's a spouse who is sick, or kids who are sick, or they are worried about something. We have over five years of data about the power of prayer, which is pretty important.

This morning, my inspirational message was about an event my wife and five members of my company participated in. They walked sixty miles last weekend—twenty miles a day for three days—to raise money for breast cancer research. It was amazing. I went down and waved them all in as they came. There was a ceremony, and 7.6 million dollars was raised. There were over three thousand people walking, and many of the walkers were dressed in pink. They were cancer victors—people who had overcome cancer. There were even men walking with pictures of their wives who had died from breast cancer. I thought it was incredible.

There wasn't one mention in the major San Diego papers on Monday. I said, "Isn't that just something." We have to be an island of positive influence because all you see in the paper today is about Michael Jackson and Scott Peterson and Kobe Bryant and this kind of thing, and here you get all these thousands of people out there walking and trying to make a difference, and nobody thinks it's news. So every morning I pump people up about what life's about, about what's going on. That's what my Chief Spiritual Officer is about.

WRIGHT

I had the pleasure of reading one of your current releases, *The Leadership Pill*.

BLANCHARD

Yes.

WRIGHT

I must admit that my first thought was how short the book was. I wondered if I was going to get my money's worth, which by the way, I most certainly did. Many of your books are brief and based on a fictitious story. Most business books in the market today are hundreds of pages in length and are read almost like a textbook. Will you talk a little bit about why you write these short books and about the premise of *The Leadership Pill*?

BLANCHARD

I developed my relationship with Spencer Johnson when we wrote *The One Minute Manager*. As you know, he wrote *Who Moved My Cheese*, which was a phenomenal success. He wrote children's books, and I was a storyteller.

My favorite books were, *Jonathan Livingston Seagull* and *The Little Prince*. They are all great parables. I started writing parables because people can get into the story and learn the contents of the story. They don't bring their judgmental hats into reading. You write a regular book and they'll say, "Well, where did you get the research?" They get into that judgmental side. Our books get them emotionally involved and they learn.

The Leadership Pill is a fun story about a pharmaceutical company that thinks they have discovered the secret to leadership, and they can put the ingredients in a pill. When they announce it, the country goes crazy because everybody knows we need more effective leaders. When they release it, it outsells Viagra. The founders of the company start selling off stock and they call them Pillionaires. But along comes this guy who calls himself "the effective manager," and he challenges them to a no-pill challenge. If they identify two non-performing groups, he'll take on one and let somebody on the pill take another one, and he guarantees he will out-perform by the end of the year. They agree, but of course, they give him a drug test every week to make sure he's not sneaking pills on the side.

I wrote the book with Marc Muchnick, who is a young guy in his early thirties. We did a major study of what this interesting "Y" generation—the young people of today—want from leaders, and this is a secret blend that this effective manager in the *Leadership Pill* book uses.

When you think about it, David, it is really powerful on terms of what people want from a leader. Number one, they want integrity. A lot of people have talked about that in the past, but these young people will walk if they see people say one thing and do another. A lot of us walk to the bathroom and out into the halls to talk about it. But these people will quit. They don't want somebody to say something and not do it.

The second thing they want is a partnership relationship. They hate superior/subordinate. I mean, what awful terms those are. You know, the "head" of the department and the hired "hands"—you don't even give them a head. "What do you do? I'm in supervision. I see things a lot clearer than these stupid idiots." They want to be treated as partners. If they can get a financial partnership, great. If they can't, they really want a minimum of psychological partnership where they can bring their brains to work and make decisions.

Then finally, they want affirmation. They not only want to be caught doing things right, but they want to be affirmed for who they are. They want to be known as a person, not as a number. So those are the three ingredients that this effective manager uses. They are wonderful values if you think of them.

Rank-order values for any organization is number one, integrity. In our company, we call it ethics. It is our number one value.

The number two value is partnership. In our company, we call it relationships.

Number three is affirmation, which means being affirmed as a human being. I think that ties into relationships, too. They are wonderful values that can drive behavior in a great way.

WRIGHT

I believe most people in today's business culture would agree that success in business is everything to do with successful leadership. In *The Leadership Pill*, you present a simple but profound premise, that leadership is not something you do *to* people, it's something you do *with* them. At face value, that seems incredibly obvious, but you must have found in your research and observations that leaders in today's culture do not get this. Would you speak to that issue?

BLANCHARD

Yes, and I think what often happens in this is the human ego, you know. There are too many leaders out there who are self-serving. They're not serving leaders. They think the sheep are there for the benefit of the shepherd. All the power, money, fame, and recognition moves up the hierarchy, and they forget that the real action in business is not up the hierarchy—it's in the one-to-one, moment-to-moment interactions that your front line people have with your customers. It's how the phone is answered. It's how problems are dealt with and those kinds of things. If you don't think that you're doing leadership with them, rather you're doing it to them, after a while they won't take care of your customers.

I was at a store recently (not Nordstrom's, where I normally would go) and I thought of something I had to share with my wife, Margie. I asked the guy behind the counter in Men's Wear, "Can I use your phone?"

"No!" he replied.

"You're kidding me," I said, surprised. "I can always use the phone at Nordstrom's."

"Look, buddy," he said, "they won't let *me* use the phone here. Why should I let you use the phone?"

That is an example of leadership that's done to them not with them. People want a partnership. People want to be involved in a way that really makes a difference.

WRIGHT

Dr. Blanchard, the time has flown by and there are so many more questions I'd like to ask you. In closing, would you mind sharing with our readers some thoughts on success? If you were mentoring a small group of men and women, and one of their central goals was to become successful, what kind of advice would you give them?

BLANCHARD

Well, I would first of all say, "What are you focused on?" I think if you are focused on success as being, as I said earlier, accumulation of money, recognition, power, or status, I think you've got the wrong target. I think what you need to really be focused on is how can you be generous in the use of your time and your talent and your treasure and touch. How can you serve people rather than be served? How can you develop caring, loving relationships with people?

My sense is that if you will focus on those things, success in the traditional sense will come to you. I think you become an adult when you realize that you are here to give rather than to get. You're here to serve not to be served. I would just say to people, "Life is such a very special occasion. Don't miss it by aiming at a target that bypasses other people, because we're really here to serve each other." So that's what I would share with people.

WRIGHT

Well, what an enlightening conversation, Dr. Blanchard. I really want you to know how much I appreciate all this time you've taken with me for this interview. I know that our readers will learn from this, and I really appreciate your being with us today.

BLANCHARD

Well, thank you so much, David. I really enjoyed my time with you. You've asked some great questions that made me think, but I hope are helpful to other people because as I say, life is a special occasion.

WRIGHT

Today we have been talking with Dr. Ken Blanchard. He is the author of the phenomenal bestselling book, *The One Minute Manager*. Also, the fact that he's the Chief Spiritual Officer of his company should give us all cause to think about how we are leading our companies and leading our families and leading anything, whether it is in church or civic organizations. I know I will.

Thank you so much, Dr. Blanchard, for being with us today.

BLANCHARD

Good to be with you, David.

Few people have created more of a positive impact on the day-to-day management of people and companies than Dr. Kenneth Blanchard, who is known around the world simply as "Ken."

When Ken speaks, he speaks from the heart with warmth and humor. His unique gift is to speak to an audience and communicate with each individual as if they were alone and talking one-on-one. He is a polished storyteller with a knack for making the seemingly complex easy to understand.

Ken has been a guest on a number of national television programs, including *Good Morning America and The Today Show*, and has been featured in *Time, People, U.S. News & World Report*, and a host of other popular publications.

He earned his bachelor's degree in Government and Philosophy from Cornell University, his master's degree in Sociology and Counseling from Colgate University, and his PhD in Educational Administration and Leadership from Cornell University.

Dr. Ken Blanchard

The Ken Blanchard Companies
125 State Place
Escondido, California 92029
800-728-6000
Fax: 760-489-8407
www.blanchardtraining.com

CHAPTER TEN

The Role Of Happiness In Wellness
Zeina Ghossoub

DAVID WRIGHT (WRIGHT)

Starting as a clinical dietitian twenty years ago, Zeina Ghossoub has since trained as a wellness executive and life coach. She guides individuals, publishes books and numerous articles, gives seminars and lectures, appears on national and international television shows, owns and operates a premier wellness center, and is completing her doctoral studies in counseling. She is a member of the International Coaching Federation and is becoming a master's wellness coach. She is the highest credentialed coach in the Middle East and is affiliated with world renowned coaches like Dr. Cathy Greenberg. She brings years of experience and a wealth of unsurpassed knowledge in wellness coaching.

Zeina, welcome to *ROADMAP to Success*.

What is success in wellness?

ZEINA GHOSSOUB (GHOSSOUB)

Success in its simplistic terms is the achievement of a goal. Whether that goal is defined by an individual or by society, success defines one's arrival at that expectation or demand or need or desire. With some goals, success is only measured when they are truly met. With wellness, success is defined through the process, the journey, and through becoming "well."

Wellness is a state of being. The World Health Organization (WHO) defines it as free of disease in mind, body, and soul. However, wellness is more than just the absence of disease. Wellness is a description of a state of existence that touches on several factors including social, mental, emotional, financial, physical, and spiritual parameters. Wellness is also a Dynamic, not a Static state of being. So the question then becomes how is wellness and its success defined in those terms? Is someone well when he or she accomplishes or reaches his or her goals that are set by those parameters? All of them? Some of them?

For me and many of my clients, "success" in wellness terms means for each in our own state being happy healthy, secure, able, confident, focused, and determined. It is not a haphazard collection of emotions because each one is linked and all are complementary as well as supplementary.

The hard part of being well is that it does involve so many variables. This is not just dealing with achieving a physical goal (lose weight, eat right), or a financial goal (make $500 thousand a year and plan for retirement), and so on. It involves the consideration of all the parameters discussed. The way I picture the human being is as follows:

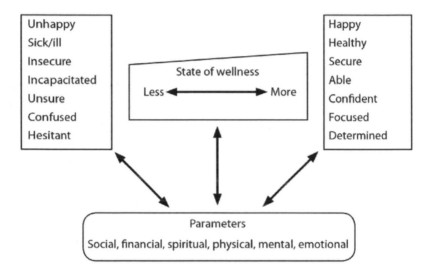

WRIGHT

Why is the concept of wellness so important?

GHOSSOUB

Wellness is a universal concept with a personal application. It is a right for all individuals. If you think about all the issues that concern us and are important to us, none touches all of us in all aspects of our lives as wellness does. It is an all-encompassing state of being.

To illustrate, let me give a small example that deals with one aspect of wellness. Take an athlete who is preparing for a race or an event. The more the athlete is rested, trained, hydrated, mentally prepared, and emotionally focused, the better the outcome and the result. It is no different here. Substitute the athlete's event with one's life, and his or her preparation with one's overall wellness, and you can see the link and the importance. We are at our best when we feel well and are full of positive energy and are achieving our goal.

To fully answer this question of importance, I simply have to ask the obvious: how does it make you feel when you feel "well"? There is no greater or more important or more vital goal for us.

WRIGHT

What does it mean to be successful in wellness?

GHOSSOUB

The beauty about wellness is that it is a standard that has some universal guidelines and it is also flexible enough to include personal- and person-specific parameters. If you consider the parameters we have discussed, then being successful in wellness is having achieved or accomplished all of them. But success in wellness is the journey itself, not the destination. This may seem as a cliché but it holds true here.

Universal parameters include the following:

From the physical health standpoint: not being overweight, exercising, watching your cholesterol and blood pressure, not smoking or drinking excessively, avoiding drugs, eating healthy and nutritious foods.

From the psychological standpoint: avoiding anxious and stressful situations, being calm and serene, avoiding drugs and stimulants, seeking the support of friends and loved ones, and being true to yourself and others.

From the financial standpoint: Having a steady income, planning your future and investing in it, being on solid ground financially, avoiding debt and minimizing expenditure. Basically, having a balance sheet that reflects a positive balance where income is more than spending.

From the spiritual standpoint: Being true and safe and satisfied within your beliefs and religion and convictions. Having a clear conscious and peace of mind.

From the emotional standpoint: Being happy and fulfilled in your relationships with your friends, family, and loved ones. More importantly, it means being happy with yourself.

WRIGHT

How does success in wellness reflect on us and our lives?

GHOSSOUB

To answer this question, I would like to go through the spectrum that I have outlined before. As individuals, we pass through times when we are not well at all and feel like failures in our endeavors. We feel we are at the bottom when it comes to our own abilities, achievements, confidence, and all self-being. Everyone has had one of those days. And everyone knows how it feels to be in those situations. Contrast that to feeling "great," feeling like one can conquer the world, overcome any obstacle, reach any goal, and achieve almost the impossible.

In sports, there is a saying: "winning cures all." In life, things are no different. Success and, more importantly, the feeling and acknowledgement of success puts us in the best possible position in life. It fills us with so much positive energy that all aspects of our lives are affected. When one is successful in anything but specifically in wellness, he or she is more tolerant, more determined, happy, secure, connected, loving, forgiving, willing, passionate, and more generous. People who feel successful usually have an air of self-confidence about them that others immediately recognize and want to emulate. Those who are successful are an immediate source of inspiration and guidance. They are asked about their ways and their "secret to success."

Success lifts us and those around us. The key issue with success in wellness is that it touches all aspects of our lives. And that is key! People could be successful at their work, yet suffer from a physical ailment or harm because of their own negligence and mistreatment of their own bodies. How do they feel their success? People can have the best romantic relationship, but feel distant and disconnected in their spirituality and religious beliefs. How successful are they? And are they able to truly feel all they can?

Success in wellness may seem like a daunting task. At first, it may be. As human beings we are taught to focus on one or two factors at any one point in our lives.

Growing up, in childhood and adolescence, we focus on school and studying and learning and achieving good grades. In college, we are taught to focus on discovering who we are through education and experimentation and to maximize the physical abilities of our bodies through sports and exercise. In early adulthood, we are focused on finding work and having an income and building relationships that are supposed to last a lifetime. In mid to late adulthood we are supposed to focus on securing our future as retirees and be wonderful parents. We are also reminded that our health is important and that we should take care of it. Sadly, that reminder comes from medical personnel and from our own bodies that suddenly show us the price of neglecting a healthy way of living for so many years. In our elderly years we learn to try and sit back and relax and be grandparents and get ready for the next journey and after life. But has this approach worked? The answer comes from all of us. And if it has, then we should be at a much better place now than we were years ago. Are we?

Success in wellness means knowing how to achieve our goals at the same time. It may seem too much to handle, and at first, it will be. Why? Because we lack the experience and the guidance to do so. People who came before us did not do this. They were taught and they are trying to teach us their own ways. These are the same ways that have led us to where we are. As a coach, one recognizes the client's abilities and helps him or her achieve his or her respective goals. As a wellness coach, the goal becomes success in wellness.

WRIGHT

Is wellness achievable?

GHOSSOUB

The simple answer is yes. The more complex answer is the process of how. I cannot stress enough how success in wellness is more about the journey than about reaching the goal. If you think about all the factors involved and how they need to be achieved to get to total wellness, then you can imagine the magnitude and complexity involved.

The road map to achieving wellness is defined by each one of us. But it also helps to consult with experts. Given what we have talked about, the professionals in the field who are of value for us include physicians (and others in the medical field), clinical dietitians, financial advisors, spiritual leaders, wellness coaches, and other experts in their respective fields. They all serve to let us know what the guidelines and the recommendations are. Often, individuals will receive steps and instructions that help them reach their respective goals. A doctor recommends losing weight, stopping smoking, and taking medications. A financial advisor advises on how to invest one's money and how to plan for the future. A spiritual leader will try to guide us in our prayers and direct our thoughts toward what is spiritually and religiously righteous and moral.

But if these were enough, then we would all be well or on the road to wellness. The truth of the matter is that most of us are not moving in the right direction. Obesity and its related diseases are on the rise. People are facing more financial crises every day. We are more distant spiritually and religiously than we ever were. The levels of stress, anxiety, and depression are at an all-time high. People blame wars, politics, financial status, and the economy as well as other factors for these hard times.

It seems, paradoxically, that we know more about what a healthy existence is and less about how to get there.

WRIGHT

Are there gender differences in successful wellness?

GHOSSOUB

As adults, there is a gender difference in the hierarchy stratification of priorities and goals.

For men, usually work and financial security are at the top of the list. That is followed by family and relationships. Next come physical, mental, and spiritual health. Most men who are successful in their careers and are *aware* complain of their failures as fathers and husbands, their shortcomings in their health, and their distance from their religion. Most of the time, the complaints about them come from their spouses and loved ones because they are so engrossed in their work and being providers that other things like simply spending quality time with their children is sacrificed. Many men feel inadequate as fathers, they are frequently impatient, and relegate themselves to being financial supporters and enablers while depending on the wives/mothers for proper guidance and raising the family. Men are frequently confronted by their physicians and other health care providers about their declining health and by their mid forties onward men are at risk for heart disease, obesity, high blood pressure, and other medical ailments. Spiritually they also suffer and frequently turn more to their faith and religion as they age and as time becomes more precious and less available.

Women often place family above all. Their children are at the top of the list. Taking care of others without knowing how to take care of one's self comes at a price: neglecting your own self and well-being. Women are under pressure—societal and familial and self-inflicted—to be the best mothers, wives, and workers. No matter the society, a woman feels she is judged by her ability to be all of those. One of her most primal instincts is to take care of her children and to ensure their survival and success. That is one of the greatest of all instincts. As a mother, I identify with it. But it has left many women sad and sometimes bitter when they realize that a huge part of their lives has been spent doing this while neglecting other aspects that include their own dreams and self-fulfillment.

Women are under greater scrutiny when they work and it is expected that they produce just as their male counterparts, all while not being given equal societal and political and economical support and opportunities. That is a recipe for stress and anger and a sense of betrayal. Women also take their physical and mental health for granted and by the time they are reminded of the importance of these elements, they are trying to minimize the damage and "turn back the clock."

In the end, the reality is that we can do so much more with our lives in being successful in our own wellness.

WRIGHT

What are some strategic steps to achieve wellness?

GHOSSOUB

If there was one step that could highlight or be the most important, it would be this one: Wellness is a state of being that involves all aspects of our lives. These aspects are tied to each other, complement each other, supplement and support each other, and drive each other.

The second point of emphasis is a reflection of the first one: targeting all aspects of our wellness ensures the most in achieving wellness and maintaining it.

I have mentioned earlier that wellness is a journey that involves so many factors. To tackle all these factors at the same time, one has to have the mentality and the ability to outline several goals and try to achieve them at the same time. The argument often heard is that people have a limited source of energy, time, and commitment. People often focus on one or two goals at the most at any single time in their lives. That is true, but it is not because we lack the ability to focus on several goals. A few simple ideas and concepts to remember are the following:

1. Wellness is a state that involves all aspects of our lives.
2. Wellness is an achievable state.
3. Wellness needs to be desired and strived for. It does not come easily and is not handed to us.
4. Wellness is a state that is multidimensional and varied in its forms, but has one or two basic paths that can be followed to achieve it.
5. The basic path for wellness starts with an understanding of the concept and the will to achieve it.
6. The path to wellness involves identifying one's own personal goals through all its components.
7. The path to wellness is about finding a strategy that works for one goal, and then using that strategy to reach all other goals.

8. Strategies of success are different for different individuals, but are common in their motivation.

9. Identifying "what works" depends on the individual. He or she can best answer that question.

Wellness coaches work with individuals to identify their strength, recognize their weakness, outline their successful approaches, define their goals, and use that information to help them achieve success in wellness.

WRIGHT

What is our role in our own success? What must or can we do?

GHOSSOUB

The answer to this question may be self-evident by now. We are at the center of our own success story. We often blame others for our failures—loved ones, coworkers and superiors, people in the medical and financial fields, circumstances, geo-political situations, economical realities, or spiritual leaders. It ultimately comes down to us as individuals. Success, in any situation, involves:

- Identifying the reality
- Recognizing one's own strength and ability
- Outlining limitations and weaknesses
- Defining achievable goals
- Taking ownership and command of one's path
- Controlling the elements to the best of one's abilities and what the environment will allow
- Assuming responsibility
- Seeing and avoiding obstacles
- Developing the will to achieve
- Being relentless and persistent
- Keeping goals realistic and achievable
- Connecting with support systems
- Utilizing all available resources
- Seeking help and guidance
- Minimizing error
- Maximizing ways of success

WRIGHT

What are the positive and negative forces that shape our success in wellness?

GHOSSOUB

The connection between success and wellness is a self-propelling circle. They are both intertwined and together propagate their own existence. People who are well often succeed more and people who are successful often feel better and are more "well." Identifying positive and negative factors can be generalized and personalized.

Positive general forces: These include physical health. People who are healthy, eat well, and exercise right, often feel more empowered and better about themselves. A sound mind in a sound body is very true. With good physical health, people usually are more productive and happier. Other positive forces include loved ones who are understanding and supportive. An appreciative supervisor, an enabling firm, and an accommodating occupation are all positive attributes. Religious and spiritual support and strengthening one's faith contributes tremendously.

Negative general forces: In general, these include the opposite of the above forces.

Private forces: Those are identified by each one of us. As individuals, we have certain people we try to avoid, places we would rather not go, situations we deem stressful, realities we are uncomfortable with, and abilities we lack. There are also events we know that boost us. In each one of the factors of wellness, we have probably identified our strengths and have seen our successes. For example, we know what sports to participate in to exercise, how and where and when to pray, what we are good doing at work, and our own personal best characteristics.

These forces shape our everyday lives. They determine whether we truly feel "well" and happy, or feel "unwell" and unhappy. This brings us to a very important topic: the role of happiness in wellness.

Happiness is a consequence. It is a byproduct of a situation or a reality that has been reached, is being lived, or is identified and recognized and resonates with one or several characteristics that define us as human beings. Success leads to happiness. Happiness is an essential part of wellness. If you think of what makes happiness feasible, you need to try and identify what states of existence make you happy.

One of the most important feelings that leads to happiness is the sense of achievement, which happens to define success. Once we realize we have achieved a goal—any goal—there is a sense of gratitude, fulfillment, comfort, and security that may ultimately culminate with a smile in our heart and on our face. That smile reflects a happiness that is as deep, serene, and as profound as the goal that has been achieved and the effort made to achieve it. Happiness is also a dynamic state. There are degrees of happiness and it is not a state we are always in, but one we are privileged to achieve.

Happiness is part and parcel of wellness and success in wellness. Look no further than yourself for proof. Of all the elements of wellness we have spoken about, choose any one of them and remember how it felt to achieve it. Now think of how it would feel to achieve so many goals on all aspects. Happiness begets wellness and wellness increases the ability to feel happy and appreciate it. Wellness does not imply happiness. It simply propagates it, makes it more achievable and more appreciated, which in turn makes wellness more enjoyable and self-fulfilling.

Happiness is defined by each one of us. Although achieving goals in general makes us happy, what kinds of goals, to what extent they are achieved, and how they are achieved give each one of us a unique outlook on happiness and its meaning. Happiness may sometimes be the only guide to knowing that you are leading a successful life. True happiness, although hard to find, is not impossible. Happiness is linked to true wellness and success in wellness. It is an indirect barometer of how successful we are when it comes to wellness in general, and any goal in particular.

There is one very important aspect of happiness that is at the core of who we are. We have to be true to ourselves—really true to ourselves. This involves being honest, brave, and understanding who we truly are. Many of us pretend to be happy to ourselves. That false state of happiness will only lead to a dissatisfied life and a state of dysfunctionality and illusion that will leave us empty, unhappy, unfulfilled, and unwell.

WRIGHT

Why did you become a wellness coach?

GHOSSOUB

As a human being, I have searched for success in general, and wellness in particular, all my life. I am no different from everyone else.

One day, eleven years ago, I was about to leave my clinic where I used to work as a dietitian, and one of my patients commented on how tired I looked. No specific comment, nothing out of the ordinary, and certainly nothing I had not heard before. Physically I was exhausted. My focus was less than adequate and I was emotionally drained. I felt I was being pulled in a thousand directions. At that point, a question popped into my mind. Why does it have to be so hard? And that is when it hit me. There has to be an easier, more productive, more efficient, and a better way of living.

As I sought answers, I found out that very few people had them. Some would give recommendations, and others would outline requirements and facts, but no one really knew how to make it work, how to encompass all aspects and, most important of all, how to guide! We are on our own I felt. Life does not come with its own trainer. Instead, it provides resources, clues, and opportunities. There is no secret book of life that tells us how to achieve happiness. There are outlines and guidelines for the afterlife. There are recommendations for being physically healthy. There are ways to become financially independent. There are books that tell us how to love, whom to love, and when to love. But how do you bring all of this knowledge together and make it a functional, achievable, and tangible way of life? Where is the proverbial "yellow brick road"?

Most of us spend a lifetime trying to find it and when we finally think we have amassed enough experience, knowledge, and wisdom, we find ourselves often too old or too tired to do anything about it. Rod Stewart sings a song that has the following lyrics: "If I knew then what I know now . . ."

As a wellness coach, I want people to know now. They need to be aware now, not later. Happiness and wellness and success in wellness are achievable goals. We all have the wisdom to identify those goals and the ability to get to them. Let us enjoy the journey!

Starting as a clinical dietitian twenty years ago, Zeina Ghossoub has since trained as a wellness executive and life coach. She guides individuals, publishes books and numerous articles, gives seminars and lectures, appears on national and international television shows, owns and operates a premier wellness center, and is completing her doctoral studies in counseling. She is a member of the International Coaching Federation and is working toward becoming a Master Wellness Coach. She is the highest credentialed coach in the Middle East and is affiliated with world renowned coaches like Dr. Cathy Greenberg. Zeina brings years of experience and a wealth of unsurpassed knowledge in wellness coaching.

Zeina Ghossoub

Vie Saine
Medical & Health Center
Antelias–Main Road–Hage Center-8th Floor
Lebanon
Tel/Fax: 00961-4-413280
Mobile: 00961-3-998313
zeinag@viesaine.org
website:www.viesaine.org

CHAPTER ELEVEN

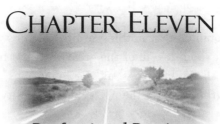

Professional Passion
Biagio Sciacca

DAVID WRIGHT (WRIGHT)

Today I'm talking with Biagio Sciacca, known to his friends as Bill. Bill grew up in the coal mining district of Northeast Pennsylvania and holds a bachelor's degree in Philosophy and Sociology, and his MBA, as well as his PhD in Business Administration. In addition to developing his career in business and entrepreneurship, he taught at the university level and has been teaching since 1982. He recently took a full-time academic post at Penn State University, one of the top ten research universities in the world, where he lectures in micro- and macroeconomics, marketing, leadership, strategic management, and interpersonal skills in business.

In addition to his academic post, Bill owns an award-winning consulting and training organization, he owned a chain of donut and ice-cream franchises, and several businesses in the automotive car care industry. His consulting company touted several thousand clients, from locally owned firms to multinational Fortune 500 companies.

Bill divides his free time between doing research in creativity, Southern Italian cooking, writing fiction, and writing and recording his own songs with guitar. He is also a certified spin instructor.

Bill Sciacca welcome to *ROADMAP to Success*.

BIAGIO SCIACCA (SCIACCA)

Well, hi, David. Thank you; it's great to be here. I really want to thank you very much for having me, I appreciate it.

WRIGHT

It's my pleasure. So tell me, what do you mean by professional passion?

SCIACCA

David, I have the opinion that nothing in life happens without some level of passion. I mean, think about it—all of the great works of human kind, all of the scientific discoveries, all the buildings, all the inventions, all the discoveries in general—what do you think caused them, David, mediocrity?

WRIGHT

I don't think so.

SCIACCA

I agree, everything I just mentioned was the result of passion—passionate people get things accomplished. The interesting thing is that passionate people do not achieve greatness because they want to achieve greatness, they simply have no choice. Greatness is a by-product of their passion and the pursuit of one's chosen endeavors.

WRIGHT

Wow, that's powerful stuff Bill. So if you do what you're passionate about, greatness will come?

SCIACCA

Yes, that's what I tell my students all the time. Do what you love and the money will follow. It works the same for what you said—do what you're passionate about and the greatness will follow. I appreciate your saying that; actually I learned something from you today. Now, I don't want to give you any more complements because I'm sure the capitalist in you will surface and you're going to invoice me for giving me that knowledge.

WRIGHT

If it were only that easy! It sounds to me as though you're trying to analyze passion and apply that principle to management and leadership, right?

SCIACCA

That's exactly what I'm trying to do David. Why should the passionate pursuit of an endeavor be limited to writers, artists, and musicians? Why not bankers, accountants, managers, and executives?

WRIGHT

I agree, why not?

So how do you go about isolating the principles that you have mentioned?

SCIACCA

Good question, let's start with a simple equation, V1 + V2 + G = WP.

WRIGHT

Well, I have to say, even though I was good at math I never really liked it, so would explain that equation?

SCIACCA

Absolutely, it's simple. It basically means that vision plus values plus goals are equal to your work plan. Now, David, I've got some bad news for you, there is another equation that we're going to have to unravel before we understand passion, but let me explain the parts of this first one to you.

The first V stands for Vision. Companies have vision statements—they pay consultants hundreds of thousands of dollars to assist them in working out a vision statement, but how many of the executives who need to execute that corporate vision statement have a personal vision statement that they execute on a daily basis. For that matter, how many people in general have a personal vision statement?

WRIGHT

I bet not a lot.

SCIACCA

Yes, not a lot at all. When I teach leadership I tell my students that vision is direction, goals are momentum; but what is the use of having goals and moving with good speed if you're moving in the wrong direction?

WRIGHT

Not much.

SCIACCA

Exactly. So the first thing you need to do is understand what your life vision is. All great people have a life vision, even if they don't have it written down and study it daily. Steve Jobs, for example, said that he wanted to make a ding in the universe. Now, wow, that's a powerful vision statement.

WRIGHT

I'll say. Tell me, Bill, do you have one?

SCIACCA

Of course I do, David. I consider myself to be an extremely passionate person so I need to have a vision statement as part of that passion.

WRIGHT

Will you tell us what it is, or is it too personal?

SCIACCA

It's personal, but the readers of this book laid down their hard earned cash to glean some of the wisdom contained within it, so I owe them my best. Here's my personal vision statement: the vision that I set for my life is to elevate myself to an unprecedented level of happiness. I do that by developing only deep, meaningful drama-free relationships, but mostly by offering myself in a service capacity—helping others however I can to achieve their goals and dreams, thereby assisting me in the attainment of my goals and dreams. I do this through education and training on life skills, values, and goals. I have the energy for this because I constantly work my body so that it remains healthy and fit and I work my mind so that it remains sharp and focused.

I live my life by my standards, by my set of values, by my beliefs. My behavior must be consistent with that set of standards and values and beliefs. What is important to me and how I may influence others is through writing, teaching, traveling, cooking, playing guitar, reading, speaking, fitness, and thinking.

What is most important to me is waking up each morning and feeling happy and content with life so far, and with a childlike wide-eyed wonder for what the day will bring. I differ from a child, though, because I know that I am the architect of my today, the builder of my future, and the constructor of my conscious choices that will lead me to that level of happiness that I spoke of.

I ask once and I give thanks often. I have deep gratitude for my successes, as they are enjoyed now, and my failures, as they are learning experience for future actions. I choose my destiny by my behavior; I am responsible to me.

David, I read that every morning, every night, and during the day when I get a moment, I always try to keep my vision top of mind.

WRIGHT

Well, Bill, I must say that is an extremely powerful statement. How can someone reading, or listening to this, write a vision statement of that magnitude?

SCIACCA

That's a good question and I would love to answer, but first I think it's a little bit beyond the scope of this project to explain the details of that process and — second, I too am a capitalist, and that process is how I earned a portion of my income. So if someone reading or listening wants to learn how to develop a vision statement of that magnitude, well, you're just going to have to call me or visit my website at www.intelligentmotivationinc.com.

WRIGHT

Fair enough, Bill. Hey, we all have to make a living.

Keep explaining the rest of that formula, if you wouldn't mind.

SCIACCA

The second V stands for Values. We all have values, but to gain any understanding of sustained passion in the pursuit of your endeavors, you need to have those values understood and highlighted.

WRIGHT

So, tell me, do you have your values as well defined as your vision statement?

SCIACCA

You bet; it's the only way I know to keep them top of mind without the noise of today getting in the way.

WRIGHT

So let's hear them.

SCIACCA

I'll tell you a few of them. They're not in any particular order of importance, but I found that one ties into another and then another. Let me explain.

The first value is integrity and I mean that from physics not philosophy. Integrity means being whole. If something loses its integrity it becomes weak, therefore, to maintain integrity I must be number two, honest. Now, when I say honest I don't mean I'm going to come up to you and say, "Hey, David. Your butt looks big in those pants," but I will say that, in my opinion, your talk could have been more effective if you did this or you did that. What I would *not* do is sugarcoat my critique because I'm afraid of hurting your feelings. Sometimes growth is uncomfortable.

Honesty will lead me to number three, my third value—precise communication. It's hard to be honest with someone if your message is not understood. Precise communication means that you take responsibility for what you say and you take responsibility for what was heard. Sometimes you might have to ask some questions to ground clarity. Precise communication, then leads to my fourth value, which is wealth.

As I mentioned earlier, I am a capitalist, too. I believe in a free market, I believe that the government should let the free market operate with a minimum of interference, and I believe that wealth is good. In the long run, the world will pay you exactly what you're worth. I value wealth because it tells me what society thinks of me and will basically pay me for my overall level of contribution. If I attain the degree of wealth that is part of my goals program, it leads me to my next value.

The fifth value I have listed is being stress free, or at least in today's world stressed reduced. It's nice knowing that you don't need to worry. I'm always looking for ways to simplify my life. I guess I'm looking for ways to make my life, how can I put this, less exciting.

With the reduction of stress in my life, it frees my mind so that I can begin to work on my sixth value, garner knowledge. I don't consider myself to be an above average person intellectually, but I do consider myself to be tenacious in my quest for knowledge. You're either green or growing or you're ripe and rotting. I always want to be green and growing and I truly feel that knowledge is the path toward that sustained growth.

Garnering knowledge leads me to my seventh value, balance. Socrates said the middle road is the best. Excess or lack of excess leads to lack of balance, which can cause your perception to be skewed. Let me give you a couple of examples. I love physical activity, and I work out at the gym every single day, but only for an hour, not three or four hours as some members do. After I finish working out, I like to go to a local bar and grab a couple of beers with a few friends, but only a few.

Get the idea? It's balance, and if I remain balanced, I can begin to apply what I consider to be my most cherished value, the eighth one, humor. Life is fun, David, so why shouldn't it be funny? I try to get one good belly laugh a day in and afterward I feel good for a long time. It's like taking a fifteen-minute vacation.

So there you have it sir—there are my values in the condensed format.

WRIGHT

Powerful Bill, very powerful. I especially like how one value leads directly to another.

SCIACCA

David, I'm very happy you noticed that. When I work with my clients on this process of vision and values, I always use the prior value to develop the thought pattern for the next pattern; it could become a continuous stream. It became practical to stop simply because it became difficult to focus on more than, say, half a dozen or so values. Remember, this is not an academic exercise, you need to focus on your vision, and on your values every day. Your values should be a template for your behavior.

WRIGHT

Okay, we covered V1 and V2, so what is G?

SCIACCA

G represents goals. If you have a well-defined personal vision and a set of meaningful thought-provoking values, the next step is to use that information to generate evocative goals. Now, it's beyond the scope of this project to get into the nuts and bolts of the goal-setting process, but I will say that if you're interested in the goal-setting process, check on my website, www.IntelligentMotivationInc.com, and invest in a copy of a book. It's a book you published, by the way, titled *Success Simplified*. My chapter in that book is an introduction to scientific goal-setting. Also, take a look at the book I just published called *Goals Book*. It's a step-by-step guide to setting goals and thankfully it's a rather enjoyable read—it reads more like a fictional novel than it does a how-to book.

I will say this about goals—they need to be derived in such a way as to modify your behavior. Goal setting is less about what you get and more about what you become.

WRIGHT

Very enlightening. And I see that defined in the left side of the equation. So what does V1 and V2 and G equal?

SCIACCA

V1 and V2 and G equals—don't lose sight of our goal. Developing professional passion, we're building the model but we're not there yet. The right side of the equation is the WP. It represents the Work Plan. At this point we have direction, we have momentum, and we know what our end results should be. Now we need to begin to put those concepts into action, so unfortunately we need a second equation to do this.

WRIGHT

Oh no, Bill! Please, more equations?

SCIACCA

Just one more David, but it's a small one.

WRIGHT

Okay then.

SCIACCA

The WP was Work Plan + TM = P. Let me explain; we know that WP is the Work Plan, we just derived it. TM is Time Management and time management is so important to professional managers, leaders, and sales professionals, and actually anyone looking for more out of life, to begin to understand the time management process. Good time management is self-discipline, self-discipline sets us free.

Again, it's beyond the scope of this talk to get into a great deal of time management techniques, that's an entire process that takes a while to understand, embrace, and apply, but if you have your goals defined, you decompose them into daily action steps, that's really the next part of the process.

WRIGHT

Okay then, if we have our work plan defined and we are great time managers what is next?

SCIACCA

Well, it's what you've been waiting for—they are the catalyst for developing professional Passion, that is, what the P on the right side of the equation stands for. So let me recap, you need vision, values, and goals to develop your work plan, add good time management skills to your work plan and you'll begin to execute the actions that lead to the fulfillment of the things that are important to you. Your daily behavior is that of focused achievement, you're focusing on your achievement, and that is what I call passion.

WRIGHT

Well, that is amazing. What a cool way of breaking down the behavior of highly successful people.

SCIACCA

Well, thank you, sir. Coming from a person of your caliber and acumen I take that as a huge compliment.

WRIGHT

Is there anything else you can add to this picture of professional passion?

SCIACCA

Sure. If time permits, I'd like to define passion in the form of an acronym. It's a little talk that I do and the name of the talk is "The Passion Principle." The P in passion stands for Persistence, passionate people never, ever give up. The A is an abbreviation for assertiveness. Passionate people politely align the resources necessary to accomplish their program, they move their agendas forward in such a way that others know what they're doing but others don't mind because the passionate people are professional about it—they know what they want. Passionate people give lessons in decisiveness.

The first S in passion is Stubborn. Now, I don't mean that in a bad way— passionate professionals make up their minds and they stick to their plan. If you want to change their mind you'd better have a damn good argument to do so because many passionate people look at a change of course as a time and resource waster.

The second S stands for Service. Passionate people know the secret—the best way to get what you want out of life is to assist others in getting what they want. Passionate people live a life of giving and they receive in return.

The I in passion is Innovative. Passionate people are ground breakers, they're pioneers, they're very creative, they're always looking at something new, different, special.

The O is Optimism, really passionate people don't look at the glass as half full, they look at the glass as being one set of glasses, all of which can be filled.

And finally, the N in passion stands for No excuses—the buck stops with them. A problem is something meant to be overcome, and the working out of that problem is invigorating—the working out of that problem creates passion.

WRIGHT

Bill, it's always a pleasure talking with you and it's always an education. I'll bet your students at Penn State enjoy your lectures.

SCIACCA

Thank you, David. I hope they enjoy the lectures as much as I enjoy giving them.

WRIGHT

Is there anything else you would like to add?

SCIACCA

Just this David, I've taken more than thirty years of research on behavior and goal-setting and I've condensed much of that information on my website. I would hope that all will visit my website and glean some information that they can use, it's IntelligentMotivationInc.com. Now, sure, for the books and recordings there is a charge, but it's a modest charge compared with the ideas contained inside of them. Think about it this way: What is the value of a great idea? If I give you an idea, I don't lose it, I just doubled it and you can give it away and triple it. I guess what I'm saying is this, "I'm not saying that my work on my website will change your life. I am saying that I documented the best ideas that have changed my life and that, sir, is the best that I can do."

WRIGHT

Well, Bill, what a great conversation. I really appreciate your taking all this time to answer all these questions. It's been delightful for me and it's been extremely educational.

SCIACCA

David, the pleasure is all mine; thank you very much.

WRIGHT

Today I have been talking with Biagio Sciacca, known to his friends as Bill. He has been teaching at the university level since 1982 and recently took a full-time academic post at Penn State University. Penn State is one of the top ten research universities in the world. Bill lectures in micro and macroeconomics, marketing, leadership, strategic management, and interpersonal skills in business.

Bill, thank you so much for being with us today.

SCIACCA
Thank you, my friend.

Biagio Sciacca is known to his friends as Bill. Bill grew up in the coal mining district of Northeast Pennsylvania and holds a bachelor's degree in Philosophy and Sociology, and his MBA, as well as his PhD in Business Administration. In addition to developing his career in business and entrepreneurship, he taught at the university level and has been teaching since 1982. He recently took a full-time academic post at Penn State University, one of the top ten research universities in the world, where he lectures on micro and macroeconomics, marketing, leadership, strategic management, and interpersonal skills in business.

In addition to his academic post, Bill owns an award-winning consulting and training organization. He owned a chain of donut and ice-cream franchises, and several businesses in the automotive car care industry. His consulting company touted several thousand clients, from locally owned firms to multinational Fortune 500 companies.

Bill divides his free time between doing research in creativity, Southern Italian cooking, writing fiction, and writing and recording his own songs with guitar. He is also a certified spin instructor.

Biagio W. Sciacca

PO Box 1073
Pittston, PA 18640
(570)430-9303
bill@intelligentmotivationinc.com
IntelligentMotivationInc.com

CHAPTER TWELVE

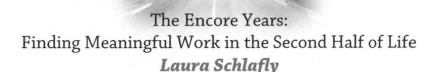

The Encore Years:
Finding Meaningful Work in the Second Half of Life
Laura Schlafly

DAVID WRIGHT (WRIGHT)

Today I'm talking with Laura Schlafly. Laura is the Founder of Career Choices with Laura, a coaching practice where she specializes in guiding midlife professionals through career detours and to investigate and then launch second act careers after they reach age fifty. With a BA in Japanese Studies from Ohio State University and an MBA from the University of Michigan, she has twenty years of hands-on, practical experience in high-tech product marketing, field sales, and small business development and turnaround.

Laura is also a private pilot, a musician, a dancer, and lifelong student of Asian cultures and languages. In her current role as a professional speaker and Encore Career Coach, she combines the skills, interests, and wealth of knowledge gleaned from her own five careers into a tailored process that helps her clients find their ideal work and uncover their core passion and purpose—with a paycheck attached!

Laura, welcome to ROADMAP to Success.

LAURA SCHLAFLY (SCHLAFLY)

Thank you, David.

WRIGHT

You've had a significant career track in marketing and sales and in small business development and turnaround. How have those experiences led to what you're doing now as a career coach, specializing in helping midlife professionals?

SCHLAFLY

Yes, that's what I do, working with midlife professionals because I am one. I always say there is one thing that is really important in changing careers, and it is being open to new experiences and learning new skills. If you look at my varied past history, you'll find that throughout my life I've explored new skills, new cultures, and built successful entrepreneurial companies. I've worked in competitive environments and I've been exactly where a lot of my clients have been. Maybe they've had a successful corporate role, built their own businesses, or lived a good life. But then something went wrong during that life or the economy soured, or they decided to completely change their course, which is what I've done.

I learned entrepreneurial skills early, watching my father repair car panels as an auto body repairman. He invented a portable sand blaster to make his job easier and it became a thriving, successful business. This experience had a long-lasting impact on my development.

Another strange and significant experience occurred when I was around age twelve. I somehow developed a passion of my own—a strong affinity for Asian cultures. It was definitely unusual for a young Ohio girl, and it influenced the choice of my college major, which was Japanese Studies at Ohio State University. I wanted to work and travel in Japan right out of college, but life had other plans for me. I eventually did study and live in Japan for five months, but when I tried to find a job using my expertise, I discovered that I was "too soon" and it seemed that no companies found value in my skills.

A couple of years later, I entered graduate school and knew that I had to focus on something that was going to bring in money, so I earned my MBA and went on to a totally different career. It was my first self-reinvention. There would be more in the years to come.

My second reinvention occurred when I stepped in to orchestrate a turnaround and sale of my family's thirty-year-old business. I left my career in data communications product marketing, and I realized it was time for another change—another change of direction. It turned out that my turnaround and profitable sale of the company was the most impactful of all my careers.

In 1990, I returned to the technology industry, this time working in field sales with products that facilitated computer networking. The companies I worked for were based in Silicon Valley. It was the day of the dot-com growth and plenty of money was to be made all around. The bubble burst when the dot-bomb occurred in 2001. That was my real wakeup call because I was laid off for the first time in my life.

But there was a silver lining and it was a time when I could do some self-reflection and redirection. I felt a strong desire to make a physical move across the country, to the Pacific Rim, so I moved to the Pacific Northwest, to Portland, Oregon. I networked like crazy and I was able to establish a business, XL Concepts, that (at last) dealt with "things Asian." XL Concepts is an advertising agency and consultancy that provides Asian language advertising to American companies looking to reach the Asian American consumer. But with the economic downturn in 2008, that business shrank, and I wondered what I was going to do next.

I turned sixty in 2009 and felt strongly that I wanted yet a fourth reinvention of myself. So I met with a career counselor, and together we did a lot of examining what would be a good use of both my interests and talents. There was a point where it all came together and we honed in on the field of career counseling and career coaching as being a good fit. I embraced the coaching concept, and became certified as a career coach. I had used several coaches in my career throughout all those years of corporate life with career strategies, moves, and changes.

So today that is what I do and I love the idea of the encore career concept because it works with people in my age bracket.

WRIGHT

What is this concept of an encore career and why is it an important issue now? Why are you championing it, making it a passion for yourself and spreading the word to others?

SCHLAFLY

There is a statistic out in the world, on the Internet and in the news media, that there are 78 million Baby Boomers turning sixty-five every year for the next eighteen years. We are a very strong force in the world—in the United States and in other countries like Korea, Japan, and certain well-developed European countries.

The concept of an encore career, which is aligned with the needs of Baby Boomers, is a term that was developed by Marc Freedman. Marc is the CEO of San Francisco-based Civic Ventures and he published a book in 2007 titled, *Encore: Finding Work that Matters in the Second Half of Life*. I surmise that the book generated this buzz around the concept of an encore career.

His original meaning of the term describes work in the second half of life that combines continued income, greater meaning, and often, a social impact component to another silo of that second half of life. You might have earned income from work that's meaningful for you this time. Additionally, this encore career frequently has a philanthropic component where you're giving back socially. Finally, there is one more component of your second half of life that would typically be of high personal interest or an avocation. This concept of life "silos" became known as a "portfolio life," from the book of the same name written by David Corbett.

WRIGHT

Are there certain trigger events that cause people to examine a second career?

SCHLAFLY

The reasons that many Boomers are starting new careers in their fifties and sixties are varied, according to reports on the phenomenon.

One major reason is the 2008 downturn in the economy. According to a 2012 annual survey by the Insured Retirement Institute, "62 percent of Boomers 50–66 believe that their personal financial situation will not improve in the next five years. Additionally, a majority of Boomers expect to retire later in life, or expect to rely on post-retirement employment income." One specific example is if you are laid off from your position due to a slowdown in sales, or maybe the company was downsized for efficiency, or perhaps there was a company merger. Another common trigger could be a health problem; these tend to show up as you enter your mid to late fifties and early sixties. A health issue might involve someone in your family, because Boomers are the sandwich generation, having responsibilities in caring for aging parents.

Another catalyst occurs when you've worked in a particular field or a particular company for a long time and it just doesn't float your boat anymore, or maybe it never did. Often it happens that the job was just something you fell into and you stuck with it all those years. I know plenty of people in that situation. They are chagrined to realize they must work longer because their retirement nest egg has diminished. However, they can't bear the thought of continuing to work at the same job; they want something that is more meaningful.

WRIGHT

So what are these midlife professionals—these Baby Boomers—doing that is different from what their parents did, as that generation approached their retirement age?

SCHLAFLY

It is a difference between what I call the old retirement paradigm and the new retirement paradigm. I think about my mother, for example, when she decided to retire from the family business at age sixty-five. Fundamentally that was a finite event. It was complete and I think she felt freedom from having to work because she designated me as her replacement CEO.

The idea of retirement emerged out of the creation of the social security program in 1935 when men were living eleven years beyond age sixty-five and women fifteen years beyond age of sixty-five. It was an ending, a freedom *from* work, with perhaps a place to retire to such as Sun City, Arizona, and you could trust your three-legged financial stool to support you.

But today we have more possibilities, with retirement being more of a gradual process. Some people prefer a phased retirement because they need to continue an income stream, and at the same time want to stay more connected and engaged. This is due to the simple fact that we're living longer after sixty-five, with men living about seventeen years longer and women closer to twenty years longer. So it stands to reason that we just want more out of our lives now that we're living longer.

On the other hand there's a scary side of this longer life. If we're going to retire at sixty, sixty-two, sixty-five, or sixty-six, and have the potential of living thirty years longer, what are we going to do with ourselves? That's the troubling question. How can we continue to be of value to our families, our community, and the world?

WRIGHT

What are some advantages that midlife people have over their Gen X, Gen Y cohorts? Where are they uniquely suited to contribute to our society today?

SCHLAFLY

Many people older than fifty are having trouble getting reengaged with the workforce, and ageism is purported to be a significant factor in their stalled careers. Still, there are industries and employers who can see several characteristics of Boomers as assets. For example, they are experienced, having plenty of accumulated field expertise in sales, service, management, manufacturing, operations, training, and skilled trades. Skilled trades have a great deal of potential, because many are trades that are not finding Gen X or Gen Y applicants. They're still very viable trades, but these younger generations often prefer to work in the service sectors, using their knowledge rather than their physical, manual skills.

Another area in which Boomers are uniquely suited is in their flexibility. They are comfortable with changing hats as the market demand dictates so they are not inflexible like some people might surmise. I think folks who are age fifty are good communicators over all, particularly in interpersonal skills. There are cases where Gen X and Gen Y workers have been accused of not having as many interpersonal skills because they heavily depend on computers and mobile phones to communicate.

Being a Boomer myself, I would mention a couple of other attributes we have in our favor. We are more willing than our parents' generation to try new skills because we've learned the value of keeping our brains active. Furthermore, we are literally forced to stay abreast of rapidly changing technology and the forces of globalization. As a final claim regarding the value of Boomer assets, take a look at their rate of absenteeism, and turnover. You'll see that it's low compared to that of Gen X and Gen Y, because the workers in those age groups are job hopping every two or three years. They want the next shiny thing or they get tired of what they are doing more quickly. The workers age fifty plus are more used to staying in for the long run.

However, I must emphasize to midlife job seekers and career changers that if you are in an interview situation with a younger hiring manager, the areas where you must make a strong, positive impression are: 1) your energy, 2) your current technology skills, 3) your appearance, and 4) your willingness to be flexible.

WRIGHT

Given these advantages, how can they discover and then leverage their talents and earn income at the same time?

SCHLAFLY

Of course there is the given of the four areas I just mentioned—showing energy, keeping up with technology, appearance, and in all around flexibility. Beyond these is where I come in to provide support and guidance as a career coach. I help my clients find work, or a career track that is truly meaningful to them at this time in their life. When they have clarity about what their work or the career is, they will be energized about that work. Even though it might not pay what they earned previously, the fulfillment is so much greater. There's a quote I like from Napoleon Hill who says that your greatest success is just one step from your greatest failure. I encourage midlife people to be open to taking a look at their next step, which is the new door that opens when another door has closed.

When I work with my clients, I start with asking them to define who they really are, which is not always readily apparent. After a long career, perhaps through twists and turns, we can lose sight of our core being. What we do is to go back in time and become a "Sherlock Holmes" in this discovery puzzle of how they showed up in the world originally. Perhaps we find that they were really destined for something else, for a road not taken into adulthood. This situation is very common to many Boomers. So I work with them, starting with enlightenment around who they are, looking at their innate strengths, core values, and doing a reconnaissance of their prior work and careers.

Another exercise is to ask them lots of questions about what matters, what matters in their work—not only what they like to do but what kind of people they prefer as colleagues or coworkers. Finally we examine the type of company culture that best motivates them. Our parents hardly ever talked about company culture—it's values, its ethics, and convenience of location for commuting. But this time around in a new career, I encourage them to be more mindful in all of these key areas that truly matter for contentment in a new career.

Our next step is to examine three major ways they can approach this new career. They can be a "career recycler," in which they apply their transferrable skills to a different field. Or they can be a "career changer," which means they are changing both their field/industry as well as their role in it. A third aspect we look at is to examine if they are suited to be a "career maker"—an entrepreneur starting their own business. These are examples of some of the processes that we go through one-on-one or in a small group to leverage their talents and earn an income.

WRIGHT

So what about you Laura? How did you discover your talents and passions that drove the several career shifts in your life?

SCHLAFLY

The most recent and significant shift started in 2009 when I turned "a certain age," and when the economic downturn diminished my Asian advertising business. I decided to work with a career counselor and ultimately discovered that working with people and their careers was actually my passion, too.

It was in the 1980s when I discovered Richard Bolles and his wonderful book, *What Color is Your Parachute?* I wanted to make a career change and I didn't know what direction to take. I would get up at 4:00 AM, go out to the dining room table, and work on the exercises in his book trying to figure that out for myself. In retrospect I see clearly now that it was a strong indication I had an interest and talent in helping others find their career calling.

That pervasive Asian interest keeps coming back and I am actively working on how I can meld that in with my career coaching. Basically, I've just continued to effect these shifts and continue to move forward, step after step. That's my story and I'm sticking to it!

WRIGHT

But in today's economic doldrums, how can others in midlife accomplish career changes at this point? So many have experienced layoffs and company mergers, health challenges, family issues, and other types of career detours that it's risky to chart a course in such turbulent times.

SCHLAFLY

Oh, it absolutely is, especially if you're still employed and you want to do an encore career as part of an exit strategy. You will need to make time in your day and in your life to explore options, which can be challenging. And I have an interesting statistic about how people are going to accomplish this if they really want to change careers or develop an encore career. A 2011 Metropolitan Life survey of people between their mid-forties and age seventy revealed that nine million were already doing an encore career and that there were thirty-one million more people who want to, but only about half of them have the financial means to do so. That is a very real issue for people. So it's important that they put pencil to paper, or hands to computer keys, to figure out if they can afford to take time out to develop a second career.

I will not make light of the reality that for many people it's going to be difficult. They must fine-tune their savings and investments to achieve the appropriate balance of their living expenses for today with whatever income sources they have. This is vital and I always encourage them, if they can do so, to work with a financial advisor to help figure this out ahead of time. During the transition from either unemployment to re-employment, or from a current job role into a dialed-back encore career, you need to plan your cash flow.

David, I say the riskiest thing is to take no risks and just do nothing. What I specialize in at Career Choices with Laura is helping people in midlife find their strengths-based direction and their passion in order to get them beyond inertia, to be active, connected, and exploring something exciting to begin.

WRIGHT

What other strategies are available to get people back into the workforce and be productive again as they look ahead to the typical retirement age?

SCHLAFLY

As a framework for discussion, let's use the three career strategy categories of "career recycler," "career changer," and "career maker."

For a "recycler" who has the skill of commercial truck driving and wants to continue driving but not long distance, he might look at a job opportunity that is locally based. Yes it will pay less, but this driver wants to contribute to the benefit of his local senior population by driving buses and vans for adult living communities, for example. That's called "career recycling"—using transferable skills.

The second career strategy category is for someone who is willing to take on much more risk, doing a career change. They're going to be out looking to undertake something completely different. For example, they are determined to have their dream career, so they've committed to diverting from what they did before in *both* their field *and* their role. In the current economy, this strategy requires more time, effort, and self-awareness. In this case, a wise plan would be to work with a career professional like myself to guide them through a self-discovery process. This includes a reconnaissance of their prior work experience, their dependable strengths, values in life, what matters in all aspects of their work, their interests, passions, and personality type.

Once they embrace this enlightening picture of who they really are, I find that it's often an "ah-ha" moment that expands their vision to a full range of career choices and roles. Then, when they take that information from the discovery phase, the next step is to research some choices, narrow down the field, and start talking to people who are already in the role that interests them. One option is to shadow someone who does that kind of work. Another is to do an internship or temporary job to see if you like it. This is what they call informational interviewing. Find out from somebody who's actually doing the job what they think of it.

Once you narrow that down, then you enter the real guts of a full-fledged job search for a new career and a new role in your career.

Then the third and last main area to expand on is actually being a career maker. That is where you become an entrepreneur. I work with people who want to take that road. They could start a new company, buy an existing one, or invest in some kind of franchise that gives them a business model and support in marketing and other aspects. These are the three different ways for "encore-preneurs" to make a significant change in how they approach work in their second half of life.

WRIGHT

So what are some popular encore career fields and jobs currently? Are there any jobs cropping up there that serve the seventy-eight million Baby Boomers turning sixty-five at the rate of ten thousand a day for the next eighteen years?

SCHLAFLY

You're not going to get rid of us very easily! We have such a wide age bracket. I think the range goes down all the way into people who are forty-eight years old, the youngest of the Baby Boomers. Marc Freedman wrote a book called *The Big Shift* in which he issues a call for converting America's looming midlife crisis into an opportunity to forge a new map of life. It includes a new stage between the end of the middle years and the beginning of retirement and old age. If those in this age range (which is not precise) take action, their "encore years" could become a fulfilling destination. The seventy-eight million people flooding into it is a human capital solution to much that ails us in this society. As we confront significant challenges in areas like education, the environment, and health care, this windfall of talent could help carry us toward a new generation of solutions.

In the 2011 MetLife Foundation survey I previously referenced, it highlighted that the number one field in which 30 percent of people are currently working in encore careers is education. Another 25 percent are finding jobs in healthcare and 25 percent are working in the government sector. As a side note, based on what we hear in the media, we tend to think that there are many workforce and funding cuts in government, especially at the local and state levels. But that's not the broad case because there are still many new opportunities cropping up in government. Another 11 percent of Boomers have encore careers in nonprofit organizations, and 5 percent in for-profit. A growing segment of about 4 percent of encore career seekers are examining the emerging sectors of environment and sustainability.

Within all of these popular areas, we find that there is an "age wave" focus attached, where younger Boomers serve the market of older Boomers.

Let me give you a couple of examples. An encore careerist can be a healthcare or patient advocate. There is a growing need for this specialty due to the huge increase in the aging Boomer population. I wish I had found someone like this early on for my mother as her healthcare needs increased, resulting in overlapping providers and services.

There are more needs for fitness trainers who are in the fifty plus age range because of the growth of age sixty plus clients. We will need more audiologists for the hearing impaired. I don't know if modern medicine has yet found a way to stop deafness from happening! How about a "senior move management" service? Many seniors are not looking to "age in place," and so they need a specialized service to help them move from their big home to a smaller home, then perhaps into an assisted living facility.

Another growing "age wave" niche is the "Senior Real Estate Specialist." A Real Estate agent obtains training to get a certificate for this specialty in order to know how to work with an aging population that needs to find a home with a single story floor plan or has the potential to be upgraded with special devices for physical disabilities. Another remodeling contractor could create a niche in doing "aging in place" modifications to a home.

Adult living communities need recreation directors who understand and know how to engage with the senior residents and create interesting and lively events. Financial planners could specialize in investment advising and planning for retirement.

And last but not least, we will need more funeral directors because no one escapes that need!

These are some very realistic examples of popular encore career fields and new, emerging specialty fields, which follow the Boomer "age wave."

WRIGHT

So how are you personally helping raise awareness of the value of encore or second act careers?

SCHLAFLY

First, in the obvious way by creating a focus in my coaching practice on helping midlife professionals move through career changes to discover and then begin their own encore career. I am launching a larger campaign to educate this midlife group through my public presentations and workshops. I love public speaking. I've been doing presentations locally for people who are in that age bracket and who are looking for more than just a re-do of their prior job. They are looking for a real change. My goal with public speaking is to bump up my engagements, create a broader scale, larger audiences, and take it to another level.

A valuable resource for raising awareness is my blog where I write about all aspects of career change, and put that out in the world to people who have an interest in getting more specifics and how-to's.

I have joined AARP as a volunteer and I will be working with them on a larger level on some of their campaigns and presentations they take into the communities on topics around aging in place, long-term care, and financial and medical support for women over sixty.

Also on the volunteer side, for about three years I've been doing coaching for job searchers with Dress for Success in their local Portland, Oregon, Career Center. Dress for Success provides clothing for women who are in need of outfits to dress appropriately for their job interviews. And finally, I am getting myself into the media with articles, this book chapter, and guest blogging for non-profit organizations targeting job seekers looking for an encore career.

I give people complimentary time with me to discuss their work/career transition to see how I might be able to help them find more meaningful work in their new life chapter. Finally, I continue to develop new programs for my business that will appeal to a range of people.

WRIGHT

What is the future as you see it for yourself? What is your own plan to continue to contribute to your community, society, and the world and remain connected and vital?

SCHLAFLY

That is a powerful question and it struck me personally recently when my mother died. She was ninety, so it was not unexpected at that age. I see that more and more Boomers are becoming adult orphans. It catches us off guard. We knew it was coming, and suddenly it happens. It's a time for deep reflection that can become a catalyst for both life and career change. We realize that we're "next in line," facing our mortality. It's forcing us to become more mindful of how we spend our time on a daily basis.

I've had the book by Stephen Covey, 7 *Habits of Highly Effective People*, on my shelf for at least fifteen years and I'm finally reading it. This book is helping me assess the paring down of several things in my life, to live with more purpose, observe everything I do, and have it be intentional. I'm getting rid of stuff, taking a lighter load both physically with the things I've collected through the years, and working on having less stress on myself. I look at my relationships with friends throughout the years and there are times I find that I'm working too much with my head down in my business while neglecting friendships.

When your last parent passes away, you start to realize that you and your friends of the same age range need to be bonding together more and looking for mutually supportive ways of living, especially if you're single.

I also recommend that continued learning and growing is a must for people as they age. What I would do is continue to contribute and remain connected, get further education, especially if you're still working in your field, and if you live near a university or community college check out the discounted rates that many are offering to seniors. With the recent popularity of MOOC's (Massive Open Online Courses) lifelong learners can attend high quality classes from any location. Learn and grow with things and activities that you've always wanted to know about but you never had time for. Just keep shifting as needed, you're stepping over hot coals sometimes, but you've got to just keep walking and jumping.

For me, my next shift is to bring coaching together with more global needs in the rapidly growing Pacific Rim. I want to apply my Asian language skills in Chinese and Japanese with my coaching in a unique way that promotes career growth, facilitates understanding the different business cultural protocols, and improves business English skills. So that's what I'm doing, that's my future, and I'm so excited to be moving forward to it!

WRIGHT

What a great conversation, I'm in that group of people you're talking about.

SCHLAFLY

I won't ask you how far in you are.

WRIGHT

Way far—I've been thinking about these things for a long time and it's really been helpful for me.

I've learned a lot here from you today and I'm sure that our readers will get a lot out of this chapter. I really appreciate your being in the book and for taking this time with me today to answer these many questions.

SCHLAFLY

Oh, I've just so enjoyed our time together because it's a topic that I have a lot of passion and energy around, as they say.

WRIGHT

Today I have been talking with Laura Schlafly. Laura is the Founder of Career Choices with Laura, a coaching practice where she specializes in guiding midlife professionals through career detours and to investigate and then launch second act careers after they reach fifty plus. In her current role as a professional speaker and encore career coach, Laura combines her skills and interests, plus the wealth of knowledge gleaned from her own five careers, into a tailored process that helps her clients find their ideal work by uncovering their core passion and purpose and getting a paycheck, too!

Laura, thank you so much for being with us today on *ROADMAP to Success*.

SCHLAFLY

I'm totally delighted; thank you, David.

Laura Schlafly is the founder of the Lake Oswego, Oregon-based business, Career Choices with Laura. She inspires and guides Baby Boomers and mid-career professionals to investigate and then launch "Second Act" careers after they reach fifty plus.

With a BA in Japanese studies from Ohio State, an MBA from the University of Michigan, and being a serial Boomer entrepreneur herself, Laura has twenty years of hands-on, practical experience in product marketing, field sales, and small business development. Laura is also a private pilot, musician, dancer, and life-long student of Asian cultures and languages.

In her current role as a Professional Speaker, Author, and Encore Career Coach, Laura combines these skills and interests, plus the wealth of knowledge gleaned from her own five careers, into a tailored strategy that helps her clients uncover their own core Passions and apply them to a motivating career with Purpose and a Paycheck attached.

Laura Schlafly

Career Choices with Laura
PO Box 2346
Lake Oswego, OR 97035
971-208-5852
Laura@CareerChoicesWithLaura.com
www.CareerChoicesWithLaura.com

CHAPTER THIRTEEN

Create A Wildfire In Your Workplace:
Get Rid Of Dead People Working And Get Fully Engaged,
Happy Employees
Dr. Sherry Blair

DAVID WRIGHT (WRIGHT)

Today I'm talking with Dr. Sherry Blair. Dr. Blair is a highly sought-after professional coach/consultant, positivity leader, professional speaker, and published author. She is the author of *The Positivity Pulse: Transforming Your Workplace*. As Founder and CEO of ISIS Innovative Specialists Inspirational Services, Sherry inspires and motivates individuals, teams, and organizations by assessing, applying, and encouraging positive psychology and the evidence-based practice of the Science of Happiness at work.

WRIGHT

She is a graduate of Rutgers University with a Bachelor of Arts degree in Psychology and Women's Studies. She went on to obtain her master's of science in social work with a concentration in policy analysis and international social welfare at Columbia University. She is duly mastered in industrial and organizational psychology, and she holds a PhD in Management, supporting her vision to make changes at the macro level in leadership. Dr. Blair is an accredited provider of the Science of Happiness at Work through the iOpener Institute for People and Performance.

Dr. Blair, welcome to *ROADMAP to Success*.

SHERRY BLAIR (SHERRY)

Thank you; I'm honored to be here.

WRIGHT

Create a Wildfire in Your Workplace: Get Rid of Dead People Working and Get Fully Engaged Happy Employees is an unusual title. I can't wait to get into this. So what is the most important strategy for business success in leadership?

SHERRY

At the core caring about your employees, business partners and the people you serve are what I believe make a difference. Making a difference and being able to measure the outcomes is what many organizations are striving to give to their employees. It also is important that you give them the processes where they can work on achieving their own potentials as well, which is at the core of the Science of Happiness[1] at work. Once you have this foundation, that's when you're creating win-win situations by facilitating their personal and professional development.

Understanding what makes an individual happy at work is an extremely valuable commodity for organizations. *Helping people discover what makes them happy at work is a commitment that demonstrates you care about them.* When people know you care, they actually care about you and in return they care about what they're doing. Overall that supports the philosophy and the sustainability of workplace relationships.

WRIGHT

Positive psychology and happiness at work sounds Pollyannaish and fluffy, so what is your response to that critique?

SHERRY

Interestingly, the business case of Happiness at Work recently made the cover of the *Harvard Business Review*[2]. The most successful and powerful thought leaders throughout time have pondered about the good life, so it's not a new concept but behind that terminology *there is a substantial amount of research that demonstrates sound reasons for increasing positive emotions, character strengths, virtues and values in our relationships.* Interestingly when *Authentic Happiness,*[3] the positive psychology modern day movement, emerged, Marty Seligman, who has

---

[1] Jessica Pryce-Jones (2010), *Happiness at Work: Maximizing your Psychological Capital for Success.*
[2] *Harvard Business Review* (Jan–Feb 2012). *The Value of Happiness: How Employee Well-Being Drives Profits.*
[3] Dr. Martin Seligman (2003). *Authentic Happiness: Using the New Positive Psychology to Realize Your Potential for Lasting Fulfillment.* Free Press: New York, NY.

sold millions of books based on happiness, was not particularly fond of using the word "happiness," he says that his editors thought it would be a good thing—people would subscribe to that and they have, millions of readers later.

I would only have to point skeptics to the incredible success of Southwest Airlines as an example[4]. Their success is due to the culture of caring they have developed since the start and it was important to build a company in which people not only loved to come to work, but also thrived. They have a culture where every employee is *all in*—no "Dead People Working."

Any company that would like to have employee engagement, a solid bottom line, and be a great place to work where highly qualified people are clamoring to be hired would do well to study this model. I have, and what I do is help leaders achieve the kind of culture that fully engages employees and has many benefits for the individual as well as the productivity and profit of the company.

When employees feel seen, appreciated, and valued, they are happier, bring their best to work, and as an added benefit they are also happier at home. It's a win-win situation!

Positive psychology turns our focus to what is psychologically strong and teaches us how to use strengths to help people move toward change. The most powerful way that we increase positivity and happiness is through the combination of the Science of Happiness at Work and the use of an approach called the Nurtured Heart Approach (NHA),[5] which we call the *"how" of achieving a positivity pulse in your workplace*. The techniques are very powerful and specific. The Science of Happiness at Work is evidence-based and focuses on not only what an organization can do for its employees, but specifically what individuals can do for themselves.

For example, when I work with companies, teams, and individuals to help them achieve their potential, I discovered that, initially, people were reluctant to focus on their own personal strengths. Perhaps it comes from traditional teaching where being humble and having humility is revered. But organizations are learning that when we focus on what helps us achieve our happiness, people feel more energized to overcome challenges and become more resilient when facing increasing job demands.

---

[4] Jackie and Kevin Freiberg (2003). *Guts: Companies that Blow the Doors Off Business As Usual.* Doubleday Business: New York, NY.
[5] Howard Glasser (2011). *Notching Up the Nurtured Heart Approach: The New Inner Wealth Initiative for Educators.* Nurtured Heart Publications: Tucson, AZ.

When people take action using our precision tools and step-by-step plan to discover what makes them happy and what enhances their strengths, not only do they benefit, but so do their organizations.

WRIGHT

What are the most frustrating things that employees, managers, and leaders discuss with you confidentially about their workplace?

SHERRY

So many organizations are dealing with increasing job demands with decreased job resources. This is leading to poor outcomes, not just with profits and the inability to meet the mission of the organization, but in the engagement of employees as well. Leaders and managers are trying multiple initiatives to increase these outcomes, but don't know exactly where to put the resources of time and money in order to improve the outcomes.

In today's tough economic climate, getting measurable outcomes is the key to not only survival, it is a mandate. *Research has demonstrated that to achieve those measurable outcomes, you have to look at how the proportion of job demands meets the job resources that one has.*

Let's start with job demands. Every company has them. Demands come from clients and the people they serve or the need to make a profit. Each day, individuals and organizations have those demands. In order to be successful in meeting job demands, you need job resources. Job resources are what an organization provides for an individual. For example, a resource may be tactical, such as an IT system or proper work space. A job resource can also be an excellent manager or administrative assistant. In short, a resource is given to an employee by the organization.

When a person or a team is given the right amount of resources to meet the demands, measurable outcomes happen. *Unfortunately, every day, it seems that organizations are dealing with increasing job demands and decreasing job resources. People are feeling overworked, underappreciated, and demotivated to perform as a result.*

WRIGHT

So what are companies doing?

SHERRY

Often, they are trying to provide a new concept or a new initiative in an attempt to create enthusiasm. Employees perceive that a new concept or initiative may create more work, or they have seen similar initiatives before that have been tried and failed or even fallen to the wayside. There are multiple reasons why change initiatives often fail.

First, they are often done without properly measuring what the pain points are for employees. It is like throwing antibiotics at an illness without the proper diagnosis, hoping that it will cure what ails the organization.

Second, it only concentrates on what an employer can give an organization, not what employees can do for themselves. We call that their personal resources. This is why you may have two employees that have the exact same resources, the same job demands, and even the same boss, and have two different outcomes. The two employees have two different levels of personal resources.

Third, rarely does the initiative provide a precise road map for what leaders can do to help individuals. They try various types of recognition programs that rarely have measurable outcomes. Again, the issue is often that they do not properly assess or evaluate before they act. So they spend enormous amounts of time and money to achieve the outcomes.

The essence of the Science of Happiness at Work is helping individuals find out how exactly how to increase their levels of personal resources, regardless of what job demands or job resources they may encounter. *Increasing the personal resources of an individual, team, or organization will have a direct result in improved outcomes.*

WRIGHT

You recommend that organizations change their culture. Why is preparing your organization for change important?

SHERRY

Change initiatives fail and that contributes to dead people working. They fail because there is no preparation for the change or a plan for sustainability. There is a staggering 70 percent failure rate[6] if you don't prepare for the change, or if you are working on something that isn't the exact issue. So, if you're looking at it from a business perspective, *why would you invest funding into an initiative that has a 70 percent chance of failing?* Unfortunately that's what happens commonly,

---

[6] John Kotter (2008). *A Sense of Urgency.* Harvard Business Press: Boston, MA.

particularly when we refer to the soft skills—the people and performance initiatives—not the hardcore technical skills.

As an example, I'll get brought in as a consultant and begin with observing the workplace and getting introduced to the staff. I can actually feel the negative energy from the "dead people working." I can feel that they're disengaged by their lack of attention and their body language. I can see they're somewhat clustered together or even isolated and immediately sense the toxicity in an energetic way. I'd bet you could, too, if you were there. The more positive people pretty much find their own space.

Once I tune into that vibe, whether negative or positive, it feels to me like a pulse in the air, so to speak. I like to call it the "pulse" and I relate that to a heart rate. Either we have a nice, steady, healthy beat—what I call a *"positivity pulse"*— or we have a crazed, stressed, chaotic pulse. In the case of dead people working, we pretty much have a flat liner. Some of them are angry, they have a lack of faith, they feel it's a complete waste of their time to sit through something they feel will go nowhere, judging from their past experiences with training.

Although the intention is well-meaning from the managers who have heard this great idea, the initiative falls to the wayside and nothing substantive follows because they have not prepared themselves or their teams for change. When the employees get back to their departments, often there is no support or worse, their immediate manager tells them they are not going to do it this new way. And *Boom!* just like that, the employees get discouraged and nothing changes and the training dollars were mostly wasted. Employers can avoid this and work swiftly to start *eliminating the negative pulse and increasing a positivity pulse by being strategic, preparing for change by making a sound investment into people and performance, and having an implementation plan with support for the new initiative.*

WRIGHT

What does it mean to have dead people working?

SHERRY

It means that people are not spending as much time doing what they are paid to do—they have checked out and stayed for various reasons. These reasons may include the economy is bad, they're waiting for tenure, they're waiting to retire, lack of alternative opportunities, or they're just plain unhappy in their job and holding out for the paychecks. They're at work physically but completely disengaged, they lack motivation, they do not work well in a team, and they do whatever they need to do just to get by.

Astonishingly, *unhappy people at work only produce about 48 percent of the workday* while *happy people produce more than one and a quarter times more than unhappy people.*[7] It's interesting because a great deal of attention and money are invested in measuring engagement. People can be engaged in work but if they are not happy they will not be optimized and they won't produce at their highest potential.

I focus on happiness at work, but we need to address what we, as leaders, are doing when we have dead people working.

WRIGHT

Is there a personal benefit as well as a business benefit to increasing positivity and happiness at work?

SHERRY

Absolutely. I believed that if you're happy at home it would stand to reason that you would be happy at work, but studies have revealed just the opposite of that, if you are happy at home it does not mean you'll be happy at work. *Conversely, if you aren't happy at work there is a higher chance that you'll be unhappy at home in your personal life.* There is also a true health benefit and a cellular change when we increase positivity and happiness in our lives but especially within the workplace.

We have a hormone called oxytocin that is in every cell of our body; when it's increased we get more brainpower. The fun part of it is that it is the bonding hormone that is attached to romantic love and sex and all that wonderful stuff. If you expand the notion of that positive bonding hormone, it creates positive health, it's really good for us, and it does create long-term health benefits and flourishing at a cellular level. So it's a love and bonding hormone I know that rocks the Pollyanna cradle again, but when we think outside of the romance piece of it and expand the definition, it definitely makes sense to get more of it and we're all better off for it.

WRIGHT

Will you explain for our readers and listeners "psychological and social capital" and the power behind increasing that at work?

---

[7] Jessica Pryce-Jones (2010). *Happiness at Work: Maximizing your Psychological Capital for Success.*

SHERRY

Sure, I am an advanced trainer and a Certified Nurtured Heart Approach Specialist. Moving away from the psychological jargon, we call it our "inner wealth"[8] and although this approach was developed for children, for transforming a difficult child, this application is extremely powerful not only in the workplace but in any relationship. *Using it in your daily moment-to-moment language increases more productive relationships with adults.* We encourage the use of it in virtual communication such as texting and e-mailing and it really does make such a difference.

Inner wealth is psychological and social capital, and making those deposits into an individual account, is like making deposits into the company's account or a team's joint account. The outcomes are stronger relationships and an increase in performance and productivity.

Psychological capital is essentially the pool of resources in our mind that builds over time when we experience positive things and we achieve our goals. There are recent studies revealing that we experience a *"broaden and build effect"*[9] and that really comes in handy when faced with crisis, adversity, or rejection. It's comforting to know when you have it, and although I've been eating, drinking, and breathing positive psychology for close to a decade it's always a fantastic feeling when you experience it in real life. It's one thing to absorb all the disciplines intellectually, but living it and feeling it makes all the difference.

Recently, in a business relationship, I had an idea and it wasn't very well received. I was okay with it and I realized after receiving an e-mail that I could have reacted in an emotionally unhealthy way, and I may have a number of years ago because I would have been more concerned with other people's approval, which can be irrational. Although I think the use of e-mail is misused and comes across as strong with a lack of caring, I still handled it well and was not in the least unnerved about the rejection. I said, "Wow I really have this broaden and build affect. It's okay." It's a state of mind where you're able to handle things with more dignity and grace and truly be more open-minded and compassionate to another person's position or decisions. You get that, in some instances, it's not about you as a person but rather your idea, and it's possibly even for the greater good. I realized shortly after, that because I stated what I needed in terms of structural organization and efficient communication, the universe was looking

---

[8] Howard Glasser (2011). *Notching Up the Nurtured Heart Approach: The New Inner Wealth Initiative for Educators.* Nurtured Heart Publications: Tucson, AZ.

[9] Barbara Fredrickson (2009). *Positivity: Top Notch Research Reveals the 3 to 1 Ratio That Will Change Your Life.* Three Rivers Press: New York, NY.

out for me as well because I was too busy to add in more work that would get me off balance between work and play.

One of the reasons I love positive psychology and the application of NHA as the "how" of the positivity pulse is because it's like using Miracle Gro in life. *Psychological capital embodies optimism, hope, resiliency, motivation, confidence, and energy. You have a better buy-in and willingness to believe in yourself and your abilities.*

WRIGHT

How does social capital work?

SHERRY

Social capital flows in more of an enriched way when individuals have more psychological capital but it's not built in a day. It's like developing a higher level of consciousness—it takes time and it evolves with a concerted effort. Just like any other strong healthy relationship we need tune-ups over time; like a car, you can't keep running it without taking care of it. We need to make sure we take care of it but we need it daily.

Social capital is also systemic and it's very intertwined in many ways. It's about connection and relationships, being interconnected among self, groups, and communities, and it's the flow within and to and from all these relationships. I like to think about that as a river where there is input and output and there are all kinds of energetic connections in-between.

When we have psychological capital, social capital flows and they are both constituents of human capital, which again is not another new concept, it's been around since the eighteenth century. *Prioritizing human capital by increasing psychological and social capital is not only good for the individual but tying it into business strategies it has shown to increase financial capital.* At the end of the day, we need nourishment in the form of human capital nutrients—psychologically, spiritually, emotionally, and socially to thrive and to flourish.

WRIGHT

So how would I increase psychological and social capital? I mean what specifically can I do and how quickly can I make it happen?

SHERRY

I am glad you asked that because I know everyone wants that quick fix. We have a little bit of that we can offer but it does take much more than a onetime speaking engagement or a three-day training event. It's something that needs to be nurtured over time as I mentioned. Some of my clients have an innate personality and have psychological and social capital, and they practice the strategies so easily because it is like having permission to be who they really are at their core being.

For others, it takes practice and they might need a little more support to fully incorporate the behavior changes. That's the beauty of Positivity Pulse. Some have a short training and that's all they need, and others prefer some coaching to make it a habit—a way of being. Our step-by-step plan guides the process.

Cultivating the culture—a culture of positivity and happiness—takes practice and it takes more for some than others, some people are just quite naturally optimistic and that's a personality factor, while others are quite naturally a little bit more cynical or a lot more cynical. When I say "naturally," I mean genetically.

Taking a "capital temperature," helps you find out what's really going on. That is a first step. As much as I like to rely on my intuition and do not need to rely on a psychometric measure for what I can already sense energetically, I know that intellectually measuring something and being able to pinpoint the location of the cancer is like going in with an ultrasound or a MRI. *We get straight to the core of that infection and, in turn, that helps us arrive a lot quicker to a solution to start a transformational process.* You can actually measure the change. After all, it's all about sustained change, right? We have the tools to measure these things before our training and say, six months or a year later for individuals, teams, and entire organizations.

It's about change and you need to prepare yourself and your team or organization. It's not easy for many people to change whether personal or professional. A first step is to help others to create the vision, remove obstacles, develop a team you know you're going to do this with, and get people to buy in just to name a few.

So for the workplace, looking at it through a developmental lens, know that you're going to go through those phases and growing pains. I look at my business developmentally and I think we need to look at that when we're trying to make change. We have to look at it developmentally and nurture it appropriately as we move forward. If it's an older, more established business, we need to be honest about how staying stuck in an old way of doing business will no longer keep us competitive.

We have a means for specific and targeted actions for pinpointing where the weaknesses are in our pipeline and identifying what makes people happy at work. There is a way to do it that we haven't been able to tap into before; *it's measuring what is happiness at work, and that answers the question as to whether or not people have a sense of pride, trust, and recognition for starters.*

A recent conversation in *The Wall Street Journal* came out about the *Five Drivers to Success,*[10] which was developed out of the iOpener Institute in London. *It was discovered that these are the things that are important to include, based on the voice of the employees and management teams—contribution, commitment, conviction, culture, and confidence, and at the heart of that is achieving your full potential.* These strengths are encircled by having pride, trust, and recognition as I mentioned.

You need to look at where you are in offering those things with your teams or within your organization in order to get more happiness at work and to increase psychological and social capital. We can measure this for individuals, teams, and organizations and take that "capital temperature" over time.

The quick fix is in using NHA where we use recognitions as a way to reflect a person's strengths and positive behavior. You can start right away by shifting the way you see things and start noticing the "greatness" or positivity in others. If people show up on time, we never notice that because we say, "Well heck, they're supposed to show up on time, that's what they get paid for." But if you change your view about that and notice that showing up on time has an inherent value in the choice to get to work on time and what it says about a person's character, you're changing the energy immediately.

---

[10] *Wall Street Journal* (Sept. 11, 2011). *Five Drivers to Success.* New York, NY.

Here is an example: "Hey good morning. Thanks for getting here on time we've got a full workload. I want to jump right in; thanks for being punctual and responsible and committed to this project." What did that cost me? It took me only a few seconds to say. That's a very easy way to jump right in but there are incremental steps you need to take to help change your way of thinking so that you determine and notice the qualities you want to applaud both within yourself and others. Although it is a way to jump right in to see an immediate energy shift, leaders need to continue to cultivate the initiative for sustainable outcomes.

WRIGHT

Is it really possible to increase an individual's state of happiness?

SHERRY

Here's where I'll default again to the power of research and outcomes. I'm very intuitive and think out of the box and some people like to say "in touch with my bohemian self." But I have a great deal of respect for knowledge and the power that it brings. *We have a 40 percent ability to change, 50 percent is a given in our DNA, so genetically that's who we are and 10 percent is life events.*[11] *That's powerful* because a lot of people believe that our life events can affect us in such a more drastic way, as if it has more power over us. Knowing that we have a 40 percent capability to change is empowering. Think about it this way: *If I said, "Give me $1,000 and I will show you a 40 percent return on your investment, you would be "over the moon." You would increase your capital by 40 percent.*

We've also found that the worst cynic can even be less cynical. So even though we have the Debbie Downers and the Doubting Daves all over, we're still able to increase their range. It's not that they will become optimistic overnight or at all, they might not ever become optimistic; however, *they might become a little less cynical. Teaching them ways to harness some of the cynicism and not be enslaved to it or infect others with it is a positive outcome and helps to create more of a positive culture.*

WRIGHT

So what else would you recommend for creating a more positive environment?

SHERRY

I can't stress enough the need to plan for change; that vision needs to be set. I am very driven by identifying first what the values are, I know a lot of people

---

[11] Sonja Lyubomirsky (2008). *The How of Happiness: A New Approach to Getting the Life You Want.* Penguin Books: New York, NY.

want to jump in and say what are our operations, what are our policy and procedures and how are we going to do this?

Firstly we need to identify the values—what values do we want to have in this organization for how we do business, for how we treat each other, how do we want that in our lives, in our family lives and our personal life? How do we want to be treated, how do we want to treat others? *Conveying and identifying what those values are and creating a buy-in to those values is crucial. Every decision thereafter intentionally upholds the values.*

I love Ken Blanchard's work in *Servant Leadership*[12] for how he conveys this. That's been something I've taken and run with for a number of years and have taught others how to do it. From your values you create your rules. The rules uphold the values. *You need to become determined to increase overall well-being for yourself and others and it takes a lot of practice, it's not easy.* Sometimes, when you get busy or things seem to be going well, you lose that momentum but when you do it's important to get back on track and *you need to give yourself and the team credit for getting back on track—recognizing is what we teach.* No one is going to be perfect in applying new knowledge all the time, you can lose it, it can easily be lost. But when you notice you are being more consciously aware of where you are, in terms of relating to others. You do have to make an effort to get outside your comfort zone until it becomes a habit, but in a deeper way, it becomes who you are.

To achieve a positivity pulse in the workplace we use techniques embodied in NHA[13]. There are three stands that help facilitate this transformation in the best way. *We teach how not to energize negativity.* For fun I always talk about my Roman Catholic upbringing but I like to say that when there is negativity or toxic people around me, I imagine myself throwing holy water and holding up my arms in sort of a crucifix saying, "No, no I can't get into that energy." I'm saying that in a fun way, just to be a little dramatic about it, we have to make a refusal—even if it's listening to gossip for example, that's engaging in negativity because you're not shutting it down. If someone asks you to be deceitful or to lie for them you're engaging in negativity.

Secondly, *we teach how to relentlessly energize the positive.* Think about it this way: when someone comes to work on time, we may not have noticed that before, but now we can create success because there that person is being successful, there

---

[12] Ken Blanchard (2003). *Servant Leadership.* Thomas Nelson: Nashville, TN.
[13] Howard Glasser (2011). *Notching Up the Nurtured Heart Approach: The New Inner Wealth Initiative for Educators.* Nurtured Heart Publications: Tucson, AZ.

the person is, being punctual and showing up. All of that that says a lot about them and their character, so you just take those few seconds to say that and add on the values associated with that desired behavior.

The third stand is having *a clear set of rules and boundaries and that code of conduct, which is driven by the values I was discussing and upheld by consistent consequences.* We need to clearly and unenergetically enforce limits. I think being consistent is hard for us—all of us—and I think a lot of us have a tendency to look the other way or to avoid conflict and confrontation or listening to somebody when you need to make a referral to an employee assistance program. Sometimes you're not really upholding the policies, you're not helping them by enabling the behavior, either. So we need to be clear about that. *There is one little caveat that goes with this: sometimes it means removing people, places, or things in your life,* particularly if they're not ready to take that journey with you. So it's not easy, it does take an effort. Metaphorically, this is the wildfire you create by refusing to energize negativity to include facilitating change that may result in the dead people leaving. Like a natural wildfire, burning off the dead weight allows room for the fully engaged, happy employee to flourish.

WRIGHT

So why does it matter to have positive relationships at work?

SHERRY

Well, relationships are everything. We are social beings and being interdependent is in our fiber. Even people with true social challenges with or without a psychiatric disorder want relationships, even when we think they don't want it because they have problems with social behaviors, with eye contact, or conversations. They still want relationships and they still cherish and value it. The most lonely people often want relationships; we human beings are very social. *When we have positive and healthy relationships we flourish.*

Think about influential leaders—an American president, for example. A president can't be a president alone; a president has a cabinet and advisors. Although a president can be a movement by himself, he's more of a force when he's synergistically working with everyone in a productive, positive, and healthy way.

As I mentioned before, when we're in positive healthy relationships it's actually good for us at a cellular level, but we can also be taken down by dysfunctional, unhealthy, energy-sucking relationships. When you are telling yourself negative things and telling yourself negative things about others, then you're relating in a negative way and that creates the opposite cellular effect. We install toxicity within our brains and within our entire being. *So health-wise it makes sense when we become more conscious of building those relationships and making it a true practice.* We find compassionate ways to communicate and manage ourselves even in challenging times.

Knowing that the ultimate goal is to be solution-focused, we need to value relationships. Even though it's uncomfortable for us to talk about something, at the end of the day we're doing it because we value the relationships. Valuing the relationship indeed preserves and strengthens the relationship.

Positive relationships result in being happier and being happier at home and work, at a deeper level is within our hearts and that's what it's all about.

WRIGHT

Well, what a great conversation. I have learned a lot here today, Sherry, and I'm sure our readers will as well. I thank you for taking all this time with me to answer these questions; it's really been a delight.

SHERRY

Thank you, I appreciate it.

WRIGHT

Today we have been talking with Dr. Sherry Blair. Dr. Blair is Founder and Chief Executive Officer of ISIS, Innovative Specialists Inspirational Services. She inspires and motivates others by applying and encouraging positive psychology. Sherry uses her skills to teach others how to build productive teams and effective caring communication to achieve results and resolve conflict. Teaching others to speak from their hearts is a key component of the work she does.

Dr. Blair, thank you so much for being with us today on *ROADMAP to Success*.

SHERRY

Thank you.

Dynamic, passionate, and powerful are some of the adjectives audiences use to describe sought-after speaker Dr. Sherry Blair as she spreads her message of positivity around the globe. Since becoming one of the first three hundred in the world to be trained in the Authentic Happiness Positive Psychology Coaching Program under the tutelage of Dr. Martin Seligman almost a decade ago, Sherry is wholeheartedly committed to transforming organizations and companies into flourishing workplaces.

Using her prodigious skills and cleverly drawing on the latest research in the field, Sherry inspires from the heart and gives others the tools to develop leadership, build effective teams, and use compassionate communication to measurable positive outcomes. She serves on both the Research/Ethics and Global Summit Committees for the Nurtured Heart Approach under the leadership of Howard Glasser. Her first book, *The Positivity Pulse: Transforming Your Workplace,* is being released in Spanish this year as well as an Action Guide with her Positivity Pulse Business Partner, Alletta Bayer. Sherry is also releasing a powerful action guide to influence teens to start change and develop leadership— *Tribal Warriors: Life Skills to Optimize Well-Being for Teens.*

POSITIVITY
PULSE

Sherry Blair

www.drsherryblair.com
Blog: www.positivitypulse.com

CHAPTER FOURTEEN

Alpha Sigma Decisions
Mauricio Espinosa

DAVID WRIGHT (WRIGHT)

Today I'm talking with Mauricio Espinosa, business owner, leadership coach, and consultant for more than fifteen years. Mauricio has worked with executives in the United States, Mexico, Colombia, Venezuela, Brazil, Argentina, the Dominican Republic, and Puerto Rico. Through these years he has developed different training programs and coaching services, helping business and individuals reach their goals.

Mauricio focuses his programs with a high level of energy, motivation, and leadership where all participants engage easily with his concepts. The ability to make things easy to understand work on a daily basis is one of the many qualities that make Mauricio one of the most recognized leaders today.

Mauricio, welcome to *ROADMAP to Success*.

MAURICIO ESPINOSA (ESPINOSA)

Thank you; it is my pleasure to be here and share this time with everyone. What a tremendous opportunity for everyone to share knowledge.

WRIGHT

Tell me, why do businesses or people feel trapped or stuck at times?

ESPINOSA

Most of the time, when people or organizations feel trapped or stuck or don't see the outcome or the finish line, is because it is difficult to understand which part of their journey or the road they are on. Let me explain, imagine we are on a road trip. We are driving together and you as the passenger take a nap. When you wake up I ask you to drive but I don't tell where we are, how long you napped, if I changed directions. Then I go ahead and take a nap. How would you feel?

We have to understand that it is a global world that we live in today. Our lives depend not just on our decisions, but we also depend on the decisions other people or other entities make and we are sometimes changing journeys or paths. Not knowing that many times we are already on a different direction than we were planning, if we had planned. Now take into consideration that most people really don't have a plan of where they are heading, so it's very difficult to not get trapped or get stuck.

WRIGHT

How can anybody start visualizing his or her path or journey as you mentioned?

ESPINOSA

Is it easy? I will say no, otherwise everybody would have one, and it is not that is hard to do, it just takes time, determination, and discipline. And time, determination, and discipline are probably where the difficulty comes in. It is important to pause in our lives and question where are we heading? Where are we at this particular moment in our lives and how did we get here? When we do this and invest the time in looking at events and decisions that have shaped our journey, we will start to understand ourselves and our patterns a little more.

Then it comes a more philosophical question: what do we want to get out of this time on Earth, basically? That applies to individuals or businesses. Sometimes most businesses do take that time at the end of the year and they do their budget and planning and it just stays there as if all was about sales and expenses. It is no wonder why we don't see that many business grow, or prevail through time. Statistics show that 66 percent of new establishments were still in existence two years after they started, and 44 percent were still in existence four years after. Lack of planning is one of the biggest reasons, followed by lack of a mentor or coach, lack of business education, and the list goes on.

We very rarely take the time to stop and do an analysis of our lives. The four main influences or spheres in our lives are: family, work, social, and self. The changes we have gone through, even in the last three months can make a significant difference between where we are and where we want to go. It all comes down to making what I call alpha and sigma decisions.

WRIGHT

How do we identify if we're part of an alpha or a sigma decision?

ESPINOSA

Every day we make thousands of decisions. That is a constant in human behavior; however, not all decisions are the beginning of something and that is what I like to call an Alpha decision. These decisions are for our own journey and not part of someone else's journey. I named it alpha because it's the first decision we make that will lead us into something.

An example is: If I decide today that I want to get a new puppy, that is an alpha decision. There are a lot of sigma decisions, or decisions that add to that initial decision. Those sigma decisions are: vet costs, food costs, who's going to take care of the puppy, who's going to take him out for a walk—all those can follow the decisions resulting from the alpha decision.

The importance of this is that most of the time we are part of a sigma decision in somebody else's alpha decision. We all intertwine in each other's journeys. As I write this chapter I had made different Alpha decisions; however, I am in the sigma decisions of other authors who are in this same book. We may play a role or a character in somebody else's picture or we may be playing our own role in our own life following an alpha decision.

The importance of these is that if we don't take the time, we will find our journey in someone else's. It is more comfortable to make sigma decisions (following somebody), but to make an alpha decision carries with it more responsibility. Questions are: am I part of my own decision? Or, am I being part of somebody else's decision? Once we understand where we are, it will give us a sense of freedom. We can get out of that trap or that stuck feeling that we sometimes feel.

WRIGHT

Being able to see the whole picture helps with the process. How can anyone visualize their path better?

ESPINOSA

When you feel that you are trapped, when you feel that you are going in circles, or that you are doing the same thing repeatedly and you just don't feel like you're getting ahead of the game, you need to take some steps back and try to imagine that you are a director and main character of your own film. Try to identify who are the lead characters who will help you in your movie. People involved in your life play a specific role in your progress in life.

As a director, you have to visualize the outcome—how you want the movie to end. When you do that, you can tell all the actors what they need to do and whether or not they see the result. In our lives we need to see where we want to be and in what role each of the individuals around my life is playing. For example, if it's my personal life, we can be talking about spouses, children or parents, and friends. If it's business we can be talking about our manager, the stockholders, employees, salespeople, vendors, so on. Everyone plays a big role in our life.

WRIGHT

If every character plays a specific role, communication must be a very important quality to develop; can it be learned?

ESPINOSA

Communication is the most important part of this process. One of the elements in communication that we need to understand is listening and paying attention to what's going on. Listening doesn't mean just listening to words, it's being aware of everything around us. It can even be an emotion we need to be aware of from others.

Yes, it can be learned.

I call it a state of awareness. If we live in a state of awareness, where we listen to our own body, our own reactions, and if we start listening to not just the words we hear but also other people's expressions, movements, and what they're doing and how they're doing it, it will help us to communicate better with them as far as how we want them to play their specific role in our lives.

For example, if I am communicating with my spouse, I might tell her what her role is in my life. She can tell me how she wants me to play my role. It doesn't mean it's the same movie, but they're complimentary to each other. So yes, it is very important to learn how to communicate.

Let's go back to the director role of our own movie. Imagine if all actors would come together after they read and memorize their script and they are left alone with no direction. What do you think will happen? Same thing in your life, or my life—how many times have you heard, "Well, he [or she] should have known? If he [or she] had known, why didn't they act or do what was expected"? This involves communication and expectations. If I do not communicate what I want from people in my life and my journey, I shouldn't expect anything.

WRIGHT

When you are referring to directing our lives, our journey, there are always unexpected situations or unforeseen events. Will you tell our readers how to deal with them?

ESPINOSA

Yes, there will always be the unexpected. When these events or situations happen, the first thing we notice is the different state of emotions we are in. They trigger our emotions on a different level and the reason is because they move us out of our journey or they move us out of our path in life, so we feel shaken.

One of the first things we need to understand is which emotions were triggered and why they were triggered. Sometimes we feel anger at the situation, when the anger truly comes because we were unable to obtain something because of that event. The anger could be because we didn't foresee what could happen. Many times, emotions involve the situation, not people.

If we stop and look at each one of the unexpected events, we'll see that they have nothing to do with a person, but with the outcomes we were expecting that did not happen.

Tying emotions with decisions is crucial in our lives, especially when it comes to an Alpha decision. This is probably the most difficult part and one of the big reasons people feel more comfortable making sigma decisions. It is easier to be in somebody else's journey and complain about it.

WRIGHT

I can see how emotions are a big part of an individual, but do we have to deal with business emotions?

ESPINOSA

Oh absolutely, and the big reason that businesses have to deal with emotions is because a business does not conduct itself—people inside the business make it successful or not, and the people inside the business have emotions. If an unseen event comes along that makes the goal unobtainable, it is possible that disappointment will hit and the team breaks down. If they're not strong and they're not identifying their emotions at that point, they might stop from achieving further successes or, even worse, they might start spreading that emotion of defeat in the business, which will have a snowball effect. The moment managers identify that there is an emotional trigger, they should address the problem and work with the team members to diffuse it.

We see this often with great sports teams. These teams have talented people, yet they don't succeed.

WRIGHT

When you consider emotions, goals, the unexpected, alpha, and sigma decisions—business and personal—how can we balance them?

ESPINOSA

That is one of the biggest questions I get all the time—how to balance all these. We need to understand the four elements we work with. Imagine a compass. Your head is the north, your feet are the south, and east and west are your arms. The north represents family. The south represents work. On one side represents our social life, and the other side we're represents our own personal life.

Those four elements are always going to be pulling us in their own directions. Here is where the concept of balance comes—our lives need to be *emotionally* in balance. Be careful to understand that balance does not apply equally to these four elements all the time; what I am saying is to make sure all of them are being taken care of during your day, week, month, and year.

How about goals? Are they work goals or personal goals? Where are the ones for yourself and your social life? Are you communicating them to everyone? If the elements are not in balance, then it is no wonder why we don't feel in balance.

WRIGHT

So if I understand you correctly, there is not that much difference between a person and a business when it comes to planning?

ESPINOSA

If you take the film illustration and move it to a company, your family are your "employees." How are your decisions affecting your employees? The top is your work and your financial goals, whatever you want to achieve in your market. Then you have your market share on one side and you're going to have your revenue on the other side. You want to make sure that all of those elements are getting attention as far as your goals and your vision of where you want to take your business. That's going to help you to see if you need to make an alpha decision, if you need to start something, or you need to follow it with a sigma decision in a plan that has already been in place.

And that's important because you need to know it's a matter of starting something new. Sometimes we just need to add to something that we're doing, which is going to help, once we start looking at the balance of the person or the business.

WRIGHT

In your opinion, what is the most important part of the plan?

ESPINOSA

There are two: Identify the emotions and Alpha Decisions. First the emotions—we need to identify how the emotions are being triggered on a personal level, or on the business part. Emotions are like the speedometer in a vehicle. It tells us how fast we were going or how slow we're going. If our emotions are positive, energized, and full of what I am—my capabilities, my potential—then I can go faster. Now, if our emotions are not in balance—feelings, I can't rely on others, I don't feel secure in what I'm doing—I'm just hitting problems one after the other, but I'm not identifying the reasons. As a team or as a person I'm going to be going nowhere and I'm not going to be able to relax. So emotions are extremely important, whether you're planning for yourself, your family, or your business.

Once we capitalize on emotions, it will become easier to identify if we need to make an alpha decision or a sigma decision. Am I starting something, or just adding or complementing something already started? Sigma decisions can be part of one of my own or other's Alpha decisions made in the past; the important part is to know where I am and what kind of emotions can I expect.

Are all these going to happen the way I expected them to be *absolutely* not; however, being prepared will make it easier to adjust and make more decisions.

WRIGHT

How about accountability—how do you incorporate accountability in the process?

ESPINOSA

One time I heard that whatever is not written doesn't exist—whatever is not on paper you're not committed to; I really believe that. I can say I'm going to do a lot of things, but if I don't take the time, the five minutes to write down a plan to at least visualize it better with a drawing, then most likely it's not going to happen. It will stay as a dream. The difference between a dream and a goal is to set a time for it.

I must write it down and incorporate everything in my plan for my goals, determine what decisions will be making, understand the difference between an alpha decision and a sigma decision, how to follow those up, what my emotional triggers are, and what are the consequences of those emotions, how I deal can deal with them, whether it's on a personal level or on a business level, and what's the outcome of those on my bigger plan or on my goals—what's the finish? If I cannot sit down and write it down and put it down and then review it every so often, then we're going to still feel trapped. Accountability is important, not to anybody else but yourself; and, again, if you don't write it, then you are cheating yourself.

WRIGHT

On the bottom line, I think what I hear you saying to our readers is that you're teaching and training people to unleash their potential, is that right?

ESPINOSA

That is absolutely right. The potential that we humans or business sense we have inside, I really believe that if we just utilize about 15 to 20 percent of it, our outcome would be impressive. Once we are pushed, once we are coached, we're guided to get better results and we feel more in balance and fulfilled. We frequently see that humans and businesses are surpassing every single idea for what people are able of doing. There were many world records broken at the Olympics this year. We see reports on the stock market and how some companies are doing what nobody else was able to do. We see the technology bringing new things to the marketplace, and new research. We see potential every day and it's amazing. We see children today, four or five years old already working on computers. When I was that age, I don't think I was even off the baby bottle. So the potential that we have, the more we feel it, the more aware we are of what we're capable of doing, the better we're going to be able to unleash it and be surprised by ourselves by what we can do.

WRIGHT

Most successful men and women I talk to always say that they had support from someone in the background. I remember a wise man told me one day that if I were walking down the road and saw a turtle sitting on top of a fence post I could bet he didn't get up there by himself. Is there anybody in your life who has made you the person you are?

ESPINOSA

Oh there are many people in my life who have contributed to my character, starting from my father and my mother to different mentors. I think there is a good number of them from whom I have learned. This includes people I have sat beside and listened to. I've observed their actions and the way they do things.

There is no way anyone can be a successful person alone. We always need somebody. We always need their inspiration. If we're religious, we can get inspiration from God or from nature or our children or anything else. Having someone to inspire us is something we need to look for.

When I was finishing high school I had the pressure of making a decision about what I wanted to do with the rest of my life. A great man asked me, "What do you really like? And don't play games. What is really what makes you happy? Think about it, find it, and do that for the rest of your life." Guess what? I did and I love doing it. That person was my grandfather Jose.

WRIGHT

This has been a great conversation. I really appreciate your taking all this time with me to answer all these questions. I've taken copious notes here and I've learned a lot. I'm sure our readers will also.

ESPINOSA

Well thank you very much. I'm hoping that we can send a good message and readers can get something valuable from of this.

WRIGHT

Today I have been talking with Mauricio Espinosa; business owner, leaders coach, and consultant. He has worked with executives here in the United States, Mexico, Columbia, Venezuela, Brazil, Argentina, the Dominican Republic and Puerto Rico. He focuses his programs with a high level of energy, motivation, and leadership; where all participants engage easily with his concepts. The ability to make things easy to understand and work on a daily basis, are one of the many qualities that make him one of the most recognized leaders today. Mauricio thank you so much for being with us today on Roadmap to Success.

ESPINOSA

My pleasure and thank you.

Mauricio Espinosa is an international business and life coach, consultant, trainer, and business owner. He has trained more than eighty-five hundred executives in sales, management, leadership, finance, and operational strategies. Discover your passion and welcome success with Mauricio and his coaching. Coaching is an advanced, collaborative methodology that helps an individual or organization improve on goals, growth, performance, and effectiveness. Mauricio is about achieving authentic results; he holds you accountable and expects tangible outcomes. With him you develop new skills to be more efficient and productive, personally and professionally. You end procrastination and take control of your life and career or business. If you are in need of direction, instruction, motivation, and support, either for yourself or your team, to achieve accomplishments and ensure success, then integrate coaching into your life and business.

Mauricio's primary customers are automotive dealerships. Most of them rank top in their own market or within their own franchise. Some other major companies that have retained his services include Volkswagen of Mexico, General Motors of Mexico, Nissan of Mexico, Toyota Puerto Rico, and Scotia Bank in Mexico.

He has developed different programs and several seminars, workshops, and leadership training classes. He is a motivational speaker, recognized by the automobile industry in Mexico and the United States. Mauricio oversees more than one hundred different companies in management, finance, and operational performance. He works directly with CEOs and managers through onsite visits, teleconferencing, and with the use of technology to achieve the fundamental pieces of the process.

Mauricio is a frequent guest speaker at numerous conventions and conferences each year in Mexico and the United States. He also shares his knowledge writing for various publications in North America.

In addition to his expertise, Mauricio is a highly regarded, and very successful, Coach and Mentor.

Mauricio Espinosa

G20, Incorporated
+1.913.940.1618
Twitter: @coach_mau
Facebook.com/g20inc
Skype: mau_espinosa
mespinosa@g20inc.net
www.coachingg20.com
www.coachmau.com

200

Chapter Fifteen

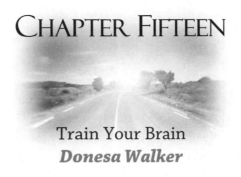

Train Your Brain
Donesa Walker

DAVID WRIGHT (WRIGHT)

Today I'm talking with Donesa Walker. Donesa is the owner and Executive Director of three Learning Rx Centers in Northwest Louisiana. Donesa is a cognitive skills and brain training expert who has accomplished several significant research studies in this field, as well as many years of experience training and raising the IQs of individuals with ADD, ADHD, dyslexia, reading and math disorders, traumatic brain injury, Alzheimer's, stroke, and many other issues that inhibit cognitive skills progression for all ages and all walks of life.

Donesa has a Bachelor of Arts in Elementary Education, Early Childhood Education, with a minor in French and Spanish from Evangel University Springfield, Missouri. Following her BA coursework, she received her Master of Education in Educational Administration from Texas A&M, and her Master of Education Reading Specialist Degree from the University of Texas.

Donesa, welcome to *ROADMAP to Success.*

DONESA WALKER (WALKER)

Thank you. I am so excited to be sharing my passion about training the brain with you and your readers!

WRIGHT

Define cognitive skills for our readers.

WALKER

Cognitive skills are the underlying skills necessary to make learning faster and easier, as well as more efficient and effective, so they positively impact all aspects of life, such as walking, talking, driving, and everything we do in the thinking process.

WRIGHT

What are the types of cognitive skills?

WALKER

The primary types of cognitive skills deal with our attention and focus, processing speed, working memory, auditory processing, and visual processing. Auditory processing is the underlying skill necessary for reading and speech, and visual processing is the underlying skill for comprehension, driving, learning new information, building things, and seeing visual pictures while being able to encode them in our mind.

Also, humans have long-term memory, which is so important because we carry knowledge from one time of learning to the next time of learning. We use logic and reasoning for test-taking tools and our ability to do mathematical processes and understand consequences for our behavior. So the various types of cognitive skills are what generate our makeup as human beings.

WRIGHT

Is there research-based evidence supporting the benefits of cognitive skills training?

WALKER

There is a multitude of research whose data significantly asserts that cognitive skills training can actually change the way the brain functions and grows. The science behind cognitive skills training has been cited by quite a few people, and recently in the *Brain That Changes Itself* (Norman Doidge, MD). Researchers have been aware of the benefits for quite some time, and recent research demonstrates that learning disabilities and other issues can be predicted as early as age four. If early cognitive intervention takes place, people who experience those struggles may never actually get the symptomology of those learning disabilities.

WRIGHT

Hmm, that sounds interesting. I've only heard of the right and left brain. Are you talking about right and left brain integration or anything like that?

WALKER

Right and left brain integration was some of the leading science that delved into how cognitive training works, so we have learned that each half of the brain does not function alone; rather, there are many neural pathways that connect across the right and left hemispheres. Auditory processes that were previously thought to be primarily on the right side of the brain actually function with the left side of the brain, so that people who have, let's say, a traumatic brain injury or damage on the right side of the brain can actually learn speech and some other skills again using the left side of the brain also. That science is called neuroplasticity, which means taking different parts of the brain cells that are not being used and harnessing them for alternate use.

For example, we had a student who was born hydrocephalic; as such, he was born with less one-third of his brain. His parents were informed by professionals that this infant would never walk, talk, read, write, or have any basic or executive processing skills. Yet, even with cerebral palsy and his other cognitive limitation, he qualified for the Paralympics. Following intense cognitive skills training, he is reading and writing on grade level and is a highly functioning individual. We can see through this and hundreds of other similar examples that the neuroplasticity of the brain is incredibly dynamic. Through the use of new cells that are produced through neurogenesis, those with learning disabilities are able to harness thousands of new cells as they grow and create dendrites in the brain.

WRIGHT

So how can you tell if a child or adult has a cognitive skills weakness?

WALKER

There are several methods of determining cognitive skills deficiencies. Sometimes it's fairly obvious because the individual is functioning slower than others. Other times an individual's processing speed may be lower than the norm. Most of the time, the average person functions with some type of cognitive skills weakness, just as some people are strong in math but not reading, and vice versa. We just consider this the norm and feel that we cannot change how we are. This is untrue. Some people assume that they are specifically left-brained or right-brained and are wholly unaware that those skills can actually be grown and cultivated through cognitive skills training.

The most effective and comprehensive measure of cognitive skills strengths and weaknesses is with a thorough cognitive skills assessment. These tests can be given by psychologists and some educational specialists, as well as through the company I work for, LearningRx, in which we dispense the Woodcock-Johnson. This assessment is an intensive and all-inclusive cognitive skills battery, and can be delivered at any LearningRx Center, nationwide. Any of these centers can test your cognitive skills, develop a plan to enhance your strengths, and strengthen your weaknesses. There is also an online cognitive skills screening called the Gibson Test, which indicates if there are any significant weaknesses or difficulties in cognition.

WRIGHT

So what is cognitive skills training; how does it work?

WALKER

Cognitive skills training, or what we call brain training, seeks to retrain areas of the brain that are weak or performing inefficiently. LearningRx is the primary and premier one-on-one brain training company, with brain training centers throughout the United States. By teaming clients one-on-one with a personal brain trainer who takes them through a program of intense sequences of mental exercises, we are able to dramatically change how the brain performs.

Intense cognitive skills training is a radically different approach—and gets radically different results—than online or video brain training games. Games played online, via video or even on your phone, are good for mental flexibility and can help maintain the health of existing cognitive skills, but are not proven to produce dramatic or lasting changes in the brain. In fact, the largest study ever conducted on this issue concluded that while players get faster at playing the games, gains do not translate into real life scenarios. In contrast, LearningRx programs are clinically-proven to create scientifically documented improvements that translate into real life.

Just as intense physical exercise builds muscle and reshapes your body, intense mental exercise builds neural pathways and retrains your brain. And in both scenarios, the most effective strategy for dramatic, life-changing improvements is to work with a personal brain trainer who has the experience and training to challenge you, hold you accountable, and get you the greatest gains possible.

The parents of John—a thirty-five-year-old LearningRx client who sustained a severe traumatic brain injury in a motorcycle accident—explained it like this: "We hired LearningRx instead of subscribing to another brain training website for the same reason we hired a professional physical therapist instead of handing our son a workout video."

WRIGHT

Is this a long-term process?

WALKER

The length of the process depends upon the weaknesses of the skills. What we see is that in as little as three to nine months, LearningRx can make a permanent change in the brain that will follow that person throughout his or her life. For instance, we can have an individual who has struggled with learning disabilities throughout his or her life. That person is given an intervention and experiences cognitive enhancement; that growth and those gains that the person experiences continue to follow him or her. People with learning disabilities can even increase that growth through continuous work on those skills.

For instance, when you learn to ride a bike, you always know how to ride that bike; however, you may be a little shaky if you're not using it often and you have to re-practice those skills. But once it's a learned skill—once you have trained the brain to do those procedures and skills—your brain is going to perform in that manner; the body must keep performing in that manner in order for it to continue to grow in that manner.

WRIGHT

So why is strengthening cognitive skills important for both children and adults?

WALKER

Cognitive skills are the underlying skills necessary for all thinking and processing. We live in a world that is so fast-paced; everything we're doing requires multitasking abilities. In this high-stressed and predominantly technological culture, our cognitive skills are often dumbed down. When we are stressing ourselves out and spreading ourselves too thin, not getting the proper amount of rest and nutrition, then we're actually taking away from our brain.

To enhance our brains and direct them to work in a faster, more efficient manner, we need to train those skills. For example, to prepare for a marathon, one would create a strict practice schedule. Someone would be unable to compete in a thirty-mile marathon without a consistent practice regimen.

WRIGHT

I'm having a little trouble figuring out the difference between cognitive skills and academic skills. Would you explain that?

WALKER

Absolutely. Academic skills are based on cognitive skills; the cognitive skills are the underlying skills for growth. A simpler way to say this is to look at how your body completes the walking process. We use certain specific muscles to walk that we do not use for other activities. The same thing happens in cognitive skills and academics. Academics is the performance or application of what the cognitive skills ability is. If one learns easily, then the ability to move forward academically is enhanced. If one struggles to learn new materials and must review information repeatedly, then there is certain to be an academic struggle. If one has a weak short-term memory, causing one to have to constantly relearn information, then academic progress will be significantly impeded.

Long-term memory is equally important; for instance, when we are driving, we must consistently recall the rules of the road. Short-term memory is included in this process, as we must constantly recall what is around us, the conditions of the road, where we are going, and where we have been. We must use visual processing in preparing ourselves for reaching our destination. All of these skills affect every different part of our lives, from sports to decision making, to our speech and how we present ourselves, to every skill that involves thinking.

WRIGHT

So how can cognitive skills training help?

WALKER

Cognitive skills training can help everyone; there is no one who cannot benefit from cognitive skills training. Just as anyone can benefit from exercise, anyone can benefit from cognitive skills exercise, which will assist in any task that requires thinking skills no matter what the age (Please see the statistical chart at the end of this chapter for a visual representation of what LearningRx can do). In an elementary age child or preschool age child, cognitive skills training will assist him or her not only be better at sports and swimming and all the activities done as little children, but also in the child's academic environment currently and in the future. The training will help the child in being able to learn more easily and efficiently. Cognitive skills training will reduce frustration for parents, caregivers, and teachers, and most importantly, for the child.

As a college and career type person, you may want to be able to get into a fast-paced career that is going to make the most money. Companies insist that they will hire only the sharpest people out there—people who learn quickly and easily are able to implement new technology and ideas and people who are able to think outside the box. These will be individuals who can think on their feet and make decisions on the spur of the moment and adults who are able to balance many things at the same time, essentially expert multitaskers. All of these skills rely on underlying cognitive skills that decline as we reach middle age. The next generation is following closely behind. Nowadays we see more and more grandparents and great grandparents raising children, having second careers, being able to go on and do things in life that they want to do such as travel and learn new languages. All of these great things will enhance their ability to live a healthier and more fulfilling lifestyle. Having a healthy, efficient brain is essential to this.

WRIGHT

I always heard that IQ can't really be increased that much; it stays fairly the same all your life. What is IQ? Can it be increased, and if so, how do you do it?

WALKER

IQ is probably the biggest debated issue and here we'll get a lot of interest because IQ is the Intelligence Quotient or the general intellectual ability of a person. It's measured by a number, in specific, which is an average of your cognitive skills abilities. We all have some weak skills and some strong skills; the more strong skills you have, the higher your IQ, the more weak skills you have, the lower your IQ. If you change your skill set, then you automatically change your average. The key is to remember that an IQ score is not just one score, but the average of multiple individual skills. So if you boost some of your underlying cognitive skills, you boost your average and therefore your IQ increases. That means if I can change the way I think and become a faster, more efficient thinker with better memory, for example, then I can increase my IQ.

WRIGHT

So if you learn more about math, would that increase your IQ?

WALKER

Well sure, if math was a struggle area for you and you were weak in that area, then it could potentially boost your IQ; however, just saying, "I learn more about math," well, math is an academic knowledge so it's not going to boost your IQ unless it is a weak area your brain has shied away from and not developed as far as logic and reasoning. If logic and reasoning is weak, which is one of the underlying skills necessary for good mathematical processes, then it is very possible that by boosting your ability to think logically and do reasoning better, then you can actually enhance your ability, not only in math, but a boost in IQ, as well.

WRIGHT

So the trick, if you want to increase your IQ, is you'll first have to discover your weaknesses?

WALKER

Absolutely, and that's the biggest key—going in to get the testing, just to know. Here is the thing that has always boggled my mind: If we're having dental issues, we do not delay a visit to the dentist to have those issues resolved so we can feel and look healthy. We want our eyes so we can see, so we take care of our eyes and get our glasses, our contacts, and all of those things taken care of. So if cognitively we have a weakness, why have we always just assumed, "Oh well, I'm just not good at that"? Why don't you find out why you're not good at it and then change it? Just as you enhance your vision, your hearing, or your health, you can enhance your overall thinking and memory abilities.

WRIGHT

I have been talking to a lot of coaches in the United States and Canada recently in some books that we're doing, and it's hard to understand how training is different from tutoring.

WALKER

Brain training (also known as mental or cognitive skills training) is different from tutoring at a very basic level. Tutoring is simply re-teaching material that a student missed the first time it was presented. The hope is that the material will *stick* this time. Here is how to tell if tutoring will work for your child.

If you've ever sat down with your child and gone over, or repeated, school assignments and he or she immediately *got it* and needed no more help, then re-teaching or tutoring will work. But, if simple explanation did not solve the problem, or if a few days later the problem persisted or was repeated, there is most likely an underlying skill weakness that tutoring or re-teaching cannot correct.

Until the underlying skills required to learn are strengthened, tutoring can only produce temporary progress at best. Struggles will re-emerge because the root of the problem—weak cognitive skills—has not been addressed. If your child faces recurring problems with each new academic year or challenge, training (rather than tutoring) is your best answer.

Brain training provides you and your student the chance to get to the root of the problem and literally rebuild his or her basic ability to read and learn with specifically designed and delivered training exercises. To understand the advantage brain training has over tutoring, consider how different your expectations would be if you enrolled in a twelve-hour lecture on piano basics versus twelve hours of piano practice with a good one-on-one piano coach. In the lecture you would be receiving information about the piano—*you would be tutored*. In the piano practice, you would end up *actually playing* the piano—*you would be trained*. Tutoring increases *information*. Training *builds skill*.

WRIGHT

What about those folks who say, "I know my child is smart; why does he or she struggle in school, and why does it take hours to do his or her homework"?

WALKER

This goes back to the same thing whether you're an adult who's struggling at your workplace or a child who is struggling in school. There is probably an underlying difficulty that is creating the anxiety or the inability to learn efficiently. Maybe the child's attention is drifting. We are seeing more and more of this as we move into this fast-paced world where we're relying a lot on television delivery and streaming media to provide us most of our information. We're not using our "thinking caps" as much as we should be and actually developing those skills.

When we struggle, it's because new information that is coming across to us is not grasped, analyzed, and synthesized into our self as quickly as it needs to be. The best thing to do with that is to identify what's causing that problem, whether you are eighty or eight. It's important to know what's causing you to have struggles with memory, focus, attention, or learning anything efficiently.

WRIGHT

Won't regular schoolwork and homework build cognitive skills?

WALKER

Actually, regular schoolwork at home is to practice academic skills. Academic skills are the learned skills that you have; it is the skill that is informational knowledge. If we think of it in terms of a filing cabinet, when you are at school and you are doing homework, they're giving you information to file away in your filing cabinet. If the cabinet is locked, the wheels on the drawer won't work, or you have no filing system set up, you're going to be just as lost when the information gets presented the first time as you are when it's presented the fiftieth time. You need to have a system in place in the brain that actually files that information efficiently and retrieves it fluidly.

WRIGHT

Very interesting. Would you tell me a little about the LearningRx?

WALKER

Yes sir, I actually own three local franchises called LearningRx in the northwest corner of Louisiana—the Shreveport/Bossier area. LearningRx is a premier cognitive training facility that does one-on-one, professionally delivered training. When you come into one of our centers, we cognitively test to see where your strengths and weaknesses are, then we identify where those strengths and weaknesses are. After that we develop a plan to enhance those skills to overcome those weaknesses and make them into strengths so that you can build your skills to become faster and more efficient in your learning.

We work with many, many people across the nation such as Olympic athletes who need enhancement so they can be faster at processing information around them. It's highly imperative that you take off as soon as that gun sounds. It's important to know exactly when you're supposed to do something and be able to perform very quickly and efficiently. This holds true for people who are just on the learning grounds of it, such as children and parents who are struggling at the school level and clients who want to be more competitive in the market.

One of the great stories I have is about Miss Virginia, who, as an eighty-something beautiful lady, had a stroke. She'd always been a businessperson with a great memory, and she had so many great things going for her. She went to the doctor and was told that the stroke would be the beginning stages of Alzheimer's for her, and that "you're going to need to go into a step down clinic." Miss Virginia did not want that—she did not want to be on medication and be dependent—so she decided that brain training was the best for her.

She stepped in and we did brain training with her and in nine weeks she was able to test from the 77th percentile of brain function up to the 93rd percentile brain function on her neurologist's tests. He was stunned to the point where he wanted to write up a report on the medication until she told him she had decided not to take medication, but to do brain exercises instead.

WRIGHT

My mother and my wife's mother both had Alzheimer's and both died with Alzheimer's. I was very interested, when I was introducing you, that you mentioned cognitive skills and brain training that have actually helped Alzheimer's; is that true?

WALKER

Yes, it is very true. We've had several clients who've been diagnosed with dementia. Alzheimer's is one of those diseases we don't know a whole lot about, but we're learning more all the time. We're learning that certain people have certain genes that incline them to have these weaknesses. We're learning how important diet and exercise is to the brain and how important it is for our cognitive functioning long-term. One of the best ways to stave off dementia of any type is to actually do intervention that actually retrains memory. When you're retraining memory you're invoking new cells into the area that is stagnating and dying or being choked off by Alzheimer's disease.

WRIGHT

That is very, very interesting.

I appreciate the time you've taken with me this afternoon to answer all these questions. I have really learned a lot here today, and I just hope that you and others, especially the researchers, get more into this retraining the brain; it looks like it might solve a lot of our problems here in this country.

WALKER

Let me tell you, this is one of the things I'm very passionate about. I do believe that we can start at a grassroots level and change some of the inabilities. We have so many people who are illiterate or unable to function efficiently, and it is affecting our workforce, our unemployment rates, and our country's economic system.

Dr. Sandra Chapman just did a study on "Brainomics," as she coins it—the study of economics and weak cognitive skills in our society and how much they're costing us in lost wages and lost time on the job because they affect so many things in learning. Think of how many times we have to retrain employees when, if we had trained them the first time and they had grasped it, we would not have to be spending that money to do it again.

The economic impact of what brain training does is huge for us long-term as a society. If we would learn that and start doing this kind of training, then just like the obesity epidemic, we're in the same place cognitively. We're introducing things that are causing our children to spend more time not thinking for

211

themselves, and because we have all these things that are thinking for our children, we're creating an epidemic that we need to intervene and turn around.

WRIGHT

Can the seventy-plus folks take advantage of cognitive skills and brain training?

WALKER

Absolutely. We have quite a few in our center right now who are getting enhancement. We have a whole group of, Baby Boomers—everybody in my dad's age and on—who are working on these skills to become better and more efficient at their learning process because they have so much to give to our society. They have been giving for years, but have so much more to give. As age tries to wreak havoc on the brain, there are things that they can do to actually beat that back and be able to be smarter, quicker, and more competitive in the environment that we live in.

WRIGHT

Well this is really, really interesting. As I said, I really do appreciate you taking this time with me and I'm so glad you're in this book; I know it's going to be an excellent chapter.

WALKER

Great! Thank you so much for allowing me the opportunity to share my passion with you.

WRIGHT

Today I have been talking with Donesa Walker, MEd. She is the owner and Executive Director of three LearningRx Centers in Northwest Louisiana. She is the proud mother of two young boys, she is a faithful wife to her husband, and a staunch supporter and member of her church and community.

Donesa, thank you so much for being with us today on *ROADMAP to Success.*

WALKER

Thank you, David. I enjoyed our visit and hope I challenged your brain.

Donesa Walker, MEd, is the owner and executive director of three LearningRx centers in Louisiana. She is the proud mother of two boys, faithful wife to her husband, and is a staunch supporter of her church and community. Donesa is a cognitive skills/brain training expert, having accomplished several significant research studies in this field. She also has many years of experience training and raising the IQs of individuals with ADD, ADHD, Dyslexia, Reading and Math disorders, Traumatic Brain Injury, Alzheimer's, Stroke, and many other issues that inhibit cognitive skills progression for all ages and walks of life.

Donesa has a BA in Elementary Education/ECE with a minor in French/Spanish and an MEd in Educational Administration/Reading Specialist at Texas A&M. She has twenty years of teaching and administrative experience, as well as one year as Dean of Online programs at Louisiana Baptist University. Further, she spent seven years as District Reading Specialist, nine years as a Master Reading Teacher, and has been Owner/Executive Director of LearningRx franchises in Shreveport/Bossier City, Louisiana, for more than three years. Donesa has been the number one Franchisee in Nation in 2010, in the top five national franchises in 2009, and top ten for 2011.

Donesa Walker, MEd

LearningRx
8856 Youree Drive
Shreveport, LA 71115
318-797-8523
d.walker@learningrx.net
www.learningrx.com/Shreveport
www.learningrx.com/bossier-city

CHAPTER SIXTEEN

Drive Smart And Enjoy The Ride
Christine Corelli

DAVID WRIGHT (WRIGHT)

Today I'm talking with Christine Corelli, an international business speaker and author of five business books including the best-selling *Wake Up and Smell the Competition*. Her latest release, *Capture Your Competitor's Customers and KEEP Them*, sold out the first print run in just two weeks and is still selling strong. To her credit, she's had more than two hundred articles featured in leading publications on topics related to competitive excellence—sales, cutting-edge customer service strategies, dynamic leadership, profit-rich growth strategies, and personal success. She has shared her business savvy as a featured guest on numerous television and radio interviews, including CNBC.

Christine, welcome to *ROADMAP to Success*.

Christine, you are known as a very savvy businesswoman. What, in your opinion, are the things that attribute to success?

CHRISTINE CORELLI (CORELLI)

There are many things that attribute to success. First, let's define success, as its definition is different for every individual. My belief is that it's not how much money or how many nice possessions you have. It's simply having the feeling of a sense of accomplishment in life. It's about enjoying what you do to make a living, having a good quality of life and, of course, having financial security. It's also about being blessed with family and friends you love and being loved by others. Let's not forget good health. If you don't have good health, you have nothing.

As for business success, what I've been sharing with audiences for many years is that your ability to achieve success is not dependent on how smart you are, how much money you have, or that you excel in sales and marketing. It's *how you think*.

First and foremost, you have to know what you want and whether it's achievable. If you're five foot two and you want to be a professional basketball player, you're setting yourself up for disappointment. Many people dream of being professional athletes, movie stars, or recording artists. They can have the greatest belief in themselves, but if they don't have the talent, their dream will not come true.

Likewise, if you want to start a business, you have to be realistic and take a good, hard look at your chances to achieve success in that business. For example, if you want to open a specialty retail store in a strip mall and think you can compete with major discount retail stores, you're likely to go broke.

Next, if there's a need for what you want to sell or offer, you have to believe in yourself and make a conscious decision to be successful. Decide to win. Be purposeful, resolute, and uncompromising in that belief.

Willingness to work hard will be next. There's just no substitute for hard work. I don't know many people who work only eight hours a day and accomplish great things. The most successful people I know spend their time on sales-related activities the majority of the day. Additional hours are spent honing the skills they need, and studying their industry and their competitors. These activities are done after hours. I'm not saying these individuals are "workaholics." You can't feel successful if you don't make time for family, friends, working out, and other activities that keep your life in balance. Interestingly, many successful people work hard and play hard. They have learned balance.

Then, there's that positive attitude. If you are not positive, you will never be able to achieve success in business and enjoy life, too. But positive attitude alone cannot replace hard work, skills, and old-fashioned perseverance. What it does do is fuel a "can-do" attitude, which is something we need on the road to success.

On the lighter side, positive attitude is a like anti-wrinkle cream. Although it's not exactly a fountain of youth, it can make you feel younger. A survey conducted by *Prevention* magazine found that people with a positive attitude said they looked and felt younger than their age. In fact, they were even told by others that they looked younger than they were. If that isn't a good reason to stay positive, I don't know what is! Want a face-lift in ten seconds? Smile. You'll not only look younger and feel better, but you'll make everyone else around you feel better, too!

WRIGHT

Christine, let's talk about starting a business. It has been said that it takes from to three to five years to establish a business. Based on your experience working with many start-up businesses, what is your opinion on that?

CORELLI

Unless you have a break-through idea, something innovative and new such as Pierre Omidyar's eBay. Omidyar came up with the idea in 1995 for the now amazingly successful on-line auction and shopping site. Another great idea came from the first person who opened a walk-in medical clinic. Now, you see them everywhere. The truth is, few people can start up a business and see a profit before three to five years.

I've seen many new business owners set their expectations too high. Even if you have a great idea or there's a high demand, and you excel in sales and marketing, it takes time to get established and patience to see a profit. Another reason it takes time is that almost every business owner makes a few mistakes along the way. Many find they make decisions and then have to shift gears quickly, such as changing their sales and marketing strategies, redesigning their products, or adding value to their offerings. It takes time to find what works!

WRIGHT

Tell us how you started your business.

CORELLI

For many years I had made my living in the performing arts in concerts and industrial shows. Motorola approached me at an event and asked me to represent their company at the Consumer Electronics Trade Show, one of the biggest trade shows in the world. I said, "What's a trade show?" They liked my personality, and gave me a script. I memorized it, delivered it well throughout the show, and I was off to a new career in in the trade show arena creating and delivering presentations for major corporations in a wide variety of industries. I enjoyed the excitement of the competitive environment where so many companies were all vying for the attention of potential customers. Working forty trade shows a year gave me valuable insight into management and sales styles as well as what makes for an effective corporate culture. It also taught me about our volatile marketplace and its ever-changing inhabitants. I observed what works and what doesn't work.

Eventually, I became a trainer and saleswoman for an international training and development company. I learned a lot. In 1993, I met a woman through a friend who specialized in women's business development. Within ten minutes she said, "You should become a professional speaker!" Shortly afterward, I made the decision to start my own business. I always tell people I started it on "blind faith" and an iron will. At that time, if anyone told me I would become a published author of five business books and speak at conferences throughout fourteen countries I would have told them they were crazy.

WRIGHT

What would you say would be the biggest contributions to the success of your business?

CORELLI

One of the best ways to be successful in any business is to learn from people who are already successful in your chosen field. I approached many of the most successful authors and speakers in my field. Amazingly, many were more than happy to help. I asked questions, learned, listened to their opinions, then made my decisions.

I took many courses including an intense public speaking workshop to hone my skills. I also read dozens of business books and studied the works of Ken Blanchard and Deepak Chopra. I "internalized" Chopra's *Seven Spiritual Laws of Success*. I still have that book at my bedside.

WRIGHT

So having said that, in your opinion, how important are communication skills in achieving success?

CORELLI

Business experts have stated that 85 percent of an individual's overall career success is in direct proportion to his or her ability to communicate. I believe that 85 percent of your overall success in *life* depends on your ability to communicate. You have to sell your ideas, express your opinions, express your wants, and needs, and influence people to follow your lead. I teach the "C's to Effective Communication"—confident, concise, convincing, compelling, and caring.

WRIGHT

And what would you say about interpersonal skills?

CORELLI

If you come across as likeable, friendly, genuine, and sincere and show a genuine interest in others, you definitely have a better chance of success in anything you do.

WRIGHT

What are the biggest obstacles people face? What can hold them back from achieving success?

CORELLI

Obtaining financing and the economy can be an obstacle. Not having the funds to add staff when you really need to can also be an obstacle. If you have a great idea and are talented but you don't have selling skills, that's a major obstacle!

Many obstacles are those we create ourselves. For example, far too many business owners don't create a *business plan*. If you "wing it" you impede your ability to achieve success. You need an accurate road map to get you where you want to go with goals, tactics, and strategies to help you arrive at your desired destination. Lack of creating a business plan will not take you where you want to go.

The next thing is lack of preparation planning itself; many people go on client appointments without being prepared. They didn't learn as much as they could about the client before the meeting. Some don't plan their day by prioritizing and executing the most important tasks first. They make a few phone calls and read their e-mails (including the jokes) first, without digging into what's going to put money in their pocket.

A major thing that can hold people back is lack of organization. I see so many people who are not organized. I tell my audiences, "Get organized!" Your alternative is to *agonize,* over all we have to do on any given day and worry about something you might forget. If you don't track and control all your to-dos, and every detail of every project, you won't get the results you want.

Lack of discipline would be another. Discipline is what it's really all about. You must be disciplined to make those phone calls, to pay attention to sales and marketing, and be willing to do what you know you need to do when you don't feel like doing it. That's what I call discipline.

Fear of failure can also hold people back. A lot of people just are so afraid to fail; they don't want to try anything new and are unwilling to take a risk. My experience has taught me that you have to be willing to take a risk. Before you do, gather all the information and opinions of people you know and trust and obtain their opinion on what you want to do. Then, make that decision.. Then I always tell my audiences that taking risks, supported by reason and careful thought, can be a force of unlimited potential.

Lack of energy can hold people back. We can't always manage our time. We must invest in healthy living, healthy eating, and getting enough sleep. You cannot achieve success in anything you do without having a very high level of energy. And, boy, is that the truth in the world we face today where people have too much to do, too little time, are they're overworked and understaffed. You have to bring a high level of energy to your team, your job, your business, and to your family as well. So you have to learn how to manage that energy through healthy living, sleeping enough, eating healthy B vitamins, green leafy vegetables, and good food.

And here's the biggest obstacle—lack of execution. People come up with great ideas, but they don't know how to execute them. Recently I had a conversation with an executive who held a retreat a few months ago. I called him to ask how it went.

"Well, really good, I think," he replied, "But you know, it's been six months and I realize that we haven't implemented them. We don't execute."

Knowing what you should do and doing it are two very different things. Think about the times people attend a seminar or read a book and say, "Wow! That was great. I got so many good ideas." Then, it's back to business as usual. I'd say 95 percent of those people do not implement those ideas.

WRIGHT

So given that, what advice would you give to people who would like to start their own business?

CORELLI

Examine the pros and cons before you move forward. In today's world, being gainfully employed and having a steady paycheck and benefits is not a bad thing. Not everyone can handle the highs and lows, peaks and valleys of being a business owner. What about being responsible for other people's salaries? Can you handle it?

One of my clients is a highly successful and prosperous owner of an equipment finance company. One day over lunch, we discussed the pros and cons of entrepreneurship.

"The positive side," he said, "is being your own boss and the sense of accomplishment you feel when business is thriving, profits are high, and your salespeople are happy with their commissions. These make entrepreneurship worthwhile. The negative side occurs when business hits a slump and you experience anxiety."

Although he has more than sufficient funds in his personal bank account to retire, he feels an obligation to keep the company going so that his partner and employees can stay gainfully employed.

"It's not easy being responsible for the welfare of so many people," he said. Then he made a statement that stuck in my head, "Owning a business requires controlling your anxiety."

Starting a business requires clear thinking. Is there a market for what you want to sell or offer? How well are you set financially? If you're willing to take that risk, jump in, do it, and keep your nose to it.

The other piece of advice is this: When they first get started in business, the tendency is to start spending money all over the place, thinking "this is going to get my business going!" Every investment that you make in your business must give you a return on your investment.

WRIGHT

How about hard-working business professionals who want to advance in their company?

CORELLI

I'll demonstrate what I refer to as organizational leadership. Act like a leader, even if you don't have a title. Display initiative beyond your job description. Make suggestions on how to increase productivity, profitability, communication, and teamwork. Identify any service flaws that exist. Demonstrate your ability to keep others in a positive state of mind.

If you want a management position, ask for one early on. If you know there is an opening, tell your boss and your HR department, "I would like this management position very much, and am confident I can add value to the department." Show enthusiasm, but refrain from coming across as overly enthusiastic.

Today it's really tough out there as far as the job market is concerned, but if you're not happy, get out whenever you have the opportunity and find something you really enjoy doing. Find a place to work where you enjoy going to work every day.

WRIGHT

You've worked with executives and managers in leading organizations. What advice can you give to today's managers?

CORELLI

Great question because I'm passionate about this! Display dynamic leadership! Remember whose job it is to keep people motivated—yours!

Motivate your employees by making them feel they are working *with* you, and not *for* you. If they feel they are working for you, you'll have a bunch of robots who go through the motions of their job and never put their heart and soul into their work. Motivate them by appreciating their hard work, bringing out the best in them. Ask questions such as, "What do you think about—" "What's your opinion on—" "How can we streamline—" "What would make it work?" And if you're brave enough, ask them these two questions, "What would you do if you were me?" How can I be a better boss?"

On the road to success as a leader, imagine yourself as the professional car driver—you're only as good as your pit crew. A pit crew can make or break the driver. They train consistently. Give your employees the training they need. So hire the best people, provide them with the training they need. Be absolutely the best boss you can be and make it a great place to come to work each day. Ask yourself this question each day: "Would you work for you?"

WRIGHT

You mentioned that in 2013, you'll be celebrating twenty years in business and you're still writing books, creating new presentations, and speaking all over the world. What drives you?

CORELLI

In many of my presentations, I use the analogy of a professional race car driver. I ask audiences what a professional driver uses for fuel. I get many different answers, but the one I'm looking for is "the love of the race. " They love racing! That's their fuel. I love what I do and I love the thrill of the drive.

Not everyone has a job that they love. But if you can learn to love it, you will be far better off. And if you can't love it, then focus on what's good about your job and think of it as a steppingstone to something greater.

WRIGHT

The road to success can be long and hard. What do you do and what do you recommend others do when the going really gets tough?

CORELLI

Business is tough these days—very tough. It's not so much the familiar saying, "When the going gets tough the tough get going." When things get really tough is when you turn inward. Tap into your inner strength, the spiritual side of yourself, and you will find the courage to keep going.

Never lose hope for a better future, as every day is a new beginning. You never know what new opportunities a new day can bring. There have been many times in my business when the economy tanked, budgets were cut, and the phones stopped ringing. It was tough. But each time, business would come back. Nothing's easy. If you can tell me a job-role or business that is easy, let me know because I'm going to go do it.

WRIGHT

A very wise man told me many years ago that if I were walking down a country road and I saw a turtle sitting on top of a fencepost that I could bet my bottom dollar it didn't get up there by itself. So as you look back on your business life, and in your life, who are the people who have put you where you are today?

CORELLI

I think all of us have someone in our lives who believed in us before we believed in ourselves. For me it was my aunt. When I was very young, she put her arms around me and whispered in my ear, "I believe in you. Go after what you want in life and *fight* for it." Her picture is in my office next to the picture of my parents.

I also had many mentors. I was very fortunate to have a highly successful sales trainer as a mentor who taught me to think like a business owner. "It's not what you make, it's what you keep." There was a women's business development consultant who directed me to this profession. I had an association executive who heard me speak, and opened many doors for me. I had a high-school friend who mentored me as well. He listened to my ideas and gave me advice for many years. He still does. But there is one person who may be most responsible for my success.

When I was working for the training and development company, the sales manager wanted his staff to spend a significant time of the business day cold calling, with a minimum of *forty calls per day*. The remainder of the day was to be spent on physical appointments in front of customers. He'd emerge from his office several times an hour to make sure he'd see the sales staff was either in the act of dialing, or engaged in a conversation. If it was too quiet, he would come out

223

from his office and bang his fist on someone's desk and say, "Folks! The phones are too quiet today! No calls coming in, means not enough calls going out!" Let me hear you on those phones!" He was tough, but he was right. It was never easy making call after call, but it was a part of my job to do it.

As time passed, I became grateful for that experience and can attribute much of my success to that tough manager. When I started up my own company, I was already disciplined to make those daily forty cold calls. Within three years, my business was profitable and my colleagues were asking how I was able to get established so quickly. "How many calls are you making per day?" was what I asked.

WRIGHT

You have shared a great deal of wisdom today on how to achieve success in business, but what about success in your personal life?

CORELLI

First of all, you need to have one! I see far too many people who are working long hours. If you're successful in business but your kids never see you or you're not living the life that you want to live, then you can't say that you're successful. If you don't have a great group of friends, and time for your family and doing the things that bring you joy (as Deepak Chopra says) you're not successful. What are the things that bring you joy and keep that life in balance? If you don't have them, then you're not going to have personal success. Life is going to pass you by.

Focus on doing for others, and learn something new every day. Learn to love to learn. There are so many people who have settled for a life of mediocrity. They don't have goals. They coast through life like a ship from port to port. I refer to them as "Coasters."

Permit me to describe them. Coasters go home from work at night and usually stick to a familiar routine. They like going to the same places and doing the same things. There's nothing really wrong with this, but I feel that because they are not very adventurous, they often settle for a life of mediocrity. I believe that if you approach life tentatively, you reap only a portion of its gifts. The Coasters of this world may be living their lives in black and white when they could be living them in vibrant Technicolor. Could it be that some might simply lack the courage to let the colors emerge—to feel them, absorb them, and be inspired by them? Unfortunately, they may never achieve any great accomplishments because they are comfortable where they are.

When faced with any type of change in their jobs or their lives, they don't always respond well, or may even be complacent. I believe this is because they do not like coming out of their comfort zone. They are the ones who are content to meet the company's sales quota every month. They expect no more and no less of themselves. They are the ones who get in on time, take their coffee breaks, and leave on time regardless of customer commitments. They will politely fix any problems a customer brings to them, but will rarely proactively contact a customer to find out how the product is working. They are content with their merit raises, and neither complain about nor expect promotions, bonuses, or "exceptional" performance ratings. They will agreeably attend training seminars, but rarely look for ways to apply what they've learned.

See what I mean about "coasting? A little "excitement" in their lives might do them some good. Perhaps if they'd only look for it, they'd find it.

The other thing I'm big on is passion. Passion is vital to your success. It is the engine that never stops moving you forward, no matter how great the challenges are that you face. Passion gets you back up the hill when you experience a valley of disappointment. Passion helps drive you to overcome any odds when others swear that you have little hope of succeeding. Passion is what keeps you moving forward in the right direction, no matter what roadblock comes your way.

Passion cannot be purchased or attained by reading a book. It is an inner drive that is ignited deep within you, proving that you believe as much in your work as yourself. Passion is enthusiasm.

Don't let the economy or anyone else ever steal enthusiasm away from you. With far too many people worried about their future and seeing the glass as half-empty, not half-full, it's no wonder so few are enthusiastic about anything. What to do? You cannot always control what happens around you, but you can learn from successful people. I believe Walter Chrysler said it best: "The real secret of success is enthusiasm. Enthusiasts are fighters. They have fortitude. They have staying qualities. Enthusiasm is the bottom of all progress. With it, there is accomplishment. Without it, there are only alibis."

With this in mind, how about taking Chrysler's advice? Try putting a little enthusiasm into your work and your life. With a little effort, you may discover that you can achieve success.

One last thing: Life is short. While on the road to success, remember to enjoy the ride. I know I am.

WRIGHT

What a great conversation! I have really enjoyed this time with you, Christine, and I appreciate the time you've spent here to answer all these questions. I have been taking notes and you have helped me with some new ideas! This will be great chapter for our book, and I'm confident it will help our readers as well.

CORELLI

That's very kind of you; I appreciate your kind words.

WRIGHT

Today I have been talking with Christine Corelli. For the past two decades she has been an in-demand professional conference speaker. She is also an author of five books including *Wake Up and Smell the Competition* and *Capture Your Competitor's Customers and Keep Them*.

Christine, thank you so much for being with us today on *ROADMAP to Success*.

CORELLI

My pleasure.

Christine Corelli approaches her work with extraordinary creativity, enthusiasm, and attention to detail. She is an in-demand conference speaker, consultant, and workshop facilitator. She is a veteran of the platform with an active speaking calendar. Visit her website to review her impressive client list and credentials.

Christine Corelli

Chirstine Corelli & Associates, Inc.
6401 Lincoln Avenue • Suite 204
Morton Grove, IL 60053
847-581-9968
cc@christinespeaks.com

CHAPTER SEVENTEEN

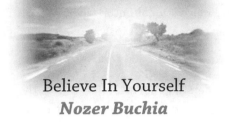

Believe In Yourself
Nozer Buchia

DAVID WRIGHT (WRIGHT)

Today we're talking to Nozer Buchia, an internationally acclaimed motivational entertainer, speaker, author, and an entrepreneur. Affectionately referred to as "Mr. Motivator," he has an inimitable style of humor and delivery and a practical approach to any situation. His straight from the heart, high energy, and passionate message has motivated many audiences worldwide and has enabled them to get out of their comfort zone and get into greatness.

With thirty-four years as an organizational builder and turnaround specialist, he uses failure as a tool to prove that success is always within one's reach. His training sessions, workshops, seminars, talks, and presentations are not only informative and educational, but extremely entertaining.

As a business coach and a life coach, Nozer mentors corporations, boards of directors, executives, and individuals to perform at their best and guides them to victory by enabling them to realize their full potential.

His pet statement is, "There is always a way, you simply have to find it; just because you cannot find it does not mean it does not exist."

Nozer, welcome to *ROADMAP to Success*.

NOZER BUCHIA (BUCHIA)

Thank you, David, it is my pleasure to be talking with you today. It is a great privilege to be authoring this book jointly with two great minds of our time, Dr. Ken Blanchard and Dr. Deepak Chopra, and mapping out successful business strategies based on my experiences in life, and in the world of business.

WRIGHT

Besides being a successful business coach and a life coach, you are a successful international speaker, motivational entertainer, author, and entrepreneur. You are affectionately referred to as "Mr. Motivator." How did you acquire this title?

BUCHIA

First of all, let us understand my interpretation of the word *motivation*. To me, motivation means *motive to action*. If you are not passionate enough to convert your motives into actions, your chances of success are very limited. It is good to have the desire to achieve, but it is imperative that one has to "act" to achieve it.

As a stage artiste, I have been associated with theatre since I was five years old. Not only do I perform plays, I also act in them, direct them, and produce them. Theatre has taught me to encourage people to perform at their best, and to raise their spirits by first listening to them, and helping them understand the impact of their role on stage and the repercussions of their actions on the audience and on the cast members, both on-stage and off-stage.

I slowly realized that people paid attention to what I said and "acted" passionately by giving their very best to the audience. They realized a change in their behavior and their acting capabilities, for finally, all their inhibitions had begun to vanish and their confidence had begun to soar. They felt comfortable enough to listen to me. As my colleague once told me, "Nozer, when you talk, we are simply mesmerized by your words and by the way in which you influence us to perform at our very best. When you speak, it all makes complete sense. And it works! We can see and feel the difference. We value your interest in helping us reach the pinnacle of our capabilities."

It felt so very good listening to all that ego-boosting talk that I started putting my heart and soul in helping people give their best. I knew instantly that my words and actions could make a difference in people's lives. I didn't realize it then, but looking back years later I now believe that the seeds of *motivating others* had been naturally but unknowingly sown along the way, and the title "Mr. Motivator" just stuck on like glue.

It is my belief that before attempting to motivate people, one has to first have immense patience to understand them, their thoughts, motives, strengths, weaknesses, and then build a road map to guide them along the path to success. They need to believe in you and accept the fact that you are working in their best interest. They need to develop that comfort feeling with you first.

It is my contention that the greatest motivational principle in life is about knowing "how." It's very important to know "how" to do the very thing you love to do, and turn it into a profitable career choice. It is about knowing "how" to build a business of your own. It is about knowing a skill and "how" to apply it in the service of others and make a successful living.

Motivating others is a responsibility that I have embraced—it is not simply an act.

WRIGHT

People rarely talk about success through failure, as you have so distinctively and eloquently done in your first book titled, *Why Entrepreneurs Really Fail: The Road to Success Always Under Construction,* which, by the way, I think is a great title. Do you really believe that we must first fail in order to succeed?

BUCHIA

Nobody deliberately plans to fail. People do unintelligent and unplanned things that cause failure. I have heard it being said many times and have also read about some people's beliefs—it is sometimes better to fail and get it over with, so that success is then within one's reach. I do not believe that is indeed how it happens. Success simply does not follow you because you once failed. If such was the case, there would be no unsuccessful person in life or business today.

You cannot script success. Success is about adapting to changing situations. It is about overcoming adversity and finding new ways to making it happen. Success or failure is not hinged on what you have done or not done, but on what you will be doing next. Success is not a straight line, David; you've got to be savvy enough to deviate and maneuver whenever it is necessary.

The first time that failure engulfed my life, I just shut myself in my room and didn't want to come out. I was afraid that the whole world would pass judgment regarding my capabilities and that I would die from sheer embarrassment. I was scared and ashamed. Fear had gripped every part of my being so much that I was scared to even think of what actually went wrong. The second time that success eluded me, I was not feeling that low or that depressed. I had learned from my earlier experience that the world did not really judge me—I judged myself.

Everybody wants to succeed. I have never met anybody who starts out to make a mess of things. At the end of the day, they all want to make a difference in their own lives and the lives of others, and want to be acknowledged for their contribution. But what most of them lack is the motivation to "act."

And talking of failure, I have failed several times in my life and have made many stupid and silly mistakes. I look back at all of those years and I ask myself, "Nozer, how could you do something like that—how could you have made such a stupid mistake?" But then I did it, for at that moment, it looked like the right thing to do. I did not plan to fail—I simply failed to plan.

Failure gives you that power and the opportunity to get up one more time and go again, as long as you believe in yourself. That's my tagline and my motto in life for all those I come in contact with: *Believe in Yourself.* If you don't believe in yourself, you cannot expect anyone else to believe in you, ever. Don't think of your failures as defeats, think of them as lessons learned.

My best credentials in life are all my mistakes!

WRIGHT

Did failure motivate you to go to your next venture, or did you have self-doubts the first time?

BUCHIA

Oh yes—I most certainly had self-doubts the first time. Looking back, it was not failure that prevented me from getting up and going on, it was ignorance. I did not know just what to do next and how to get started again. I had concerns and fears that barred me from thinking straight. I had more negative thoughts than positive ones. I just thought this was never going to pay off, and that I was making the biggest mistake of my life. Why was I doing this? Why was I trying to be an entrepreneur when I could just get a steady, secure job and not worry about failure and embarrassment? Why was I deliberately putting my family through all that risk, mental agony, and uncertainty?

But then again, I have never been satisfied with past performances and have always looked at the road ahead. I believe that successful people learn to let go of what they no longer posses and open their hearts and minds to what can be in the future. Why would I then let my past performance of failure control my life and my destiny? And the answer was clear to me. Success requires faith and belief in oneself, and a sharp, laser-like focus on the end result. That is when I said to myself, "Come on Nozer, get up and try again—this time more intelligently." And I did!

WRIGHT

You were very successful in the corporate world. You held jobs that most people would give anything to have and yet you gave up all that and ventured into the uncertain, risky world of entrepreneurship. What was the reason you took the plunge? And have you ever regretted it?

BUCHIA

We all have giant aspirations for ourselves, and possess inner desires of what we want to achieve in life. I was by no means an exception to this fact and belief. I was at a time in my career where I felt "used" and under-utilized in every way. I felt that my performance was not at its best. I wanted to, and was capable of, achieving more than what my corporate designation allowed me to accomplish.

My background, as you know, David, is growing people and corporations. I help entrepreneurs build and grow companies, sell companies, and even take companies international. My passion and skill is taking non-performing and underperforming companies and turning them around. My desire is to enable people shed their inhibitions and soar in life and in business. All this I could not achieve in the corporate world. I felt trapped.

So I took the plunge, not realizing how lonely and risky it was to venture out in this unforgiving world of business, all by myself. Trust me on this one thing, David, this world is very unforgiving, to say the least. And believe me, it has not been an easy ride. When you are in business for yourself, besides being on call 24/7, you suddenly realize that you have only yourself to blame for your tensions and failures. It all starts and ends with you and nothing else matters.

But I have not regretted it one bit, for I believe that the cause was worth making all the sacrifices in life. Being an entrepreneur has allowed me to utilize my skills and talents for the betterment of others. It has permitted me to break the shackles of corporate bondage and experience the spirit of entrepreneurial freedom. But it comes with a price. There are many sacrifices that I have had to make and many compromises that our family has had to endure. But it is all worth it!

Being in business for myself has made our family closer than we ever were, and even more supportive of one another. We talk at the dinner table each night and discuss and share ideas with one another. I say this with conviction: it has helped me immensely. To top it all, our fifteen-year-old son, Kyrus, watches me conduct business each day, and has gradually developed entrepreneurial traits of his own. My wife, Persis, and I are very proud of him and know in our hearts that he will excel in life and in business. I know he will succeed!

WRIGHT

How do you define your own success? Is there a secret road map to success and if so what is it?

BUCHIA

Success, in my opinion, is measured by the strength of your desire. It is measured by the size of your dreams and by how you handle disappointments along the way. That is what I resolutely believe.

Most importantly, in life and in business, when we lose our way, it is not typically because we lose sight of the goal or that we lose sight of the destination or even our strategy. It is because we have no road map to get there.

When we get into a car and drive to a new location, we are always thankful for all the traffic signs along the way that tell us what to do, or better still, what not to do—slow down, one way, wrong way, and so on. These signs are there to guide us and deliver us to our destination.

When a business plan fails, trust me, there are signs along the way that you have neglected to observe and reflect on seriously. There are signs that must have warned you of the fact that your plan has not worked as effectively as you had expected and that you need to slow down, stop, turn around, and not be afraid to ask for directions once again.

You need to create a new road map, a better strategy, and a more realistic business plan. Why are you going there (purpose of the business)? What do you need to make your business successful (products and services)? Are you moving in the right direction (strategy and business plan)? Do you have enough money (capital) for the trip?

You need to constantly ask for directions along the way and find role models and mentors who can help guide you. You need to stop occasionally and evaluate your path, and, most certainly, the speed with which you are traveling. These are the things that have helped me define my own success.

There are three simple rules that will help you understand and evaluate your behavior, and therefore your chances for success:

- If you do not go after what you want, chances are that you will never get it.
- If you never ask a question, the answer will always be no.
- If you don't push yourself forward, you're always going to be in the same place.

Success is neither magical, nor is it earned overnight. It is a tedious process that you engage in, day after day. Your level of success is directly proportionate to your tolerance to risk, your passion to succeed, and your never-give-up attitude.

I am entirely convinced that the day you develop clear intentions and decide firmly in your mind to set your own course is the day you start creating your own road map to success.

WRIGHT

You've had the privilege of being in leadership positions at corporations in your career of thirty-four years. Is there a certain leadership style that one needs in order to be successful?

BUCHIA

Leadership style is the behavior and the approach of providing direction, implementing plans, and motivating people. There are different styles of leadership that leaders can embrace depending on circumstances. But the critical element of leader effectiveness is choosing the right style, at the right time, under the right situation. A leader with a good leadership style understands and does what is right; a leader with a great leadership style understands and does what will sell.

Many so-called leaders choose to follow the style that instills fear in the minds and hearts of their subordinates. This style, in my opinion, originates from personal fears of survival, and lack of control. Such a leadership style is disturbing, demeaning, and does not last forever. The type of leadership style that enables leaders to be successful is where the leader coexists with their employees. As a leader, you have to earn their respect not demand it. Remember, mangers are appointed whereas leaders are selected!

People ask me this question: are your employees more important than your customers? It is a very difficult question to answer, but I always answer it this way: if I did not have my employees, I would not be able to take care of my customers. Now, some people would argue the other way around, but I don't. Customers are your external people; employees are your internal people.

My leadership style is a collaborative but situational one (versus a confrontational or fear-instilling one); I motivate people to exploit their full potential, and achieve the unexpected. My belief is that leaders do not create followers, they create more leaders. People need to be empowered to make decisions and therefore make mistakes. In my organization, mistakes are rarely punished. People are guided and helped via open communication. We gather around the conference room table and we debate, we talk, we critique. We don't critique the person but the idea, the plan. This builds employee confidence and removes the element of fear that causes individuals and organizations to fail.

Remember, leaders lead people; managers manage things!

WRIGHT

You are a business coach and a life coach. What advice would you give professionals who are frustrated with their careers and therefore their lives and want to shift into a world of entrepreneurship?

BUCHIA

We all have a choice—a choice every single day as to what we're going to do with our life and where we are going to take it. If you follow your passion and your dreams, you'll be amazed at how far it can actually take you—all you need to do is to believe in yourself and your abilities.

Never be afraid to create your own opportunities. Successful people always know where they are going, and where they're going to end up. And if you need help along the way, just ask. Remember, you are your own driving engine and you are your own brake. The only person who can stop you from achieving anything in life is *you!*

And do not worry about people criticizing your goals. If people do not laugh at your goals, your goals are probably too small.

Let us learn from the likes of corporations like Starbucks. It began as one little coffee shop opened sometime in the '70s, resulting in the largest coffee shop company/meeting place in the world. My executive assistant does not start her day well if she does not smell Starbucks every morning. And it is nothing but just plain simple coffee with the brilliant idea of convenience at every corner. And furthermore, Starbucks has quite cleverly repositioned the brand by associating it with "happening" people. If people see you with a cup of Starbucks coffee, you are considered to be "trendy." Talk of branding! Did the originators of Starbucks ever dream that it would go so far?

So, if you want to get into the world of entrepreneurship, do it cautiously. Some of the key ingredients for success are as follows:

- Determine your passion and the reason for the shift.
- Believe in yourself and in your abilities. Remember, if you do not believe in yourself, nobody will.
- Identify your strengths and weaknesses. Do not fix your weaknesses, strengthen your strengths.
- Involve your family in your decision-making process because they will be the ones most affected by your decision.
- Find a mentor who will hold you responsible for achieving what you have planned and promised yourself to achieve.
- Build a sustainable strategy. This will prevent you from doing the same thing over and over again expecting a different result.

- Study the lives of other entrepreneurs and understand what they have done to be successful.
- Assemble your own road map for success and measure your achievements from day one. This will enable you to stay on course.
- Be prepared to take risks – remember: no guts, no glory.
- Determine your exit strategy. You should know when to call it quits.

People ask me, "Nozer, is it difficult to get to the top of the ladder?"

And my answer is, "No, it is not difficult to get to the top of the ladder. What is difficult is getting through the crowd at the bottom; they will convince you that you cannot do it. And trust me, they will sound very convincing at the time. The one reason they will convince you that you cannot do it, is because they cannot do it."

As a business coach and a life coach, it is my responsibility to identify my clients' brilliance, their limitations, and their tolerance to risk. Then and only then can I attempt to assist in their creation and construction of a "healthy" perspective to life and business.

My principle—If you believe in yourself, anything is possible!

WRIGHT

You are an eternal optimist. Has this attribute contributed toward your success in life?

BUCHIA

Well, it's funny you ask me that. Yes, actually, I am very optimistic, and it is this trait of mine that has contributed largely to my success in life and in business. I believe that big doors swing on small hinges. There is absolutely nothing that you cannot do in life if you have the right attitude and the undying passion to succeed.

I also believe that the day your memories become bigger than your dreams, you are headed for the grave. I am a believer in my dreams, in my capabilities, and my abilities to convert those dreams into reality. I dream a lot; I also make things happen. It is my life's ambition to help other people realize their dreams and succeed. I believe that limits, like fear, are only an illusion, for I will never let my past experiences harm or determine my future prospects of success.

In fact, I am so very grateful for all those difficult people in my life; they have shown me exactly who I do not want to be. Their words do not predict my destiny, they simply add fuel to my entrepreneurial fire. And that is why I do not worry about the people from my past; there is a good reason they are not in my future. I cannot change the past, and my future doesn't deserve the punishment arising out of the fear of failure.

And talking of people and optimism, remember to never allow anyone to make more withdrawals than deposits in your life. If you do, you will be out of balance and in the negative. Be optimistic, but know when to close that account.

So yes, I always look at life optimistically but cautiously. Life has taught me that success is merely a frame of mind. Obstacles will steer you away from your dreams for a while, but the only one who can deter you from you goals is you!

WRIGHT

Does success have anything to do with the culture or upbringing of a person? In your opinion, would the son of a successful person be as successful as the father?

BUCHIA

Culture and upbringing most certainly have their place of influence in the life of an individual. The son of a successful businessman undoubtedly has better chances of success, for besides having a launching pad already in place with all the required support, he has had the privilege of observing the master at work. But no matter how tall your father is, you have to do your own growing up.

In my opinion, the biggest gift a parent can give a child is the ability to think on its own. There is no better and no permanent gift that can be passed down from generation to generation. So, can the son of a successful father be as successful as he is? Yes. Will that always be the case? No.

Aspects of one's culture, by all means, support the progress and success of an individual. Culture comprises of values, beliefs, and attitudes. It involves personality and it takes time to develop. Culture is the behavior that results from experiences and is especially influenced by the head of the family/community/organization because of their role in decision making and strategic direction.

It ultimately depends on the knowledge and wisdom passed down from father to son and mother to daughter. That, to me, is an obligation that parents have toward their children. That, in my opinion, is what will ultimately shape up the thinking of a child.

The father must gradually instill that difference between knowledge and wisdom, so it becomes etched in the brain of the child for relevant comparison and use in the future. As I told our son Kyrus, knowledge is realizing that the tomato is a fruit, wisdom is not putting it in a fruit salad!

WRIGHT

It has been said that people need to know their capabilities and limits if they really want to succeed in life and in business. What are your thoughts on capabilities and limitations?

BUCHIA

The only way of finding your limits of the possible is by going beyond, into the impossible. To accomplish great things, we must not only act, but dream and not only plan but believe.

One thing I have noticed is that people immediately compromise when faced with a difficult task at hand. They give in too easily because they are unsure of their own potential and therefore cannot peak their own performance. They become dysfunctional pleasers and in the process make themselves "options" in the lives of "relationship grabbers." This is exactly why people need coaches and mentors in their lives. I have learned in life never to expect anything from anyone—it is better to be surprised than to be disappointed.

Excellence arises from within. Tap into your behavior, take a good look at your passion; it only lives in your heart. We always see our intentions not our behavior. And that is precisely where the disconnect begins. People judge us by our behavior and not our intentions. We do not recognize or realize what we are good at doing—most often we just do it effortlessly. Life is like a dance; sometimes you will lead and sometimes you will be forced to follow. It all depends on the music.

Knowing one's limitations is not enough. One has to acknowledge them. And most often it is not the "load" that is the limitation, it is the way you carry it.

I hear this said often: "I cannot succeed, I am not that unique or great in anything I do." And my answer to those ignorant ones who say this is, "You don't have to be unique or great to get started, but you have to get started to become unique and great."

Challenge the status quo with persistence and perseverance. When a person says "I cannot do it," what is really being said is that the person does not know how to do it or does not want to do it. Hiding behind the belief that "I have my limitations, I don't think I can do it" is being weak. And being weak is a choice; so also is being strong.

Nothing great has ever been achieved, except by those who dared to believe that something inside them was certainly far more superior than their perceived limitations or even circumstances.

WRIGHT

So what in your opinion are the key ingredients required to build a successful road map in life and in business?

BUCHIA

My experiences have shown me these three key ingredients required to build a successful road map for success:

Risk—the risk of indignantly falling flat on your face after a failure. But if you do not take the risk, nothing is going to make any sense whatsoever. Just as a lobster, if you stand still and do nothing, you will be carried away by the current. Learn to push yourself if you want to make progress. A ship is very safe in a harbor, but that is not what a ship is built for in the first place. Even a turtle makes progress only when it sticks its neck out and pushes itself to move forward.

Are you willing to take the risk to follow your dreams? Are you willing to give it everything you've got? Are you willing to live on the boundary of failure and disaster? To me, pitiful is the person who is afraid of taking risks, for when he or she looks back in life, the person will hear the heart says: you could have made it if only you had tried a little bit harder.

Passion—the intense obsession to succeed. This is about your idea and how bad you want to win. Nothing is more powerful than an idea whose time has come. It is so rightly said that if you love what you do, you will not work a day in your life.

John Paul, founder of Paul Mitchell hair products, started with a mere $700, and went from salon to salon, trying to sell his hair products. Today, his successful corporation is the result of his passion—his passion for what he actually believed in.

Life has no limitations except the ones you make. You will encounter a wall each time you want to achieve success. These walls are only there to signify how bad you want something. No business was magically produced overnight. It is the result of that undying passion of tearing down the wall, brick by brick.

Persistence—the never-give-up attitude. Persistence is enduring continuation. Nothing in the world can take the place of persistence. We do not know how strong we actually are and how we can keep on going, until someone tries to take advantage of our weakness. A diamond is just a piece of charcoal that never gave up and handled stress exceptionally well.

We need to ask ourselves these three questions:
1. Where are we today?
2. Where do we want to go?
3. How will we get there?

People are not unsuccessful because they fail, they are unsuccessful because they give up. Successful people know where they are going and where they will end up. Do you?

Those people who are the best at what they do, took the risk for the sake of their passion and proved to the world that they would never let anyone deter them from reaching their goals.

WRIGHT

What do you think is more significant to be successful, experience or education?

BUCHIA

Can experience make up for the lack of a degree, or does a degree provide something that experience cannot? Is one more important than the other? Has the global push for higher education started to outweigh and devalue hands-on experience? These are questions that will truly have you chasing your tail. The answer is "it all depends."

Experience is what you undoubtedly earn through hard knocks in life. It is the best teacher you can ever have during your entire existence, for unlike formal education, it gives you the test first, and then teaches you the lesson. It is like a comb that you acquire when you get bald.

Education, on the other hand, lays the foundation on which a well-rounded future can be built. It is a desired requisite (especially in today's world), that routinely positions a degreed person as being far more intelligent than an experienced one, even though that may not actually be the case.

In my opinion, it all depends on the hiring manager, the task at hand, and the policies of the enterprise. The first thing to do is to learn about your chosen industry. There are some career fields where it is common for top level employees to work their way up from the bottom with little to no formal education. Then there are career fields that require industry-specific training, licenses, and certifications, which make advanced education essential.

Throughout the early years, large companies operated their own internal training and development programs. As a result, employees enjoyed long, successful careers, usually working for the same company their entire lives. The recent job market volatility has put an end to those traditions. In today's economy, workers jump ship more frequently, making it difficult for employers to invest heavily in their employees. Therefore, employers rely on job seekers to develop their own skills, thus increasing the demand for formal degrees.

Education will never steer you the wrong way. On-the-job training gives you great experience, but education is required at some point along the way. A good tactic is to gain experience and education simultaneously.

WRIGHT

You are working on a plan to establish the *Nozer Buchia Leadership Institute* for Advanced Education, Training, and Development. Will you elaborate on your vision for this venture?

BUCHIA

My dream is to endow the entrepreneur, the executive, and the emergent leader with *life-long learning.*

When I was growing up, I had very few people I could turn to who would have the desire and the experience to guide me toward my path to triumph. When I needed advice, plenty of wanna-be experts came out of the woodwork to help me with their words, but when I needed real help, real hand-holding, people slowly dwindled away, and those who were left simply gave me advice. It was very frustrating, to say the least. I felt helpless and demoralized. At times, I struggled to keep afloat, for I did not know just what to do next. I quickly realized that I should never trust the advice of those who were not affected by the end result, for they had simply nothing to lose.

There are significant demands on the world's top management to perform and to excel. When leaders participate in advanced education, training, and development, they expect much more than just information. Besides being educated with newer ideas and concepts, and failures and mistakes, they expect to be inspired and entertained.

The initiative I am working on will foster the spirit of learning through a quality educational experience in an entertaining manner. Participants will interact with successful and then not-so successful people, and will be awarded the unique opportunity to excel through interaction, evaluation, and active participation.

The institute's mission will be to increase the effectiveness of entrepreneurs and executives around the world. Through customized leadership development training, the focus will be to strive to produce a new generation of leaders who are unwavering in their commitment for personal and organizational growth.

WRIGHT

Nozer, this has truly been an amazing discussion. I can see now why you are referred to as "Mr. Motivator," what an appropriate title. I sincerely appreciate your time and the valuable insights you have so graciously shared with us. This is going to be a really great chapter in our book *ROADMAP to Success,* and I appreciate you being in it.

BUCHIA

It has been a privilege to share my experiences alongside the visions of Dr. Ken Blanchard and Dr. Deepak Chopra. Thank you, David; I enjoyed our conversation.

WRIGHT

Today I have been talking with Nozer Buchia, internationally acclaimed motivational entertainer, speaker, author, and entrepreneur. With thirty-four years as an organization builder and turnaround specialist, he uses failure as a tool to prove that success is always within one's reach. After my conversation with him today, I understand why he is called "Mr. Motivator."

Nozer thank you so much for being with us today on our journey toward a *ROADMAP to Success.*

BUCHIA

Thank you, David.

Nozer Buchia, also referred to as "Mr. Motivator," is an internationally-acclaimed motivational, inspirational, and keynote speaker of repute. He is known as a "speaker's-speaker" due to his dynamic inimitable style of humor and delivery, and his practical approach to any situation.

His straight-from-the heart, high energy, and passionate message has motivated audiences worldwide, and has enabled them get out of their comfort zone and get into greatness. His message is delivered with great passion and complete conviction, as he has lived what he talks about. His determination, persistence, and his never-give-up attitude have enabled him to be successful in life and in the world of business.

Nozer is a business coach and a life coach, specializing in coaching and mentoring executives, high profile managers, non-performing, and under-performing teams and individuals who have the potential to excel and who want to expand their influence repertoire. He is especially interested in helping individuals and corporations who believe they have reached their "peak" and cannot grow anymore. With his motto, "Believe in Yourself," he helps organizations, teams, and individuals reach higher levels of efficacy.

Nozer's executive coaching and leadership training programs have been created to maximize your success by enhancing your natural talents and future capabilities. His approach to coaching has been developed and strengthened by his decades of experience, and is personalized through individual and group events that motivate and empowers each participant to improve leadership and managerial capabilities while producing results.

Individuals and corporations worldwide have greatly benefitted from his motivational and keynote addresses, his seminars, and his leadership training sessions, as he helps formulate and communicate corporate strategy with clarity and effectiveness.

Nozer Buchia

Sugar Land, Texas, USA
832-606-1777
nozer@nozerbuchia.com
www.nozerbuchia.com